GW00372338

The Cover: The cover art, "Building More Stately Mansions" by Aaron Douglas, is reprinted with permission from the Carl Van Vechten Gallery of Fine Arts, Collection of Fisk University, Nashville, Tennessee.

About the Artist: A leading artist of the Harlem Renaissance, Aaron Douglas (1899-1979) painted murals that merged African and African-American motifs. He superimposed abstract figures using muted tones to communicate visual and spiritual depth, unity, and pride. His finest works include murals that grace the Countee Cullen Branch of the New York Public Library and illustrations of such classics as *The New Negro* (1925) by Alain Locke and *God's Trombones* by James Weldon Johnson (1927).

Marsha Woodbury, Editorial Assistant
James S. Dowling, Managing Editor
Susan Lafferty, Production Assistant

PUBLICATIONS COMMITTEE
Leigh Estabrook, Janice Del Negro, Monica Walk, David Dubin

UNTOLD STORIES

CIVIL RIGHTS, LIBRARIES, AND BLACK LIBRARIANSHIP

ð edited by John Mark Tucker ð

To Those Great Tennessee Bibliophiles
Who Made a Difference

CHARLES ELDER
Elder's Book Store

EDWIN S. GLEAVES, JR.
Tennessee State Library & Archives

DAVID MARSHALL STEWART
Public Library of Nashville & Davidson County

REBECCA SMITH
Middle Tennessee State University

EDITH UPTON TUCKER
David Libscomb University

MARVIN D. WILLIAMS, JR.
Disciples of Christ Historical Society

Table of Contents

Preface

ತಿ. John Mark Tucker ತಿ.

> The civil rights movement did not grow out of the dream of any one man,
> or woman. . . . The people who made up the Movement were almost as
> diverse as America itself. [It] was carried out by a tiny percentage of all
> those who could have taken part. And yet this small group was able to
> generate a wave that washed over the entire nation, that spawned similar
> movements in a dozen fields. (Powledge, 1991, pp. xi, xii)

The idea for this collection of papers grew out of my discussions with Donald G. Davis, Jr., Professor of Library and Information Science at the University of Texas (UT) at Austin. In the early 1990s, the Special Collections Department of the University Libraries at UT obtained the papers of James Farmer, founder of the Congress of Racial Equality (CORE). Davis had learned that these papers contained documents about libraries established by civil rights workers engaged in the Mississippi Freedom Summer project of 1964 and instantly he recognized the research potential of these materials. At about the same time, I became vice/chair and chair/elect of the Library History Round Table (LHRT) of the American Library Association (ALA) with responsibilities for the Round Table's program session and research forum for the ALA conference at Miami Beach in June 1994.

Untold Stories: Civil Rights, Libraries, & Black Librarianship thus began with Davis's interest in "freedom libraries" and my interest in planning programs for LHRT. Given the historian's impulse to revisit the past on anniversary occasions, the 1994 convention (scheduled 30 years after Freedom Summer) offered a timely forum for exploring the relationship between books, libraries, and the great social movement of our times, the American civil rights movement. I recalled having seen a photograph of a library in the community center established by activists in Meridian, Mississippi (Huie, 1965). Davis remembered that Virginia Steele, a classmate from his library school days at the University of California at Berkeley, had participated in a Freedom Summer project. After consulting Steele, Davis began to research the topic of freedom libraries collaborating with Cheryl Knott Malone.

Davis and Malone break fresh ground in the historian's attempt to tell the story of how books and libraries became essential to civil rights efforts. Emphasizing reading for political and intellectual opportunity, their paper raised further questions: What role did books and reading play in stimulating social change? How did library workers act, individually or collectively, to promote equality of opportunity? In efforts to reach out to the previously unserved, how did the library community revise its practices of recruiting and developing staff, of providing information, and of building collections? How was the library profession as a whole influenced by the drive for civil rights and, in turn, how did the profession influence those who sought to make constitutionally sanctioned guarantees more of a reality?

LIBRARIES, BOOKS, & CIVIL RIGHTS

In seeking to address questions like these, the LHRT Program Committee sought speakers to complement Davis and Malone's "Reading for Liberation." Constituted of James V. Carmichael, Jr. (University of North Carolina, Greensboro), Elizabeth I. Hanson (Indiana University), Joanne Passet (formerly of Indiana University), Kenneth Potts (formerly of Northern Illinois University), John Mark Tucker (Purdue University), Wayne A. Wiegand (University of Wisconsin), and Robert V. Williams (University of South Carolina), the Committee wanted to ensure that little-known stories would receive a fresh hearing.

We entitled the session "Libraries, Books, & the Civil Rights Movement" and added two speakers on racial integration at the University of Houston. Edward G. Holley, Director of Libraries at Houston from 1962 to 1971, had led the way in integrating the University's faculty and professional staff in 1967 when he recruited Charles D. Churchwell as Assistant Director for Public Services. In preparing his remarks for the LHRT program, Holley became intrigued by the opportunity to interview former colleagues, to re-examine internal memoranda and reports, and then to offer insight into the attitudes and actions of key participants when Churchwell became Houston's first black professional. Churchwell likewise welcomed the opportunity to reminisce; he reminded us of the complex factors influencing his decision to move to Houston, of the challenging environment he entered by joining its library faculty, and of the human emotions and reactions that could be elicited by the campus visit of a charismatic leader like Bobby Seale. We who live in the 1990s sometimes have difficulty understanding just how cataclysmic those events actually were that took place a mere three decades ago.

Our final speaker at this session was Jessie Carney Smith, University Librarian and Cosby Professor at Fisk, on the topic of "Black Women, Civil Rights, & Libraries." Smith recalled the struggles of seven black women who began pursuing library and literary careers during times much more hostile to social change than the 1960s. The obstacles they overcame in order to develop themselves professionally and to establish legacies of high achievement serve as inspirational models for faculty and practitioners beset with rapid change in our own times. The stories of these seven provide vivid reminders that serious racial progress was painful and threatening to much of the nation.

The Round Table also conducted a research forum by calling for papers on the history of black librarianship in America. The forum attracted a number of well-written, well-researched contributions. Joanne Passet graciously reviewed these and passed along her recommendations. Casper LeRoy Jordan, former professor at Atlanta University and former library director at Atlanta and at Wilberforce universities, moderated the panel featuring presentations by Rosie L. Albritton on African-American social library and historical societies, Dan Lee on the history of library services to blacks in South Carolina, and Casper Jordan with Beverly Lynch on the Association of College and Research Libraries (ACRL) projects for historically black academic libraries. These three papers (introduced below), together with the four in the program session, constituted the Round Table's official programs for 1994, and were co-sponsored by ALA's Black Caucus, Library Research Round Table, and Social Responsibilities Round Table.

The eight other essays collected here came through several avenues. Some were submitted but not chosen for an LHRT presentation either because other papers seemed more appropriate to the subject of the session or simply because the time allotted could not accommodate more than the seven papers actually presented. Some excellent submissions were not included since their subjects or methods of inquiry were better suited to another form of publication; I am pleased to note that at least one of these has already made its way into print. I also solicited papers from scholars who produce excellent work and who likely had research in progress that would enhance the collection as a whole. Occasionally I met with disappointment as anticipated manuscripts never arrived. In other instances, wonderful surprises awaited, and I have been able to include first-time as well as experienced authors. Readers familiar with some of our contributors will recognize representation from black and white alike, testimony to the powerful appeal of the subjects involved. The civil rights movement in general holds great fascination for both races; we should anticipate that studies involving books and libraries within the civil rights context would likewise attract biracial interest.

Various interwoven threads tie these essays together. One, identified by Donald Davis and Cheryl Malone, may be termed the "faith-in-books" attitude apparent at the Freedom School near Canton, Mississippi. Activists sensed that books could lead a people in their quest for knowledge and information, giving them new self-assurance, an "air of possibility." Thus, what might be achievable in the growth and development of an individual, a group of students, a community, a race, or a society, could take root in the ability to read and be nourished in the opportunity to use a neighborhood library.

Contributors to this collection also brought a strong historical consciousness to their work. Some employed the methods common to traditional historical inquiry. They read widely from scholarly books and journals, they scrutinized pertinent unpublished materials in manuscript collections and archives, analyzed those materials, and then organized their observations into narratives that challenged old perspectives and/or offered new ones. They used newer methods as well, oral history in particular. They conducted interviews, some on a one-to-one basis and some in groups; they contacted former colleagues in an effort to jog memories; they pored over discolored old files and notes; they searched for the past by questioning, discovering, remembering, and reminiscing. Their personal experiences make their stories fresh and poignant.

And they have told stories, accounts of events and people, of success and failure, of pride and pain. Thus we can read about people who taught others how to read, people who founded libraries and people who supported them, people who organized libraries and people who used them, people who wrote and edited books for librarians to add to collections, and people who demonstrated courage and skill amid the actions of others that were much less commendable. Edward G. Holley (1977), one of our contributors, has written elsewhere of his interest in "larger movements," in the "philosophical underpinnings of librarianship," and in the "institutional histories which are becoming better all the time," but that what concerns him the most are:

> the people, the real flesh and blood people whose motives were mixed, whose leadership was often inadequate, but whose accomplishments were significant. They enabled our profession to make great strides in the past 100 years. What were they like? How did they interact with each other? What views did they hold? Did they battle each other the way we do today? (p. 122)

Contributors have shed new light on old stories and have turned our attention to new ones. These authors are by no means the first to write about civil rights, libraries, and black librarianship. That literature has been growing for decades and in modern times has been enriched by Rosemary R. Du Mont, Arthur C. Gunn, E. J. Josey, Eric Moon, Annette L. Phinazee, Ann Allen Shockley, Benjamin F. Speller, Jr., and others including several scholars represented in this collection. Yet, contributors to this volume seek to add their own special testimony to the power of books and libraries, of printed words, and of the human spirit.

LEGACIES OF BLACK LIBRARIANSHIP

In "Liberty & Literacy," Marilyn Pettit discusses literacy education for blacks in the early nineteenth century. She tells what essentially has been an "untold story" of women engaged in programs that sprang from religious activity, of how libraries were created within a larger effort designed to teach black women how to read the Bible, and to help them develop high moral attributes. Her essay calls us back to the origins of those impulses that would re-emerge as powerful forces in the middle of the twentieth century. Rosie L. Albritton establishes a typology for libraries and identifies cultural organizations that served as early vehicles for black intellectual expression. These organizations, many of them historical societies, mentored early black historians and book collectors, thus playing a significant role in preserving a racial memory for future generations. Albritton's fine analysis identifies genuine heroes in African-American history.

James Hooper has examined original records from the Rockefeller Archives and one of the Rockefeller family's principal foundations, the General Education Board (GEB). Through millions of dollars of subventions, the GEB greatly enhanced education, literacy, and libraries in the early twentieth-century South. Hooper presents an important chapter in black academic library history corroborating the oft-expressed view that the philanthropist-beneficiary relationship is, indeed, both delicate and complex.

Andrea L. Williams tells the story of a library of a particular type—the black public library, scratching out a meager existence in separate, unequal, hostile circumstances. We desperately need exposure to her story, and not only hers but also the stories of numerous other libraries, accounts of which are preserved (but often ignored) in masters theses written in schools of librarianship at Atlanta University and elsewhere. Our profession is indeed fortunate that the thesis requirement came into use in library education at just the moment when the separate black public library was closing its doors and the records of its activity had not yet been discarded.

CHRONICLES FROM THE CIVIL RIGHTS MOVEMENT

The next five essays treat libraries implicitly and explicitly within civil rights contexts. In "The Ugly Side of Librarianship," Klaus Musmann plumbs the depths of the library version of those five full decades between the U. S. Supreme Court's approval of the "separate but equal" concept and unequivocal rejection of that concept (Plessy v. Ferguson, 1896 and Brown v. Board of Education, 1954). Musmann shows how librarianship reflected dominant national values, how the organized profession repeatedly wavered in its efforts even to talk about services much less implement them on behalf of black America. He discusses, for example, the incredibly short life of that 1920s entity, the ALA Work with Negroes Round Table, illustrating sharply that librarians failed for decades to serve people of color, that separate was never equal (Jenkins, 1990).

Dan Lee chronicles the resistance to tax-supported libraries for blacks in South Carolina; the contributions of philanthropists Willie Lee Buffington, Harvey Kelsey, and Julius Rosenwald; the devotion of library heroes like Susan Dart Butler and Emily America Copeland; and the courage of student activists in the 1960s. Lee demonstrates just how long and arduous a journey can be that involves significant social change, that requires groups and individuals to move from resistance to accommodation, that takes a profession and a race from segregation to integration. The next essays, on freedom libraries in Mississippi and integration at the University of Houston, have been discussed.

RESOURCES FOR LIBRARY PERSONNEL, SERVICES, & COLLECTIONS

Jessie Smith's account of the careers of seven black women highlights the work of individuals, the achievements of the flesh-and-blood people of such interest to Professor Holley. Discussed in more detail above, Smith's essay grew out of research for her landmark reference sources, *Notable Black American Women* (1992) and *Notable Black American Women Book II* (1996). Donald Franklin Joyce, arguably the nation's foremost authority on black book publishers due to his work in *Gatekeepers of Black Culture* (1983) and *Black Book Publishers in the United States* (1991), gives us a glimpse of a rare phenomenon, that of the librarian as book publisher. He uses interviews to identify the factor(s) that stimulated black librarians to enter the challenging world of book publishing. Thus, we learn something of the reference instincts of Doris Saunders, a concern for copyright issues on the part of poet-librarian Dudley Randall, and of the antiquarian interests of W. Paul Coates.

Casper L. Jordan and Beverly P. Lynch provide a retrospective of the programs of the ACRL to strengthen libraries in HBCUs (Historically Black Colleges and Universities). For more than two decades, ACRL mounted several major projects designed to further develop professional librarians through internships; compile statistics on staff, budgets, and collections; improve library-related humanities programming; and to better prepare librarians and college administrators for regional accreditation. Like essays by Holley, Churchwell, Joyce, and others, the Jordan-Lynch contribution utilizes oral history as a tool essential to the historical enterprise. Most telling is a recent letter to the editor from Casper Jordan, "I realized as I did this research that I am the only living person closely related to the project" (Jordan to M. Tucker, personal communication, 2 April 1996).

The development, accessibility, and use of collections are primary concerns in our final three essays. In Ontario, Mississauga Library System's Norman G. Kester describes the inception and the growth of African Caribbean collections of the North York Public Library, located in Metropolitan Toronto. He discusses the special attributes and responsibilities of librarians devoted to the creation and maintenance of ethnic collections. He identifies the cross-cultural issues inherent in written and oral communication in urban public library practice including collection development, readers advisory work, and community programming. Like other contributors, Kester employs interviews to elicit the insights of key participants.

Detine Bowers decries the "auction block" dispersal of the personal books and papers of one of the major literary figures of our times, Alex Haley. Having attended the Haley auction at the University of Tennessee, she describes her visceral reaction and, again out of personal experience, shows how one scholar can become involved in reclaiming the past by actively collecting the documents, photographs, and other artifacts of institutional memory. She suggests possibilities for collaboration among archives, universities, community organizations, and museums, and she emphasizes the importance of mutual respect and trust between researchers and those living and breathing individuals and groups who have become the subjects of scholarly inquiry.

Finally, Edward A. Goedeken reviews selected resources on the overall topics of this collection—civil rights, libraries, and black librarianship. Bibliographer for Libraries & Culture and the LHRT Newsletter, Goedeken concentrates on the four decades between the Brown decision in 1954 and the LHRT programs in 1994. He highlights important monographic and collected works on the history of black America, cites significant contributions to the interpretive literature devoted to Martin Luther King, Jr. and the civil rights movement, and thus provides a context for understanding the literature of black American library history, biography, and autobiography.

Readers will notice diversity in the nomenclature adopted by contributors. Words and phrases frequently used include blacks, Blacks, negroes, Negroes, African Americans, African-Americans, Afro-Americans, and people of color. These terms reflect the dynamic nature of the subject in a context that ranges from personal reminiscence to historical scholarship. While a fluidity of usage is perhaps something of a commentary on black life in America, it also represents something much more specific. Some authors have chosen the word "negro" or "black" in an effort to reflect usage common during a particular period of history as they describe it. Others have chosen "Black" or "African-American" for reasons that more closely approximate selected current scholarly conventions or ideological commitments. While the editor and the Publications Office have sought to create a uniformity of presentation, notation, and bibliographic format, we have also sought to create an avenue of unfettered scholarly communication. We are reminded of the view expressed by Fred Powledge (1991):

> I respect the desire of any group, particularly those who are oppressed, to choose the name by which they prefer to be known. I also respect the need of oppressed groups to choose new names from time to time, to mark the way stations along their march out of oppression. (p. xxi)

Thus we have permitted each author to adopt his/her own terminology, making changes simply to facilitate consistency within an individual essay. This approach has, we believe, encouraged diversity of expression just as it has encouraged diversity of interpretation.

ACKNOWLEDGMENTS

To compile and edit these essays, a delightful yet challenging process, has involved indebtedness to numerous individuals. I am most grateful to my contributors whose attraction to the topics of civil rights, libraries, and black librarianship resulted in solid historical analysis and thought-provoking oral history. Financial support for the 1994 LHRT programs was provided, in part, by a Special Allocation grant from Hardy R. Franklin, past ALA President, through the Office of Conference Services. I also want to thank John Berry of *Library Journal* for recommending the LHRT sessions to conferees at Miami Beach (Berry, 1994). My efforts in planning and implementing the sessions were greatly facilitated by Charles Harmon, formerly the ALA Headquarters Librarian and liaison to LHRT. Those of us fortunate enough to have worked directly with Harmon know that the LHRT has benefited greatly from his organizational savvy and managerial abilities.

Donald G. Davis, Jr. and Edward G. Holley understood the potential for this collection and offered valuable counsel and frequent words of encouragement. Without their interest and support, publishing these papers would not have been possible. Donald W. Krummel, Professor Emeritus of Library and Information Science at the University of Illinois, has long taken an active interest in my scholarly pursuits. Whatever editorial skills I possess continue to be nourished by his abilities as a mentor. My thanks go to Marcella Genz, who directed the Publications Office when the manuscript was accepted, Kevin Ward, who succeeded Marcella Genz, and Jim Dowling, Managing Editor of the Publications Office. All have proven to be talented, conscientious, and well-organized. I have greatly enjoyed the opportunity to work with them and their staff, and I trust that readers will conclude that our collaboration has been beneficial. I especially appreciate Marsha Woodbury, Director of Instructional Technologies, who signed on to this project as it neared completion, who was captivated by the subjects involved, and who ensured that the book became a reality. Jac Kloen typed early revisions of several manuscripts. My secretary, Pam De Bonte, has shared my enthusiasm for this project from its inception and produced numerous drafts in order to placate ravenous editorial urges. Finally, I thank my wife, Barbara Wilson Tucker, who from the very beginning understood the significance of this project, gently inquired about its progress, and faithfully supported my efforts to complete it.

REFERENCES

Berry, J. (1994). Program picks and pans. *Library Journal, 119*(10), 54-70.
Brown versus The Board of Education of Topeka, Shawnee County, Kansas. (1954). 347 *U. S. Reports* 483, pp. 483-500.
Holley, E. G. (1977). The past as prologue: The work of the library historian. *Journal of Library History, 12*(2), 110-127.
Huie, W. B. (1965). *Three lives for Mississippi.* New York: WCC Books.
Jenkins, B. L. (1990). A white librarian in black Harlem. *Library Quarterly, 60*(3), 216-231.
Joyce, D. F. (1991). *Black book publishers in the United States: A historical dictionary of the presses, 1817-1900.* Westport, CT: Greenwood Press.
Joyce, D. F. (1983). *Gatekeepers of Black culture: Black-owned book publishers in the United States, 1817-1981* (Contributions in Afro-American and African Studies, no. 70). Westport, CT: Greenwood Press.

Plessy versus Ferguson. (1896). 163 *U. S. Reports* 537 (May 18).

Smith, J. C. (Ed.). (1992). *Notable Black American women*. Detroit, MI: Gale Research.

Smith, J. C. (Ed.). (1996). *Notable Black American women book II*. Detroit, MI: Gale Research.

Liberty & Literacy

Sunday Schools & Reading
for African-American Females
in New York City, 1799-1826

❧ Marilyn H. Pettit ❧

S unday school in nineteenth-century America grew rapidly into a nor-
mative childhood experience. For some people, Sunday schools became the window for personal and legal emancipation because they
taught reading, writing, geography, account-keeping, sewing, and knitting to
girls between five and twelve years of age. Though the *Bible* was the corner-
stone, Sabbath or Sunday schools taught children and young people, then adults,
to read and write, and African-Americans were, from the beginning, a central
constituency of New York City's Sunday schools.[1]

The Sunday schools became increasingly sentimental, using *Bible* stories, inspirational fables, songs, and standardized lessons to instill in young
people a generalized Protestant catechism and middle-class moral behaviors.
The process institutionalized both the rational and the irrational in the American
Protestant religious experience and became a force that bonded children to a
denominational identity, confirming the next generation of members without
the drama of an individual public confession or conversion experience. The
Sunday-school Union, founded in 1824, unified numbers of Sunday schools
into a federalized Protestant structure, and published age-specific lesson plans
and standardized teaching materials that emphasized the unifying elements
shared by American Protestant churches (Boylan, 1988; Rice, 1917; Lynn &
Wright, 1980).

The Sunday schools began, however, as common school education in the
republic's cities; New York City's were inaugurated in 1803 for the poorest and

most vulnerable residents of the city, white and African-American female children.   Thus, between 1800 and 1830, Sunday schooling became an important matrix for the acquisition of literacy and for the use of libraries and books, particularly for African-American females.   Of equal importance, Sunday school became a *de facto* agent of gradual emancipation due to the mandated relationship between full emancipation and the ability to read (Pettit, 1991).

New York City had an African-American population of 9,008 in 1816, including 617 slaves, and 12,559 in 1825 (Rosenwaike, 1972).   A substantial number learned to read and write not in the often-praised African Free School or in entrepreneurial schools created by the black community, but in Sunday schools.   How this came about affords some insight into the little-known females who founded and managed the schools, and gives a voice and an identity to even less-well known females who attended.

Common schools in the city consisted of three types.   Entrepreneurial schools flourished, usually with boys and girls in separate classes.   Attached to churches, charity schools, a second type, schooled and catechized thirty to fifty poor children of their own congregations, and supplied them with shoes, stockings, clothing, and slates.   The oldest were the Dutch Reformed, Episcopalian, and Quaker schools, founded in the colonial period, followed in the Constitutional period by the Presbyterians, Methodists, and Roman Catholics.   A third variety was the state-funded free common schools, which began with one in 1805, but by 1820 still had only four.   They taught about 1,000 white male children who could attend on weekdays—that is, who were not indentured servants or laborers.   The African Free School, created by the Manumission Society, taught about 100 students, primarily boys, from about 1795 (Moseley, 1963; Bourne, 1870).

Within this panoply of schooling functioned New York City's original Quaker school for "poor black females," a weekday school dating from about 1798, in which: "The necessities of the poor [were] inspected [and] their children freely [partook] of learning to fit them for business" (New York Friends Society, Minutes of April 1, 1807, 1816).   The children received instruction from Quaker women such as Ann King who, in 1808, had the charge of thirty-five black and white girls "whose improvement in manner, and in various branches of learning [was] encouraging" (New York Friends Society, Minutes of May 2, 1808, 1816).

In 1810, the Quakers hired a white female as full-time schoolteacher, and by 1812 Mary Weeks Morgan of Philadelphia, a converted Methodist, began holding Sunday morning classes in her weekday classroom for the instruction of any child, of any race, of any or no church affiliation.   At the same time, Isabella Graham and her daughter, Joanna Bethune, were developing their weekday and Sunday schools that began with four in 1803 under the aegis of the Society for the Relief of Poor Widows with Small Children, founded 1797 (North, 1870; New York Historical Society, 1922; Bethune, D. & J., 1816; Bethune, G. W., 1863; Bethune, J., 1838).

These modest beginnings in New York City engendered two decades of the ascendency of Sunday school as common school; by 1815, nineteen; by 1817, twenty-five; and by 1820, forty female schools operated morning and afternoon sessions on Sundays, the one day free of labor for females over the age of ten or so years; hence the name "Sunday" or "Sabbath" schools. Several thousand "children and female adults who [could not] procure these benefits during the week" attended Sunday morning or afternoon school sessions. Some schools were sponsored, but not controlled, by particular churches (New York Female Union Society to Promote Sabbath Schools, 1820, 1827).[2]

Instruction included *Bible* reading, prayer, and exhortations from the Protestant catechism. Ineligible for seminary, ordination, or the diaconate, women prayed aloud and preached. In addition, they taught reading, writing, and other standard elements of a common school education according to the ability of the teacher. The ratio of teachers to students was two teachers per class of eight to ten "scholars," a direct contrast to the clamorous Lancasterian pedagogy of all ages and levels of students in a single room reciting aloud, often supervised by monitors hardly more advanced than the students.

The lowest classes worked at reading and spelling syllables and words of two or three letters; the highest, fifth class, read the *Bible* and spelled words "indefinitely." A sixth advanced class might be formed of class assistants who could expect to teach if the assigned teacher were absent. The Sunday schedule became a tightly woven, highly structured session of recitation of lessons, singing, and religious and moral instruction, with no allowance for disruptive behavior, but tolerant of absence to an astonishing degree, since only half to two-thirds of those enrolled could be present on any given Sunday.

The 1816 schedule called for opening the schools with prayer at 9:00 a.m., followed by twenty-five minutes of recitation and twenty-five minutes of reading and spelling tasks. Students reassembled in the afternoon for thirty-five minutes of reading and spelling, twenty minutes of religious instruction, ten minutes of singing, and another thirty minutes of reading and spelling. In between, all were dismissed to attend public worship at a church of their choice; clergymen, jealous of their traditional authority to preach and catechize, insisted on this arrangement. This plan formalized a Protestant but non-sectarian structure in the earliest Sunday schools and provided a pattern for subsequent Sunday school unions in New York and Brooklyn in 1816 by setting standards for cooperation among the denominations.

Adult females and boys very quickly entered the Sunday schools, implicitly witnessing that no other schools existed for them; it was then decidedly uncommon to school males and females together, and always preferable that boys be taught by men. Mary Morgan (Mason) noted in her diary that adult females of all ranks began to trickle into her Sunday morning class, including one "with a baby in her arms" (North, 1870, p. 97). At the end of its first incorporated year, the society had grown to twenty-five Sabbath schools for "female adults and youth of both sexes," and at their annual meeting in the spring of 1817 gently mocked the men, noting that "the weaker sex" had formed the first Sabbath School Union in the United States (New York Female Union Society to Promote Sabbath Schools, 1817).

The published report for that year indicated 5,500 students and 340 teachers in twenty-five female schools. School No. 2, conducted in rooms at Wall Street Presbyterian, had five white female adults, fifty-eight white female children, eighty-three "colored" female adults, and seventy-two "colored" female children. Some of the adults were "over forty years old," and "many who did not know a letter when they entered . . . [had] been advanced to the *Bible* class." Female Sabbath School No. 6, at St. George's (Episcopal) Church, had three white and eleven "colored" adult females plus 206 children, 100 white and 106 "colored." School No. 11, held at "Rev. Mr. Phillips's Church," had enrolled 301 of whom about one-third attended regularly; one "scholar" was a female slave who had made her public conversion speech that year accompanied by a change in some unspecified conduct. This school, initially formed at the Associated Reformed Church in Murray Street, had broken off from School No. 8, indicating racial separation, grossly different levels of learning, or too large a number in one school.

A few schools were very large such as Sabbath School No. 9, with 715 enrolled and more than half usually present. This school was sponsored by the Methodists and held in rooms at Free School No. 1 near City Hall; it was the Sunday school taught by Mary Morgan (Mason), the schoolteacher hired by the Quakers in 1810.[3] Assisting her was her friend, modestly dressed Methodist Eliza Verplanck, half-sister of Knickerbocker political figure Giulian Crommelin Verplanck. The 1817 corporate meeting invoked the late Isabella Graham's memory and affirmed a common interest with the Widows' Society and its goals, repeatedly linking the Sunday schools to the generation preceding. One of the forty-three teachers at Sabbath School No. 9 was "C G, a poor girl (who) was taught by Mrs. Graham in the first Sabbath school & got a *Bible* from her hand" (New York Female Society to Promote Sabbath Schools, 1817).[4]

All of the first Sabbath schools included black females and some schools, such as those using borrowed rooms at Wall Street Presbyterian and St. George's Episcopal churches, seemed to be almost entirely for blacks, but clearly included a few whites as well (Anstice, 1911; Stone, 1848; Tyng, C.R., 1890; Tyng, S.H., 1860). Reports indicate that roughly 50 percent of the "scholars" were black, and many of them were older adults. A black woman at Sunday School No. 15, aged forty-seven, was reported to have advanced from spelling to reading; and a black woman at No. 19, aged fifty-five, had "advanced from the first lesson to *Bible* reading." The 5,500 enrolled in 1816-17 plus 340 teachers and 50 or so superintendents accounted for 6 percent of New York City's population in 1817; 3,000 black female students constituted one-third of the 8,391 blacks numbered in the 1816 city census. Many of the women and girls, black and white, were servants, the most common female occupation, and children of servants; a woman at School No. 15 quietly told her teacher that she

> regretted much that she had not attended more regularly, but in consequence of living at service, it had been out of her power. (New York Female Union Society to Promote Sabbath Schools, 1823, p. 10)

Women of all ages attended classes, using lesson materials and a classroom structure suitable for children; one woman who attended the school at Brick Presbyterian for several years was seventy years of age in 1824. The whole spectrum of literate behavior was apparent, though many of the women's names were not reported, often indicating that their church membership resided elsewhere. Many of these older women may well have been born in Africa, importing that culture with them into the classroom. Others were doubtless already schooled and literate, but perhaps needed to log the school sessions for other purposes. Many were non-literate or semi-literate, their reading progress laborious, and their achievements noted and celebrated.

So the Sabbath-school Society flourished, founding mission-type schools in marginal areas. Clergy and laymen became gradually aware that, where females founded Sunday schools, a demand for preaching and settled clergy arose. The churches began to seek avidly their nominal constituents and the unaffiliated who were coming to Sunday school; church attendance and membership grew enormously during this period. In addition, reports noted that many male adults "pleaded" for the same schooling, suggesting that the female schools preceded the male. A few cents purchased membership in the female Society, a provision that allowed women of all ranks to participate, and a life membership, only $10, supported a fund for books and supplies. The book depository supplied spelling and lesson books, songbooks and song sheets, teachers' guides, printed copies of their constitution and rules, class registers, and reward tickets.

The goals of the society included a lending library, which made its appearance in 1823. The 1823 *Report* noted:

> A library has been recently formed for the accommodation of the four schools attached to the (Beekman Street Presbyterian) church, the usefulness of which has just begun to dawn on the minds of our beloved charge. Our school is more flourishing than it has been at any period since its formation. (p. 8)

The library's 409-volume collection was initially housed at the Philomathean Academy at 108 William Street, later at 66 Ann Street, near Brick Church. Books could be borrowed or purchased by a "schollar" who earned that privilege by making progress in her schooling. Thus, one could purchase James's *Sunday School Teachers Guide* for twenty-five cents, Bickersteth's *Scripture Help* for eighteen cents, and *Little Henry and his Bearer* for twelve cents (Gillespie, 1982, pp. 359-70; Margo & Villafor, 1987, pp. 873-96).[5] Many of these books and tracts were English or Scottish, having reappeared promptly on the market following the cessation of hostilities after the War of 1812 when the nationalistic fervor to produce American works was still in its infancy.

These female schools offered an entire culture of schooling, books, and library to a working and dependent population of black and white women and girls, which implicitly offered inclusion in a larger Christian community along with, perhaps, membership in a church. Females of nominal or no church affiliation, however, may well have been attracted permanently to a favorite teacher's church. Reading and writing in general, however, enabled and benefited these females in terms of reading handbills, newspapers, letters, accounts, bank drafts, wills, and contracts of labor and indenture. At the same time, of course, Bible reading, with exhortation and moral lessons, encouraged moral behavior. Schooling conferred additional benefits on the population of shop-girls, pieceworkers, household servants, and slaves. Small and supportive female group instruction encouraged women to become introspective about their beliefs, their values, and their behavior, thus according respect and dignity to the investigation of their emotional and intellectual attributes in matters other than religion. At the same time, the rigor of learning in the company of trained but unpaid teachers, the class schedule on the only day free of labor, and the textbook titles suggest a fair amount of intellectual effort.

Classes formed a social grouping where women and girls sang and prayed together, as in a liturgical church setting, and then recited and solved problems in small groups that crossed generational, class, and even racial lines. Evangelicalism, sometimes considered a religious expression of romanticism in America, validated the ability of untrained, and even ordinary, minds of whatever sex or race, to reason in matters of religion. The Sunday school classes, imperfectly sorted by age, race, and reading ability, established a norm of structured learning. They provided a library for urban women and girls who had limited access to books and schooling due to status, class, race, language, the demands of labor, or other social isolation (including newness to the city or lack of church membership), and conferred on them the title of "schollar."

Sunday school additionally offered opportunities for women of all ranks and both races to become instructors, to experiment with pedagogical methods, and to offer authoritative religious instruction; the records indicate that black teachers and black assistants drew other blacks to the schools. In addition, black females with diplomas from the schools began to teach. Thirty females received diplomas from St. George's School in 1826. One was Mary Freeman, described as "the fifth child from one family that has received this award"; two women of that name taught in African Free School No. 7 on White Street in the 1830s (New York Female Union Society to Promote Sabbath Schools, 1826, p. 33). A black Methodist "auxilliary" teacher withdrew from Female School No. 9 in May 1816 to "assist in the school established by Brick Church" (Methodist Sunday School Union, 1816). Catherine Ombony received her diploma in 1823 and proceeded to teach "a class of small colored children"; the graduating class of Oliver Street Baptist Church in 1826 numbered fifty-nine, some of whom were members of the African Female Tract Association.

Limited evidence indicates that some schools contained classes of blacks and whites together, older women and younger girls together, and even males and females together. School No. 20 at Harlem had seventy black students "of both sexes" in 1817; the Wesleyan Seminary on Crosby Street had one "colored adult" with a number of white children; and School No. 4 had a "colored woman aged seventy-six" in classes which were held in John Griscom's schoolroom but taught by Dutch Reformed women. Thus at a time when blacks were deliberately withdrawing into separate churches of their own creation, the Sunday schools represented an alternative. They offered instruction to almost anyone who walked in the door—many deliberately left an empty chair for a stranger— and provided a mutually supportive social setting that depressed those factors that had made women and girls different from each other in terms of race, social status, age, and occupation, and re-defined them as a community of learners and teachers (George, C. V., 1973; Lapsansky, E. J., 1980; Lerner, G., 1979, pp. 15-30).

The Sunday schools wrought other changes in New York City. Membership in the Sabbath-school Society was available to females of the middle rank and lower, a decided change from the upper classes who had founded the Widows' Society in 1797. In addition, churches erected after 1816 adapted their building designs to include long, low basements for Sunday school instruction, such as the first St. Phillip's Episcopal Church on Collect (now Centre) Street, dedicated in August 1818. Its lay reader, then deacon, then ordained clergyman, then bishop, was Peter Williams, the son of Peter and Molly Williams of John Street Methodist and Zion African Methodist Episcopal Church. The First Colored Presbyterian (Shiloh) Church, founded in 1822 by black preacher and newspaper publisher Samuel E. Cornish, originated in an "independent chapel" in a black community on Rose Street near the waterfront. Its original building housed both the black Presbyterian meeting and a volunteer fire company, both of which possessed Sunday schools in 1816. The black Presbyterians constructed their church, which allotted space for a school, at 119 Elm (now Lafayette) Street in 1824 with the help of funds from the New York City Presbytery (Allen, 1964, pp. 62-63).[6]

Teaching poor females to read and write constituted a political statement, but the Sunday schools also fostered more explicit political expressions. The Female Union gathered at a Presbyterian Church on Murray Street on April 8, 1818, for its second annual meeting, a typical ceremonial occasion demonstrating solidarity, like the meetings and parades of craftsmen, militia companies, and political parties. The women celebrated a year's progress with songs and speeches, refreshments, and awards and diplomas for graduates. That evening's program included an anti-slavery hymn of twenty verses that scans in 4/4 time, probably sung to the tune of a well-known hymn. Sung by African-American women, it included the following verses:

> The white man camewith wicked hands
>   and stole our race away
> To wander long in foreign lands
>   and far from home to stray.
> The children of that very race who
>   gave our fathers pain
> Are striving in the strength of grace
>   to wipe away the stain.

One verse revealed early involvement in newly emergent back-to-Africa sentiments:

> Who knows but yet in Afric's wild
>   A Christian black may sow
> The word of God, pure, undefiled
>   And a rich harvest grow! (New York Female Union Society to Promote Sabbath Schools, 1817, pp. 4, 5)

The hymn, sung at evening meetings where white and black females met, talked, ate, and drank, testified to an anti-slavery agenda and the common grounds on which black and white females gathered—literacy and libraries. The potential for division apparently resided in religion, so the coalition of women permitted at meetings "no discussion on controverted points of religion" (New York Female Union Society to Promote Sabbath Schools, 1827).

The unity of any federal system that cut across social and racial, as well as political and denominational, lines required strict rules, a constitution, and by-laws. The Female Sabbath School Union had five officers, a committee of eleven, and 660 paid annual subscribers; teachers were not paid. The managers were enormously well-informed and innovative, noting the need for shoes and clothing at one school, calling elsewhere for a superintendent in a new school for "colored Adults begun on Long Island" (New York Female Union Society to Promote Sabbath Schools, 1817).

Why did Sunday schools teach blacks in such great numbers and teach both whites and blacks separately and together? Literacy was the condition and prerequisite for unsupervised freedom required by a series of arcane New York emancipation laws between 1799 and 1817. The New York State Assembly made finite the condition of slavery for African-Americans born after July 4, 1799, with servitude to age twenty-eight for males and age twenty-five for females. Slavery bound slave owners into a contract for slaves' education, and the owner or his estate retained perpetual liability if manumitting a slave over the age of forty-five unless a bond were given or the freed person were guaranteed to support himself or herself. This led to the practice known as abandonment by which a slave owner legally divested himself or herself of ownership and responsibility by filing with the courts a certificate of abandonment. Babies, young people, and adults were all abandoned in this way, terminating the liability, if not the actual relationship. Older slaves, manumitted or abandoned, who were unable to support themselves, along with orphans and indigents, migrated to the supervision of the city's overseers of the poor. The Almshouse, or Poorhouse, was supported by municipal and state poor taxes, so the Corporation had a vested interest in holding former slave owners on their bonds (Klebaner, 1955; Zilversmit, 1967, see chap. 7).

The law also required that, whether the services were retained or hired out, a slave by age eighteen was to be "able to read the holy scriptures" or be given "four quarters schooling"; if not taught to read, the slave could be released from servitude at that age. Subsequent laws reiterated the literacy requirement, and laws of 1816 and 1817 specifically revised the manumission age to twenty-one years for both scxcs rather than twenty-eight and twenty-five. New York City manumission records show a gradual increase in manumissions and abandonments after the 1799 law and a sharp increase between 1816 and 1820 as blacks born after 1799 began to reach ages eighteen through twenty-one, at which point they were to have been taught to read. Several hundred manumissions took place in New York City between 1799 and 1817; manumittors included families whose politics or church government espoused anti-slavery sentiments long before they actually freed their slaves (Yoshpe, 1941, pp. 78-107).

Some African-Americans purchased their own freedom, of course, such as William Lambert, a Methodist lay preacher, who purchased his freedom for $250 in 1815. Five years later, Lambert co-founded the Bethel African Methodist Episcopal Church, along with the Reverend Henry Harden, sent to New York for that purpose by Bishop Richard Allen of Philadelphia (Yoshpe, 1941, p. 84). Bethel Church took shape in the summer of 1820 in "a school-room [on] Mott Street," and by 1822 this church had 347 members, a little over half the number of members in all the eight black churches. Other blacks purchased a family member's freedom but in so doing became legally responsible for that person; attesting to the schooling of the family member terminated the purchaser's liability. For example, Thomas Charnock, a carpenter, purchased for $400 in 1813 his sixteen year old son, George, and guaranteed the son's ability to maintain himself, deposing that his son had been "well educated in the Arts and Sciences in the City of New York under the superintendence and direction of good teachers" (Yoshpe, 1941, p. 80).

The Sunday schools' evidence of large accessions of black children and adults coincides with the climax of the emancipation laws. Schools and reading began with children, but adults quickly flooded the classes, and the names and locations of the schools are known, if not the names of all the "schollars." Thus the law encouraged manumission by rewarding manumittors in economic terms, because they could free themselves from the costs of schooling and from liability for those unschooled, and then rehire freed slaves for wages. At the same time, the law encouraged schooling because minimal literacy freed former slaves from a perpetual and galling relationship in which local commissioners of the poor possessed continuing oversight of those manumitted. Minimal literacy for both female and male African-Americans stood as the actual measure by which they sloughed off any residual patriarchal oversight from city and state and acquired true status as free men and women.

The Sunday schools thus became a magnet for manumittors, who could opt out of the paternal care of freed slaves by institutionalizing their education in such schools, and simultaneously became a magnet for slaves and freedmen since it offered common schooling on Sunday, the only day free of labor. The female schools had their own evangelical and charitable reasons for attracting new "schollars," welcomed blacks of all ages, and quickly swelled to become several times larger than the four schools of the Free-School Society (which before 1820 taught about 1,000 white males and about 100 young black males in the African Free School).

Implicit in Sunday schooling was the knowledge that society was filled with laboring children, both black and white, who could not be schooled on weekdays. School on Sunday seemed a systemic panacea for preventing or curing in these children vice, pauperism, or dependency and for promoting socialization, quasi-citizenship, and female nurturing and instruction for the next generation. The city of New York was interested in reducing dependency and generating taxpayers, and the Minutes of the Common Council recorded very practical sentiments:

> The Introduction of Sunday Schools throughout the various parts of our city has had a very salutary effect upon the minds and morals of the poorer classes of society. . . . [E]ducation . . . not only . . . prevents its recipients from being idle consumers, but promotes their becoming active producers, in the common stock of national wealth; and thus, while it diminishes the demand for taxation, it increases the supply from which Taxes are to be drawn. (City of New York, 1917, Feb. 15, 1819 and March 9, 1829)

This account of the earliest Sunday schools concludes in 1826-27, when Sunday schools began to metamorphose into agencies of churches, aimed increasingly at training the next generation of congregants in their responsibilities. At mid-decade, all schooling of a religious nature was separated from state support on newly-articulated grounds that the U.S. Constitution prevented New York state from allowing its tax revenues to be used by religious institutions.[7] In the name of democratization for white males and specifically to benefit the Free-School Society (ancestor of New York's present day public schools), the many weekday and Sunday schools for blacks and females lost the possibility of sharing state tax revenues.

I want to conclude with a comment that we continue to seek and take into custody records that bring African-American culture and life onto the stage of history, such as black and white females working together to create schools, libraries, and churches. I did not expect to find the relationship between manumission and the large numbers of black students learning to read and to use books and libraries in the earliest Sunday schools in New York City, but there it was, awaiting discovery, due to the availability of records. We can do more to promote access to them by users, and to promote the recruitment and training of African-American librarians and archivists who are alive to the research potential of such records.

But let us also continue to examine records already in custody and think of new ways to use and disseminate them; most of the records I used have been in custody for generations without much comment about female groups that literally invented schooling and libraries for black and white females in the age of mandated manumission. Compare conclusions in this discussion with the comments of a senior historian who wrote in 1981:

> [T]here was remarkably little interest in black education displayed by individual white philanthropists or by white human institutions [which displayed] general satisfaction with the activities of the Manumission Society, coupled with the availability of state educational funds for the African Free Schools. (Curry, 1981, p. 154)

We can all gain by re-examining documentary sources on several levels: those that relate the activities of black and white women in cities, particularly in religious institutions; those that record the names of males as leaders of institutions in which females—described officially as auxilliary—were actually innovative and energetic, and doing most of the work; those that give a corporate name and voice to ordinary females who seem to have been engaged in extraordinary activities; and those that demonstrate the cultural conditions for the growth of racism and, conversely, show its unexpected absence.

Notes

[1] This article is derived from portions of Marilyn H. Pettit, "Women, Sunday Schools, and Politics: Early National New York City, 1797-1827" (Ph.D. dissertation, New York University, 1991).

[2] The New York Sunday School Union, founded in 1816, was a separate white male organization that opted to serve as an umbrella society for all Sunday schools and counted the female union's students in its enumeration.

[3] Mary W. Morgan married Methodist clergyman Thomas Mason in 1817. "Brother Tommy" Mason later became the book agent of the Methodist bookroom in New York City and collected and published Methodist camp-meeting and revival songs as *Zion's Songster*. Their daughter, Elizabeth Mason North, was the mother of social gospel advocate Frank Mason North.

[4] The early reports identified only a few females by their first names or initials; later reports, such as that of 1823, named those who excelled.

[5] On children's literature, see, for example, Joanna B. Gillespie, "Carrie or the Child in the Rectory: 19th-Century Episcopal Sunday School Prototype," *Historical Magazine of the Protestant Episcopal Church 51* (1982), 359-70.

[6] Samuel E. Cornish, 1793-1858, founded and published *Freedom's Journal* and *The Colored American*, black newspapers published in New York City in the 1820s.

[7] "Report of the Law Committee on the Distribution of the Common School Fund, April 1, 1825," *Minutes of the Common Council . . . XV*, 1825-26. A broader discussion is found in Leonard W. Levy, *The Establishment Clause: Religion and the First Amendment* (New York: MacMillan, 1986); and in an older work, Evarts B. Green, *Religion and the State: The Making and Testing of an American Tradition* (New York: New York University Press, 1941).

References

Allen, J. E. (1964). *The Negro in New York.* New York: Exposition Press.

Anstice, H. (1911). *History of St. George's Church in the City of New York, 1752-1911.* New York: Harper & Bros.

Bethune, D., & Bethune, J. (1816). *The power of faith: The life and writing of the late Mrs. Isabella Graham of New York.* New York: John S. Taylor.

Bethune, G. W. (1863). *Memoirs of Mrs. Joanna Bethune.* New York: Harper & Bros.

Bethune, J. (1838). *The unpublished letters and correspondence of Mrs. Isabella Graham from the year 1767 to 1814, selected and arranged by her daughter.* New York: John S. Taylor.

Bourne, W. O. (1870). *History of the Public School Society of the City of New York.* New York: William Wood.

Boylan, A. (1988). *Sunday school: The formation of an American institution, 1790-1880.* New Haven, CT: Yale University Press.

City of New York. (1917). *Minutes of the Common Council of the City of New York, 1784-1831* (vol. 10, pp. 244 ff.). New York: M. B. Brown.

City of New York. (1917). Report of the Law Committee on the distribution of the common public school fund. *Minutes of the Common Council of the City of New York, 1825-1826* (vol. 15). New York: M. B. Brown.

Curry, L. (1981). *The free Black in urban America, 1800-1850: The shadow of the dream.* Chicago, IL: University of Chicago Press.

George, C. V. (1973). *Segregated sabbaths: Richard Allen and the emergence of independent Black churches, 1760-1840.* New York: Oxford University Press.

Gillespie, J. B. (1982). Carrie, or the child in the rectory: 19th century Episcopal Sunday school prototype. *Historical Magazine of the Protestant Episcopal Church, 51*(4), 359-370.

Green, E. B. (1941). *Religion and the state: The making and testing of an American tradition.* New York: New York University Press.

Klebaner, B. J. (1955). American manumission laws and the responsibility for supporting slaves. *Virginia Magazine of History and Biography, 63,* 443-453.

Lapsansky, E. J. (1980). Since they got those separate churches: Afro-Americans and racism in Jacksonian Philadelphia. *American Quarterly, 32*(1), 54-78.

Lerner, G. (1979). The lady and the mill-girl: Changes in the status of women in the age of Jackson. In G. Lerner (Ed.), *The majority finds its past: Placing women in history.* New York: Oxford University Press.

Levy, L. W. (1986). *The establishment clause: Religion and the First Amendment.* New York: MacMillan.

Lynn, R. W., & Wright, E. (1980). *The big little school: 200 years of the Sunday school* (2d ed.). Birmingham, AL: Religious Educational Press.

Margo, R. A., & Villaflor, G. C. (1987). The growth of wages in antebellum America: New evidence. *Journal of Economic History, 47*(4), 873-896.

Methodist Sunday School Union. (1816). *Records of the New York Methodist-Episcopal Church, 1768-1821.* Unpublished manuscript records in the New York Public Library archives.

Moseley, T. R. (1963). *A history of the New York Manumission Society, 1785-1849.* Unpublished doctoral dissertation, New York University.

New York Female Union Society to promote Sabbath Schools. (1817). *Annual report* (1st ed.). New York: J. Seymour.

New York Female Union Society to promote Sabbath Schools. (1820). *Annual report* (4th ed.). New York: J. Seymour.

New York Female Union Society to promote Sabbath Schools. (1824). *1823 report.* New York: J. Seymour.

New York Female Union Society to promote Sabbath Schools. (1826). *Annual report.* New York: J. Seymour.

New York Female Union Society to Promote Sabbath Schools. (1827). *Constitution and rules of the New York Female Union Society for the Promotion of Sabbath schools.* New York: J. Seymour.

New York Friends Society. (1816). *Minutes of the New York Friends monthly meeting, 1806-1816.* Unpublished manuscript records of New York Historical Society, Haviland Records Room.

New York Historical Society. (1922). *Records, minutes and reports, Society for the Relief of Poor Widows with Small Children, New York Historical Society, 1797-1830.* Unpublished manuscript records of New York Historical Society.

North, E. M. (1870). *Consecrated talents: Or, the life of Mrs. Mary W. Mason* (with an introduction by Bishop Janes). New York: Carlton & Lanahan.

Pettit, M. H. (1991). *Women, Sunday schools, and politics: Early national New York City, 1797-1827.* Unpublished doctoral dissertation, New York University.

Rice, E. W. (1917). *The Sunday-school movement, 1780-1917, and the American Sunday-school Union, 1817-1917.* Philadelphia, PA: American Sunday-School Union.

Rosenwaike, I. (1972). *Population history of New York.* Syracuse, NY: Syracuse University Press.

Stone, J. S. (1848). *A memoir of the life of James Milnor, D. D., late Rector of St. George's Church, New York.* New York: American Tract Society.

Tyng, C. R. (1890). *Record of the life and work of the Reverend Stephen Higginson Tyng and history of St. George's Church, to the close of his rectorship.* New York: E. P. Dutton.

Tyng, S. H. (1860). *Forty years' experience in Sunday-schools.* New York: Sheldon & Co.

Yoshpe, H. B. (1941). Record of slave manumissions in New York in the colonial and early national period. *Journal of Negro History, 26*(1), 78-107.

Zilversmit, A. (1967). *The first emancipation: The abolition of slavery in the North.* Chicago, IL: University of Chicago Press.

The Founding & Prevalence of African-American Social Libraries & Historical Societies, 1828-1918

Gatekeepers of Early Black History, Collections, & Literature

ફ Rosie L. Albritton ફ

T he rise of African-American literary and library societies between 1828 and 1874 is characteristic of the "self-improvement" movement during the early- to mid-nineteenth century. The founding and activities of these societies fits the definition of "social libraries" as described in the history of library service during the early colonial and ante-bellum periods in the United States. While white Americans were setting up reading rooms, literary and debating societies, church literary groups, and early libraries before the Civil War, African-Americans founded over fifty counterpart literary and library societies. In most major cities of this period, African-Americans were prohibited from using libraries, attending lectures, or participating in debates, and they formed their own cultural, improvement, and educational societies.

McMullen (1987) referred to these groups as "social libraries" in his study of early libraries in the northeastern United States within the following context: "A few social libraries were established by free blacks in the Northeast; however, these seem to have been general in content, similar to the social libraries established by whites" (p. 326). This statement by McMullen appears to be the only reference in the literature by "mainstream" white library historians to African-Americans organizing early social libraries in their communities.

Porter (1936, 1943, 1984) has written extensively of the existence of early African-American literary societies and reading rooms (with documentation from primary sources—i.e., minutes of meetings, newspaper articles, bylaws, charters, and letters). She does not specifically identify these groups as typical "social libraries" of any type, such as "subscription libraries" or "association libraries," nor does she attempt to place them within the context of early libraries and the evolution of American library history.

Other researchers of African-American history and literature (Bontemps, 1944; DuBois, 1899; Foner, 1983; Good, 1932; Greene, 1968; Joyce, 1975; Kessler, 1955; Sinnette, 1989; Spady, 1974; Wesley, 1952; Willson, 1969; Porter, 1936, 1939, 1943, 1971) have published findings that support the existence of over fifty counterpart African-American literary and library societies in mostly minority or black sponsored publications with limited circulation and exposure. The early African-American literary groups were also associated with many pioneering African-American bibliophiles such as David Ruggles and Robert Adger. The historical and learned societies that began during the last quarter of the nineteenth century were also heavily influenced by later African-American bibliophiles including Henry Proctor Slaughter, Daniel Alexander Payne Murray, Jesse E. Moorland, John Edward Bruce, and Arthur A. Schomburg.

The purpose of this chapter is to review the founding of these early literary and historical societies by African-Americans within the context of early social libraries of the eighteenth and nineteenth centuries as predecessors to American public libraries as defined by Jewett (1851), Joeckel (1935), Shera (1949), and McMullen (1958, 1965, 1985, 1987). In addition to citing the founding of these organized groups, this chapter also acknowledges the associations of influential bibliophiles and the impact of their activities on the preservation and establishment of unique and rare collections of African-American literature and history. Another objective is to develop a chronology of the founding of various types of African-American literary, debating, reading, and historical societies.

CHARACTERISTICS OF SOCIAL LIBRARIES

Shera (1949) defined the early social library as follows:

> Generically and reduced to its simplest constituent elements, the social library was nothing more than [a] voluntary association of individuals who had contributed money toward a common fund to be used for the purchase of books. . . . Two principal types of social libraries have been distinguished: 1) proprietary and 2) subscription, which includes association, society, and mercantile libraries. (pp. 57-58)

The social library movement began in the fourth decade of the eighteenth century. By 1775, each of the New England States had at least one such institution. By the end of the Colonial period the social library had demonstrated a strength that promised survival where earlier public library forms had failed (Shera, 1949). These libraries were regularly described as public libraries, although none of them met the now accepted definition of a public library as an institution free to all citizens.

The term "social library," used throughout the literature of library history, is defined differently among writers. While most agree that certain libraries were "social," they disagree as to whether others come within the meaning of the word. Eaton (1961) alleged that Jewett, in his 1851 report, may have been the first person to use the term. Jewett (1851) referred to "social libraries, including athenaeums, lyceums, young men's associations, mechanics' institutions, mercantile, etc."

Joeckel (1935) divides the social libraries into two groups: the first class, based on the joint stock principle, required actual ownership of the property of the library; the second class required only the payment of an annual fee or subscription. This definition, according to Eaton (1961), appears in contemporary discussions of "social libraries." However, Thompson (1952) accepts only one class of the Joeckel definition for social libraries. Thompson argues that since the young men of the mercantile libraries and young men's associations united as individuals, not as partners, and since their agreements were not like the social compacts of the early proprietary libraries, their libraries should not be called social libraries. Shera (1949) explained that the terminology has never been standardized, and that he followed Joeckel closely in *Foundations of the Public Library* as "the only one who, in print, [had] seriously considered that matter and because it is time that there be definitions that are generally accepted" (p. 58).

McMullen (1965) describes the social library as one formed by an association of people who band together to provide themselves books of a general or miscellaneous nature. Broadly speaking, the term has also referred to a library owned by people who have other purposes as well (perhaps holding a lecture series), or for a collection owned by one group for the benefit of another (as when businessmen supported and directed an apprentices' library), or for an association formed to buy books of a specialized nature (as when a social law library was organized).

The first class of these libraries, "proprietary libraries," based on the joint stock principle, involved the ownership of shares in the property of the library. The second class required merely the payment of an annual fee or subscription which entitled the user to membership in the association. Even this elementary classification is subject to some qualification since many of the proprietary libraries provided for annual subscriptions by persons who were not shareowners or "proprietors" (Joeckel, 1935). In this chapter, the term "social libraries" includes all libraries operated by a voluntary association for the use of adults and children and which contained books on a variety of subjects. This definition permits the inclusion of literary, debating, improvement, and other societies with reading rooms and/or lecture series for educational, cultural, and philosophical study. On the other hand, this definition excludes libraries belonging to religious organizations if the books were mainly religious in nature, or others of a specialized subject matter such as medicine or law; it also excludes mercantile and mechanics groups and all libraries owned by schools or colleges.

The following terms review the types of libraries associated with nineteenth-century library history:

- **Association Libraries:** voluntary associations of individuals who contributed money to buy books for common use. There might be an initial fee for joining the group in addition to the annual subscription fee. These libraries, usually referred to as "subscription or association" libraries, consisted of people grouped according to interest; debating societies, philosophical societies, social and literary clubs, groups of clerks and artisans all formed association libraries. The ladies' library associations, the young men's library associations, and the public school library associations exemplified association libraries that provided books for the people who belonged to their groups.

- **Athenaeums:** scientific and literary associations which frequently established libraries for the use of their members. Such libraries could be conducted as association libraries but were also commonly organized as proprietary libraries which sold stock to members. The name "Athenaeum" does not indicate a particular kind of library organization.

- **Circulating Libraries:** commercially operated collections of books that could be borrowed for a set fee per week, per quarter, per year, or per item read. These libraries, called "subscription" libraries due to annual or quarterly subscription charges, featured two kinds of libraries to which the term "subscription" may be applied. The difference between those libraries referred to as "subscription and circulating" and those called "subscription and association" is the difference between a business operation and a voluntary organization which provided books for its own group. Circulating libraries were sometimes part of small businesses such as millinery or stationery stores. When the businesses were operated on the basis of a charge for each book read, they were not unlike our present rental libraries.

- **Endowed Libraries:** libraries that provided books at no expense to the people who used them. These libraries might take several forms such as reference collections available to scholars only or free public libraries open to all members of a community. In this period, an endowed library met all expenses from its endowment fund.

- **Free Libraries:** libraries available without fee to the community served. These libraries might be supported by endowment, or by appropriations from the town, or by taxes levied on citizens, but they did not collect subscription fees or membership dues of any sort.

- **Ladies' Libraries:** libraries supported by associations of women. These libraries began to flourish about the middle of the nineteenth century and continued well into the twentieth. In many cases they were transferred to the city as the foundation for a free tax-supported public library.

- **Mechanics' and Apprentices' Libraries:** libraries that served young artisans, those still serving their apprenticeships, and those who had just begun to work as mechanics. These libraries were sometimes financed by the organizations which employed the youths.
- **Mercantile Libraries:** libraries intended primarily for the use of young merchants' clerks. In the beginning, membership was limited to such clerks. At a later period opened to general readers, these libraries also sponsored lectures and classes. Other libraries formed by groups of young men, such as the Young Men's Association Libraries and Athenaeums, resembled the Mercantile Libraries and are often counted with them for statistical purposes.
- **Proprietary Libraries:** libraries based on the joint stock principle involving the actual ownership of shares in the property of the library, the shares usually being transferable to others by sale or will.
- **Special Libraries:** a term that seldom appears in early works, libraries limiting their collections to a given subject. It should be noted, however, that libraries devoted to medicine and law date from an early period.
- **Social Libraries:** a term which was used to encompass a number of different kinds of libraries. Jewett (1851) used the term in his report to refer to athenaeums, lyceums, young men's associations, and mechanics and mercantile libraries. These were not free libraries but were public in the sense that they were open to any member of the community who cared to meet the requirements of dues (Eaton, 1961).

SCOPE, LIMITATIONS, & METHODOLOGY

In this section, the term "founding" indicates the same term used by McMullen (1958, 1987). In his study of the prevalence of libraries in the Northeastern states, McMullen (1987) suggests that the date of founding of a library is significant since the typical social library of this period was short-lived, and most records indicate that much more information [had] been recorded about the beginning or "births" of many libraries than about their "lives" of activities or even their demise. Sometimes the only proofs of their existence were facts about their founding. In 1958, McMullen used the term "founding" for three events: "(1) the meeting at which a group decides to form a library and elects officers; (2) the incorporation of the group [in other words, the granting of a charter]; and (3) the opening of the library for use" (p. 2). In the present study, the date of the organizational meeting was used, also declared by McMullen as the "choice . . . based on the assumption that meeting together is the act which most clearly expresses an intent to form a library" (p. 2). Therefore, the year 1828 is the beginning date for this chapter since it is the date of the first known Afro-American social library as reported by Porter (1936). The year 1918 is the terminal date for a similar reason; the literary and library societies eventually led to the founding of historical associations and learned societies and, by the early 1900s, several of these associations had been established. One of these groups, The Negro Library Association, was founded in 1914 by Schomburg and some of his associates from the Negro Society for Historical Research, also cofounded by Schomburg in 1911 (Sinnette, 1989). In 1918, members of these groups sponsored the first annual exhibition of books, manuscripts, and engravings, and published an impressive catalog, a historically significant highlight of that era for Afro-American history, literature, and librarianship.

The study involved searching and reviewing the printed literature available through the library and archival resources at the University of Illinois at Urbana-Champaign. Reproductions of bylaws, preambles, constitutions, catalogs, speeches, and other documents associated with the literary and library groups, or the bibliophiles and scholars connected with them, were located in the available printed resources. The main purpose of this research is descriptive—i.e., to identify printed secondary sources for evidence of the founding and prevalence of early Afro-American social libraries.

AFRO-AMERICAN SOCIAL LIBRARIES, 1828-1874

The rise of African-American literary and library societies between 1828 and 1874 parallels the era of social libraries in American history and of public library services in the early colonial and antebellum periods. These pioneering societies also cultivated a literary culture that nurtured the development of some of the earliest known black history collections (Kessler, 1955). During the nineteenth century, almost all libraries were established by and for whites. However, since African-Americans in nearly all Northern cities were prohibited from using libraries, attending lectures, or participating in debates with whites outside the ranks of abolitionists, blacks formed their own self-improvement societies. In the late 1820s and through the 1830s to the 1850s, literary clubs, debating groups, and library companies emerged in every urban community of the North, Northeast, and Middle States with a sizable black population. These societies were founded in Philadelphia, New York, Boston, Pittsburgh, Buffalo, New Bedford, Providence, Newark, and Washington, DC through the 1830s. In the 1840s and 1850s, they were also founded in Rochester, Schenectady, Cincinnati, Columbus, and Detroit. These organizations were known not only as literary societies but also as debating and reading-room societies. In these locations, both white and black newspapers and magazines printed reports of their activities. Porter (1936) identified forty-five early Afro-American literary and library societies: nine in Philadelphia, six in New York City, five in Boston, and the remainder spread among the cities of the Northeast. The majority of these societies were composed of men but a few also admitted women and some were for women only.

The Free African Society, organized in Philadelphia in 1787, seems to have been the first society organized by blacks. This was a group established for mutual aid rather than literary purposes. Soon after the birth of this society, other beneficial organizations appeared in various cities. Blacks also organized *Bible,* educational, welfare, missionary, and moral reform societies (Porter, 1936).

As shown in Appendix A, this study revealed the founding of close to fifty of these societies from 1828 to 1845. The names varied from reading rooms, literary societies, debating societies, moral and mental improvement societies, to literary circles. Appendix B indicates the geographical distribution of these early "social libraries" as predominantly in the northeastern states with almost half from New York and Pennsylvania.

The period from 1834 to 1839 represents the highest rate of "foundings," as twenty-four societies (55 percent of the total number documented between 1828 and 1845) were organized during this time. Porter (1936) explained some of the intentions, purposes, and motivations that encouraged the founding of these groups:

> Some of the expressed reasons for the organization of these institutions were the stimulation of reading and the spreading of useful knowledge by providing libraries and reading rooms, the encouragement of expressed literary efforts by providing audiences as critics and channels of publication for their literary productions and the training of future orators and leaders by means of debate. Thus their activities as a whole were educational. . . . There were certain existing conditions inherent in the race relations of the times which led to the establishment of these societies. . . . The presence of Negroes in white literary organizations was not wanted. . . . New institutions were formed in these places as a result of this discrimination. Thus, Negroes began to form societies of their own in which they could have fuller and freer discussions and freedom of activity and control. (p. 557)

Several societies cited regularly in the literature due to significant historical contributions include the first group established in a community, the largest membership, affiliation with a political movement, the prominence of leaders or members, publications, and recognition by the press (both white and black). Some of these "better-known" groups are highlighted as representative of Afro-American social libraries.

The earliest black literary society was founded in Philadelphia on March 20, 1828 as the "Reading Room Society" (Willson, 1969). William Whipper, one of the prominent blacks of the day, was the guiding spirit of the group. He served as secretary during the first year and on May 2, 1828 delivered a public address which was published in an 1828 issue of *The Freedom's Journal* and reprinted in Porter's anthology of *Early Negro Writing: 1700-1837.* This document reveals that the library consisted of books on ancient, modern, and ecclesiastical history, plus *The Laws of Pennsylvania, The Freedom's Journal, The Genius of Universal Emancipation,* and other similar works. The Reading Room Society collected monthly dues and an initiation fee and conducted weekly meetings when members received and returned books and read and discussed the readings. Allocations of funds for the purchase of books were as follows:

"[A]ll of the money received except that which went for wood, light, and rent was to be expended for the purpose of securing books." These books were to be placed in the care of a "librarian" who was instructed "to deliver to said members alternately such books as they shall demand with strict regard that no member shall keep a book out of the library longer than a week, without paying a fine prescribed in the constitution, unless an apology for sickness, or absence be given—those shall be the only excuses." (Porter, 1971)

In New York City, the leading group among literary and library societies was the New York Philomathean Society, organized in 1830. Porter (1936) reported that, by 1837, this society had acquired about 600 volumes for its circulating library and solicited donations of books and money for the purchase of books and for subscriptions to periodicals.

The earliest reports of literary societies for women cite the "Female Literary Society" of Philadelphia, organized in 1831. Other documented female societies include: the "Afric-American Female Intelligence Society" in Boston in 1832; the "Minerva Literary Society" in Philadelphia in 1834; the "Ladies Literary Society" in New York City in 1834; the "Female Literary Society" in New York City in 1835; and the "Sarah M. Douglas Literary Circle" in Philadelphia in 1859 (Porter, 1936; Willson, 1969; Foner, 1983). Members of the Female Literary Society of Philadelphia met every Tuesday night for the purpose of "mental improvement in moral and literary pursuits." The majority of the ladies wrote original literary pieces which were placed anonymously in a box and later criticized. A poem called "Farewell" and signed by "Ada" appeared in the *Liberator* for June 30, 1832. The Minerva Literary Society of Philadelphia had thirty ladies present at its first meeting in October 1834. The group held weekly meetings; activities consisted of "readings and recitations of original and selected pieces." The last of the ante-bellum women's societies in Philadelphia was the Sarah M. Douglas Literary Circle formed in September 1859 and named in honor of a teacher of young black women (Foner, 1983).

Kessler's (1955) description of the "Philadelphia Library Company of Colored Persons," founded in 1833 and incorporated in 1836, strongly supports the idea that these early Afro-American literary societies were synonymous with "social libraries" and among the first depositories of American black literature. The "Philadelphia Library Company of Colored Persons" was established as counterpart to the Library Company of Philadelphia. According to Abbot (1931), the Library Company of Philadelphia (1973) had its beginning in the "Junto Club" founded by Benjamin Franklin "for literary and scientific discussions, reading of original essays, poems, etc." Franklin's group, the "club of mutual improvement," paved the way for "social libraries" and "subscription libraries" in the United States. The Library Company is still in existence.

On January 1, 1833, the Philadelphia Library Company of Colored Persons was established. Willson (1841; 1969) reported the following as present and signing the constitution: Messrs. Frederick A. Hinton, James Needham

(Treasurer), James Cornish, Robert C. Gordon, Jr., John Dupee, William Whipper, J.C. Bowers, Charles Trulier, Robert Douglas, Jr., and James C. Matthews. Willson stated that these persons may be considered the founders of the first successful literary institution of this description established by colored persons in Philadelphia. The society, consisting of free black males, grew rapidly in membership. An announcement to the public concerning the society appeared in the *Genius of Universal Emancipation* for May 1833 and was reprinted by Porter in the *Journal of Negro Education* (1936). Excerpts of that announcement are given below:

> From the *U.S. Gazette*
> To the Public,
> We, the people of color of this city being deeply impressed with the necessity of promoting among our youth, a proper cultivation for literary pursuits and improvement of the faculties and powers of their minds, deem it necessary to state, for the information of our friends, where situated, that we have succeeded in organizing an institution under the title of the "Philadelphia Library Company of Colored Persons." . . . In accordance with which we most respectfully appeal to the friends of science and the people of color, for such books and other donations as will facilitate the object of this institution. . . . The following individuals are duly authorized to solicit and receive such donations in behalf of said company, as a liberal and enlightened public feel disposed to bestow.

The main objective of the Philadelphia Library Company of Colored Persons was to build up a collection of useful books on every subject for the benefit of its members and to educate the group by means of weekly lectures on literary and scientific subjects. By 1838, the library had 600 volumes and the society had about 150 members; the admission fee to the society was one dollar and the monthly assessment was twenty-five cents (Willson, 1969).

Kessler (1955) reported that the largest group, wielding the greatest influence and also organized in 1833, was the Phoenix Society of New York City. The expressed purpose of this group was "the diffusion of knowledge by means of lectures, debates, classes, reading rooms, circulating libraries, and literary production and criticism" (p. 224). The Phoenix Society, according to Porter (1936), was composed chiefly of young black men and had as its primary object "to promote the improvement of the colored people in morals, literature, and the mechanical arts" (p. 565). All persons who wished to promote the objects of the society and who were of good "moral character" could become members by paying a one dollar joining fee and twenty-five cents quarterly. The constitution and by-laws, published in 1835, were included in Porter's anthology (1971).

According to the constitution and by-laws, the Phoenix Society attempted large projects involving many duties for its members such as an attempt to raise $10,000 to erect a public building for a library, reading room, museum, and exhibition hall where black youths and others could enjoy lectures and other instruction on literature, mechanical arts, and morals. Ward societies were organized whereby members visited families within the ward and recorded demographic information for every black person including whether or not residents could read and write.   Each Ward group also maintained a circulating library for use at a moderate fee, organized lyceums, and promoted lectures on science.   Samuel E. Cornish, at one time librarian of the society, made vigorous efforts to build up the library.   He sent a letter which was printed in the *Colonizationist and Journal of Freedom* for February 1834 and reproduced by Porter in the *Journal of Negro Education* (1936).   Excerpts from Cornish's letter are as follows:

> A Library for the People of Color
>
> Messrs. Editors: Aware that you take lively interest in the subject of the improvement and elevation of our colored population, I am free to address you in behalf of a library and Reading Room lately opened by the executive committee of the Phoenix Society, for [its] benefit.   The Institution is located in spacious rooms, second story of the northwest corner of Canal and Mercer Streets. . . . The establishment of schools, of libraries, of reading rooms, and the delivery of public lectures for our benefit, I trust will be sown in good ground. . . . The time has come, which we sincerely hope our community will not stop to find fault with our oppressed people but turn their attention to their education and to the improvement of their condition.   Permit me, therefore, through your useful people, to solicit donations from the favored citizens of New York, in books, maps, papers, money, etc. . . . and I beg the benevolent ladies of our city who are first in good work not to forget us.   We shall thankfully receive from them any volumes which they may read and [lay] by, or any useful papers they can dispense with.
>
> As agent of the Society, I shall call on the wise and the good of our community—those who are blessed with all the privileges of enlightened civilization and religion, to bestow some of the blessings on the neglected and oppressed, by donating in maps, books and journals—and I pledge myself in the name of the society and as present **Librarian**, to make the best use of all gifts we may receive.
>
> Permit me to subscribe myself,
>
> Respectfully yours,
> Samuel E. Cornish
> December 7, 1833.

As a result of the above notice, a number of donations were acknowledged in a letter to *The Emancipator*, the New York anti-slavery newspaper, by Samuel E. Cornish, January 31, 1834 (Porter, 1936).

The Gilbert Lyceum, organized for literary and scientific purposes, appears to have been the first and maybe the only society to admit both males and females.   The founding meeting was held on January 31, 1841.   A series of lectures was delivered to the group, and membership was reported for 1841 as forty-one members (Porter, 1936).

Foner (1983) regarded the most noted ante-bellum Philadelphia African-American literary society as the "Banneker Institute," named after the African-American scientist Benjamin Banneker.   Founded in 1854 and constituted primarily of young men, by 1860 the institute had a library of 450 books. The Debating Society of the Banneker Institute has been noted as discussing both scholarly matters and events of the day. The institute's secretary, John C. White, Jr., kept careful minutes of its meetings and debates for many years, and these and other records have been preserved by the Historical Society of Pennsylvania. Although numerous other intellectual and moral societies were founded in Philadelphia following the birth of the "Reading Room Society" in 1828, none reached the stature of the Benjamin Banneker Institute. As of October 1854, there were thirty-seven members, four of whom were honorary. It was reported to be in existence as late as 1871. As a forerunner of the "Afro-American Historical Society," the "Banneker Institute" developed an outstanding collection of black Americana; as the institute declined, one surviving member, Robert Adger, managed to keep much of the material intact (Ball & Martin, 1981).

Robert M. Adger, a black book collector from Philadelphia, compiled one of the most outstanding libraries of black literature during the nineteenth century. His *Catalogue of Rare Books and Pamphlets* covers "Subjects Relating to the Past Condition of the Colored Race and Slavery in this Country." The American Negro Historical Society elected Adger president at the society's founding in 1897 (Josey & Shockley, 1977).

In New York City, Rochester, and other cities in the state of New York, similar attempts were made to form literary and library societies, debating clubs, and other self-improvement groups. The leading literary society in New York City, the New York Philomathean Society, was organized in 1830. The Philomathean Society was "devoted to the improvement of literature and useful knowledge." In 1837 it had acquired about 600 volumes for its circulating library (Porter, 1936).

The New York Garrison Literary Association appears to be the only society maintained primarily for black youth. Anyone of "good moral character" between the ages of "four and twenty by subscribing to the constitution and by paying twelve cents admission and one cent per week could become a member." The society was formed in early 1834.

David Ruggles, first black printer, bookseller, directory compiler, and editor of the first black magazine, *The Mirror of Liberty* (1838-1839), served on the executive committee and in other capacities for the New York Garrison Literary Association during 1834. The abolitionist press frequently printed Ruggles's trade bibliographies on the Negro and slavery (Kessler, 1955). As an officer of the New York Vigilance Committee, defender of freemen and fugitives, Ruggles compiled the *Slaveholder's Directory*, a listing of the names and addresses of pro-slavery lawyers, police, city officials, and other antagonists. Ruggles also worked for the Phoenix Society of New York and for *The Emancipator* as a traveling agent and regular editorial writer.

In 1834, Ruggles opened a bookshop near Broadway in lower Manhattan where he stocked a large collection of anti-slavery and anticolonization literature. Here he also maintained a circulating library and reading room for blacks. During most of his active public life, he led the Underground Railroad in New York City. In 1838, he sheltered Frederick Douglass after his escape from slavery, and in Ruggles's presence Douglass was married by the Rev. James W.C. Pennington (Porter, 1943). In 1845, Ruggles published *The Genius of Freedom*, the second Afro-American newspaper in the country, following James Russwurm's *Freedom Journal*. With all of these activities, Ruggles still managed to allow time to accumulate a significant body of black writing for posterity (Josey & Shockley, 1977).

In the Midwest, literary societies among African-Americans were fewer in size and number than in the East. The number of free African-Americans in the Midwest was much smaller; settlements of both whites and blacks were comparatively new in the early to mid-1800s. Many of the counties in these states were not developed until later in the nineteenth century. Records indicate that, by 1842, at least two groups with the name "Literary Society" were active in Cincinnati and Columbus; by 1845, the "Young Men's Lyceum and Debating Society" had been organized in Detroit, Michigan. Further research should reveal records of other groups in the major cities in the Midwest, particularly in Chicago, Cleveland, Toledo, and Louisville, Kentucky.

The present study revealed only one society originating as far west as Chicago, "The Association for the Study of Negro Life & History" in 1915, under the leadership of Carter G. Woodson. The other area just south of the northeastern states showing early foundings was in the Washington, DC/Baltimore area. The dates recorded for Washington, DC were from 1834 (the "Washington Conventional Society") to 1916 (the "Negro Book Collectors Exchange"). A chapter of the "Phoenix Society" and a group known as the "Young Men's Mental Improvement Society for the Discussion of Moral and Philosophical Questions of All Kinds," were also established in 1834 in Baltimore. The chronology in Appendix B illustrates the prevalence of the founding of the later historical and learned societies in the Washington, DC, area subsequent to the establishment of Howard University in 1865.

As a result of these societies, many African-Americans started private libraries and, by 1838, in Philadelphia and nearby cities, private collectors held an estimated 8,333 volumes (Porter, 1936). The lecturers who addressed these societies chose not only literary topics but also scientific and educational ones. These lectures prompted many blacks who could read to read further and those unable to read to learn how. Many of these addresses were printed and circulated widely throughout several states; some of them have been preserved in rare book collections. In addition, the evidence suggests that the lecture platform of these societies became the "workshop" and the "preparatory school" for many black anti-slavery activists.

With a few exceptions, these societies struggled to continue their activities. The existence of several societies in one city created competition for membership. Willson (1969) reported that several of the leaders of the Philadelphia societies favored a merger into one large organization. James Needham proposed a plan for "lectures by competent persons at stated intervals, to encourage men of color to become professors in particular branches of science, and to establish a library." No evidence has been found to indicate that this society was ever organized. The various anti-slavery organizations weakened the literary societies by calling constantly on society members to furnish audiences for their lectures and to serve as speakers and workers for the emancipation programs (Porter, 1936). For the most part, these societies were short-lived. Some existed actively for ten or twelve years, others not as long. In time, as a particular society had served its purpose and passed out of existence, another organization with similar purposes would be set up, such as the historical, research, and learned associations founded in the later nineteenth and into the early twentieth century. However, as a result of these early efforts, many collections were developed which included the earliest black literature.

AFRICAN-AMERICAN HISTORICAL SOCIETIES: 1875-1918

The rise of historical and learned societies began during the last quarter of the nineteenth century. A resolution, passed at the National Equal Rights Convention in 1873, stated that the time was ripe for an association which would actively gather materials for sowing the seeds of knowledge about Negro life; however, no evidence exists that action was taken in this direction until the middle-to-late 1870s (Kessler, 1955). Moss (1981) discussed the founding of the Virginia Historical and Literary Society in 1871 and the Bethel Literary and Historical Association in Washington, DC, in 1881 (considered one of the more prestigious societies of the late nineteenth century).

Additional early efforts toward developing an organized approach to the study of black history and culture occurred in 1897 with the almost simultaneous formation of the American Negro Historical Society in Philadelphia (mentioned earlier in association with Robert Adger) and the American Negro Academy (1897) in Washington, DC. The objectives of both organizations were to collect evidence and conduct research that would inform, inspire, and uplift the black race (Spady, 1974).

The American Negro Academy, the first major black American learned society, was founded on March 5, 1897. Not purely a historical society, the academy dealt with historical subjects, and most of its members were concerned directly or indirectly with sociological or historical materials. The academy maintained a membership limited to fifty persons and was listed in the *Handbook of Learned Societies and Institutions of America* (Thompson, 1908). From its establishment until its demise in 1928, the academy claimed as members some of the most important leaders in the black community: W.E.B. Dubois, Alain Locke, Carter G. Woodson, James Weldon Johnson, Jesse E. Moorland, and Arthur Schomburg.

On April 9, 1911, in Yonkers, New York, the Negro Society for Historical Research was founded with Arthur A. Schomburg as secretary and John Edward Bruce as president. The formation of this society further stimulated the collection of black literature and historical documents (Sinnette, 1989). One of the major goals of the society was "to collect useful historical data relating to the Negro race, books written by or about Negroes, rare pictures of prominent men and women . . . letters of noted Negroes or of white men friendly to the Negro, African curios of native manufacture, etc."

The Association for the Study of Negro Life and History was organized in Chicago on September 9, 1915 under the leadership of Carter G. Woodson. The group adopted a constitution and elected officers: George Cleveland Hall, president; Jesse E. Moorland, secretary-treasurer; and Carter G. Woodson, director of research and editor. The association was incorporated in the District of Columbia on October 3, 1915. The following year, the *Journal of Negro History*, a scholarly quarterly journal, was launched with Woodson as editor (Wesley, 1952). The Association for the Study of Negro Life and History emerged as the most important learned society founded by blacks as it continued to investigate, publish, and use the facts and lessons of history. Its research, educational work, the founding of Negro History Week, the *Journal of Negro History*, and the *Negro History Bulletin* evidenced outstanding success (Wesley, 1952).

The Negro Book Collectors Exchange, founded in 1916 in Washington, DC, and the Negro Library Association, known to be active in New York City from 1914 to 1918, appear to have been associated with the membership of the American Negro Academy. Sinnette (1989) indicates that the leaders of the academy, including Arthur Schomburg and other prominent black bibliophiles, were active in establishing the Negro Book Collectors Exchange and held memberships and offices in the Negro Library Association.

These early Afro-American historical societies, associations, and learned academies were among the first such organizations developed by blacks in the United States for searching out evidence of the historical accomplishments of the black community. The collections and libraries of these groups have become the nuclei of rich resources of black literature, culture, and history.

SUMMARY & CONCLUSIONS

The founding of nineteenth-century African-American literary and reading room societies between 1828 and 1874 exemplifies "social libraries" organized by blacks for their self-improvement, education, and cultural development during a period of American history when public libraries either did not exist or when they were not accessible to the black population. These early literary and library societies were also the earliest depositories for rare and unique Afro-Americana. As Porter (1936) suggests, the libraries and the members of the groups form a meaningful and significant chapter in the cultural and educational history of the American black. The results of this study suggest that the founding of these libraries as a type of social library was characteristic of the self-improvement movement in early American history.

The social library became a popular means by which local communities could supply their reading needs. This library type, representing a significant predecessor of the public library in the years after 1731, has been researched in great detail by many American library historians including Shera (1949) and McMullen (1958, 1965, 1985, 1987). Shera and McMullen showed that the Northeast provided the leadership for library development in the United States. However, these studies ignored the existence and significance of early social libraries in thriving African-American communities of the northern, northeastern, and middle states, even though these geographical locations were the major focus of research on library history and more libraries of all types were located in this region in the eighteenth and nineteenth centuries.

These libraries, reading rooms, and debating and literary societies were founded in the black communities for the same purposes as in the white communities—i.e., self-improvement and the sharing of useful knowledge symbolic of this period in American library history.

This study revealed that the founding and prevalence of African-American social libraries followed the same pattern as their white counterparts in terms of geographical distribution, chronological rate of growth, and their rather slow decline. The geographical distribution and chronological trends for both black and white libraries were directly related to population density, economic developments, and related demographic factors as explained by McMullen (1958, 1965, 1985, 1987). For example, McMullen (1958) cites eight social, economic, or political conditions which may have been related to the founding of social libraries: change from frontier to settled areas, speed of population growth, the origin of immigration, business cycles, increases in per capita income, presence of colleges, presence of lyceums, and legislation. All of these factors may have been significantly related to the rise of African-American social libraries, either as direct, indirect, or inverse influences.

The decline of African-American social libraries is somewhat more complex when compared with their white counterparts. The issue of slavery and abolitionist activities seemingly had a more significant impact on the stability of African-American societies, while the lack of availability of access to public libraries as they were gradually emerging in the last quarter of the nineteenth century, may have encouraged blacks to hold on to the social libraries. However, some of the reasons for the slow decline of social libraries, outlined by McMullen (1958), seem appropriate for those founded by blacks:

> In the United States as a whole, social libraries did not begin to decline in popularity when the public libraries first became popular around the middle of the nineteenth century. Records of the founding of social and public libraries, as well as counts of the numbers in existence at various times, show that by 1875 social libraries were more popular than ever before and were still considerably more popular than public libraries. By 1900, the public library had caught up with the social library and, in one respect, had surpassed it: among the largest institutions there were more public than social libraries. (p. 207)

McMullen (1985) suggests several reasons for the slowness of the decline of the social library and considers certain aspects of nineteenth-century American attitudes, habits, and customs as related factors:

(1) The use of the voluntary association as a means of accomplishing a social goal and as a source of personal enjoyment by its members.
(2) The sparseness of population in much of the United States, even late in the century.
(3) The nature of migration from east to west as a cause of the founding of libraries in the West.
(4) The growth of cities in the United States in the nineteenth century.
(5) The social libraries formed by one group for the benefit of another group as expressions of the general concern for underprivileged elements in society.
(6) Ignorance about public libraries and their advantages.
(7) The establishment of quasi-public [or quasi-social] libraries during the second half of the nineteenth century. (pp. 221-23)

This descriptive study of the founding of early African-American social libraries is only the beginning of further research on the roots and realities of the history of black librarianship. There is a paucity of research in this area, and results of this study imply strongly that further study should be planned on the activities of female African-American bibliophiles; the Negro Library Association; and the founding of other literary societies and reading rooms by African-Americans in urban centers of the central middle states (Illinois, Kentucky, Michigan, and Ohio) and central southern states (Georgia, Missouri, and Tennessee) prior to the establishment of public libraries in selected communities.

In conclusion, the early black bibliophiles, associated with the literary and historical societies, were drawn together by a common cause and shared a common passion for searching out evidence of the historical accomplishments of African-Americans. Their collections provided irrefutable proof that blacks could achieve. In addition, the black bibliophiles' desire to collect was not motivated solely by the need to own rare books and treasures; their passion to acquire books and materials about people of African descent was fired by a desire to share the contents of their collections with others. In most cases these black bibliophiles eventually sold or donated their collections to historically black institutions where they became the nuclei of rich resources of black literature and history. The most generally useful and rarest of the black collections is the Schomburg Collection in New York with over 85,000 volumes plus manuscripts. Howard University (1976) benefited greatly from the donation of the Jesse E. Moorland Library. Whereas, the Atlanta University resources were greatly enriched by the Henry Proctor Slaughter collection. Schomburg also helped develop the rare black collection at Fisk University. The Daniel A. P. Murray collection formed the nucleus of the Library of Congress black collection. The story of the development of black education and librarianship would therefore be incomplete, as Porter (1936) maintained, without some reference to the endeavors of the scholars, bibliophiles, and other leaders of the early African-American social libraries, literary and historical societies: gatekeepers of black history, collections, and literature.

REFERENCES

Abbot, G. M. (1931). *A short history of the Library Company of Philadelphia: Compiled from the minutes, together with some personal reminiscences*. Philadelphia, PA: Published by order of the Board of Directors.

American Negro Academy. (1969). *The American Negro Academy occasional papers, 1-22* (1897-1924) (reprinted). New York: Arno Press.

Ball, W., & Martin, T. (1981). *Rare Afro-Americana: A reconstruction of the Adger Library*. Boston, MA: G. K. Hall.

Bontemps, A. (1944). Special collections of Negroana. *Library Quarterly, 14*(3), 187- 206.

DuBois, W.E.B. (1967). *The Philadelphia Negro*. (1899) (reprint). New York: Schocken Books.

Eaton, T. (Ed.). (1961). *Contributions to American library history*. Champaign, IL: Illini Union Bookstore.

Foner, P. S. (1983). *History of Black Americans*, 2 vols. Westport, CT: Greenwood Press.

Good, C. H. (1932). The first American Negro literary movement. *Opportunity, 10*(3), 76-79.

Greene, L. J. (1968). *The Negro in Colonial New England*. New York: Atheneum.

Howard University Library. (1976). *Dictionary catalog of the Jesse E. Moorland Collection of Negro Life and History*. Boston, MA: Allyn & Bacon.

Jewett, C. C. (1851). *Report relative to the library*. U.S. 31st Congress, 1st Session, House Miscellaneous Documents, No. 50. Washington, DC: USGPO.

Joeckel, C. B. (1935). *Government of the American public library*. Chicago, IL: University of Chicago Press.

Josey, E. J., & Shockley, A. A. (1977). *Handbook of Black librarianship*. Littleton, CO: Libraries Unlimited.

Joyce, D. F. (1975). Arthur A. Schomburg: A pioneering black bibliophile. *Journal of Library History, 10*(2), 169-182.

Kessler, S. H. (1955). Collectors, scholars and Negro literature. *Midwest Journal, 7*(Fall), 222-234.

Library Company of Philadelphia. (1973). *Afro-Americana, 1553-1906: Author catalog of the Library Company*. Boston, MA: G.K. Hall.

McMullen, H. (1958). *The founding of social and public libraries in Ohio, Indiana, and Illinois through 1850* (Occasional Paper Series No. 51). Urbana-Champaign, IL: University of Illinois Library School.

McMullen, H. (1965). The founding of social libraries in Pennsylvania, 1731-1876. *Pennsylvania History, 32*(2), 130-152.

McMullen, H. (1985). The very slow decline of the American social library. *Library Quarterly, 55*(2), 207-225.

McMullen, H. (1987). Prevalence of libraries in the northeastern states before 1876. *Journal of Library History, 22*(3), 312-337.

Moss, A. A. (1981). *American Negro academy*. Baton Rouge, LA: Louisiana State University Press.

Porter, D. B. (1936). The organized educational activities of Negro literary societies, 1828-1846. *Journal of Negro Education, 5*(4), 555-576.

Porter, D. B. (1939). Early manuscript letters written by Negroes. *Journal of Negro History, 24*(2), 199-210.

Porter, D. B. (1943). David Ruggles, an apostle of human rights. *Journal of Negro History, 28*(1), 23-50.

Porter, D. B. (1971). *Early Negro writing, 1760-1837*. Boston, MA: Beacon Press.

Porter, D. B. (1984). Introduction. In R. Newman (Ed.), *Black access: A bibliography of Afro-American bibliographies*. Westport, CT: Greenwood Press.

Shera, J. (1949). *Foundations of the public library*. Chicago, IL: University of Chicago Press.

Sinnette, E. D. (1989). *Arthur Alfonso Schomburg: Black bibliophile and collector—A biography*. Detroit, MI: Wayne State University Press and New York Public Library.

Spady, J. (1974). The Afro-American historical society: The nucleus of black bibliophiles, 1897-1923. *Negro History Bulletin, 37*(3), 254-257.

Thompson, C. S. (1952). *Evolution of the American public library, 1653-1876.* Washington, DC: Scarecrow Press.

Wesley, C. (1952). Racial historical societies and the American heritage. *Journal of Negro History, 37*(1), 11-35.

Willson, J. (1969). *Sketches of the higher classes of colored society in Philadelphia by a southerner.* Philadelphia, PA: Rhistoric Publications.

ADDITIONAL REFERENCES

Bergman, P. M., & Bergman, M. N. (1969). *The chronological history of the Negro in America.* New York: Mentro Books.

Blockson, C. L. (1915). *Pennsylvania's black history.* Philadelphia, PA: Portfolio Association.

Boardman, H. (1945). The rise of the Negro historian. *Negro History Bulletin, 8*(April), 148-154.

Bolton, C. (1917). *Proprietary and subscription libraries.* Chicago, IL: American Library Association.

Bracey, J. H., Jr.; Meier, A; & Rudwick, E. (1972). *The Afro-American: Selected documents.* Boston, MA: Allyn & Bacon.

Brackett, J. R. (1971). *Notes on the progress of the Colored People of Maryland since the War* (1890) (reprint). Freeport, NY: Books for Libraries Press.

Brotz, H. (1966). *Negro social and political thought, 1850-1920.* New York: Basic Books.

Cottrol, R. J. (1982). *The Afro-Yankees.* Westport, CT: Greenwood Press.

Cromwell, J. W. (1912). *History of the Bethel Literary and History Association* (A paper read before the Association on Founders' Day, February 24, 1896). Washington, DC: Pendleton Press.

Cromwell, J. W. (1914). *The Negro in American history.* Washington, DC: The American Negro Academy.

Curry, L. P. (1981). *The free black in urban America, 1800-1850.* Chicago, IL: University of Chicago Press.

Dunlap, M. E. (1935). Special collections of Negro literature in the U.S. *Journal of Negro Education, 4*(4), 482-489.

Fishel, L. H., Jr. (1953). *The North and the Negro, 1865-1900.* Unpublished doctoral dissertation, Harvard University.

Fordham, M. (1975). *Major themes in Northern Black religious thought, 1800-1860.* Hicksville, NY: Exposition Press.

Garonzik, J. (1974). *Urbanization and the black population of Baltimore, 1850-1870.* Unpublished doctoral dissertation, SUNY at Stony Brook.

Green, C. M. (1967). *The secret city.* Princeton, NJ: Princeton University Press.

Gubert, B. K. (1982). *Early black bibliographies, 1863-1918.* New York: Garland Press.

Harris, R. L., Jr. (1976). Daniel Murray and *The encyclopedia of the colored race. Phylon, 37*(30), 270-282.

Haynes, R. V. (1972). *Blacks in white America before 1865: Issues and interpretations.* New York: David McKay.

Hirsch, L. H., Jr. (1931). The Negro and New York, 1783 to 1865. *Journal of Negro History, 16*(October), 382-473.

Jacobs, D. W. (Ed.). (1976). *Ante-bellum black newspapers.* Westport, CT: Greenwood Press.

Johnson, C. S. (1928). The rise of the Negro magazine. *Journal of Negro History, 13*(1), 7-21.

Joyce, D. F. (1983). *Gatekeepers of black culture: Black owned book publishing in the U.S., 1817-1981.* Westport, CT: Greenwood Press.

Joyce, D. F. (1986). *Blacks in the humanities, 1750-1984: A selected annotated bibliography.* New York: Greenwood Press.

Jubilee, V. (1980). *Philadelphia's Afro-American literary circle and the Harlem Renaissance.* Unpublished doctoral dissertation, University of Pennsylvania.

Lindsay, A. G. (1942). Manuscript materials bearing on the Negro in America. *Journal of Negro History, 27*(1), 94-101.

Litwack, L. (1961). *North of slavery.* Chicago, IL: University of Chicago Press.

Locke, A. (Ed.). (1925). *The new Negro.* New York: Albert & Charles Boni.

Martin, T. (1981). Race, men, bibliophiles and historians: The world of Robert M. Adger and the Negro Historical Society of Philadelphia. In W. Ball & T. Martin (Eds.), *Rare Afro-Americana: A reconstruction of the Adger Library* (pp. 1-38). Boston, MA: G. K. Hall.

McBride, D. (Ed.). (1983). *Blacks in Pennsylvania history: Research and educational perpectives.* Harrisburg, PA: Pennsylvania Historical & Museum Commission.

Meier, A. (1971). *Negro thought in America, 1880-1915.* Ann Arbor, MI: University of Michigan Press.

Meier, A., & Rudwick, E. (1986). *Black history and the historical profession, 1915-1980.* Urbana-Champaign, IL: University of Illinois Press.

Miller, M. I. (1966). *The American Negro academy: An intellectual movement during the Era of Disfranchisement, 1897-1924.* Unpublished master's thesis, Howard University, Washington, DC.

Moynihan, K. J. (1973). *History as a weapon for social advancement: Group history as told by Jewish, Irish, and black Americans, 1892-1950.* Unpublished doctoral dissertation, Clark University, Worcester, MA.

New York Public Library, Schomburg Collection. (1962). *Dictionary catalog of the Schomburg Collection of Negro Literature and History.* Boston, MA: G. K. Hall.

Paul, W. G. (1972). *The shadow of equality: The Negro in Baltimore, 1864-1911.* Unpublished doctoral dissertation, University of Wisconsin.

Penn, I. G. (1969). *The Afro-American press and its editors.* (1891) (reprint). Springfield, MA: Wiley & Co.

Porter, D. B. (1976). Bibliography and research in Afro-American scholarship. *Journal of Academic Librarianship, 2*(2), 77-81.

Rhees, W. J. (1859). *Manual of public libraries, institutions, and societies in the U.S. and British Provinces of North America.* Philadelphia, PA: J.B. Lippincott.

Rubinstein, S., & Farley, J. (1980). Enoch Pratt Free Library and black patrons: Equality in library services, 1882-1915. *Journal of Library History, 15*(4), 445-453.

Siegel, A. (Ed.). (1975). *Philadelphia: A chronological & documentary history.* Dobbs Ferry, NY: Oceana Publications.

Spingarn, A. B. (1938). Collecting a library of Negro literature. *Journal of Negro Education, 7*(1), 12-18.

Stapp, C. B. (1993). *Afro-Americans in ante-bellum Boston: An analysis of probate records.* New York: Garland.

Thompson. (1908). *Handbook of learned societies and institutions: America.* Washington, DC: Carnegie Institute of Washington.

U.S. Bureau of Education. (1876). *Public libraries in the United States of America: Their history, condition, and management* (Special Report. Part I). Washington, DC: U. S. Bureau of Education.

Wayman, H. H. (1903). The American Negro Historical Society of Philadelphia and its officers. *Colored American Magazine, 6,* 287-294.

Wiegand, W. A. (1989). The development of librarianship in the United States. *Libraries & Culture, 24*(1), 99-109.

Williams, G. A. (1979). *The A.M.E. Christian recorder: A forum for the social ideas of black Americans, 1854-1902.* Unpublished doctoral dissertation, University of Illinois.

Wright, R R., Jr. (1969). *The Negro in Pennsylvania* (1912) (reprint). New York: Arno Press.

Yeatman, J. L. (1985). Literary culture and the role of libraries in democratic America: Baltimore, 1815-1840. *Journal of Library History, 20,* 345-367.

Appendix A

Chronology: Founding of African-American Social Libraries & Learned Societies

(Including subscription libraries, reading rooms; debating, scholarly, literary, and historical societies; and other self-help organizations)

1828:	Reading Room Society - Philadelphia
1829:	New York African Clarkson Society - New York City
1830:	New York Philomathean Society - New York City
1831:	Female Literary Society - Philadelphia
1831:	Theban Literary Society - Pittsburgh
1832:	Afric-American Female Intelligence Society - Boston

1832:	Pittsburgh African Education Society - Pittsburgh
1832:	Tyro and Literary Association - Newark, NJ
1833:	Library Company of Colored Persons - Philadelphia
1833:	Phoenix Society - New York City
1833:	Literary Society - Providence, RI
1833:	Ladies Literary and Dorcas Society - Rochester, NY
1834:	Minerva Literary Society- Philadelphia
1834:	Ladies Literary Society - New York City
1834:	New York Garrison Literary Association - New York City
1834:	Washington Conventional Society - Washington, DC
1834:	Literary and Religious Institution - Hartford, CT
1834:	Thompson Literary and Debating Society - Boston
1834:	Phoenix Society - Boston
1834:	Young Men's Mental Improvement Society for the Discussion of Moral and Philosophical Questions of all Kinds - Baltimore
1835:	Female Literary Society - New York City
1835:	Philadelphia Association for Moral & Mental Improvement of People of Color - Philadelphia
1836:	Rush Library and Debating Society - Philadelphia
1836:	Debating Society - Troy, NY
1836:	Literary Society - Troy, NY
1836:	Mental and Moral Improvement Society - Troy, NY
1836:	Boston Philomathean Society - Boston
1836:	Debating Society - Providence, RI
1836:	Debating Society - Buffalo, NY
1836:	Young Ladies' Literary Society - Buffalo, NY
1836:	Literary Society - Poughkeepsie, NY
1836:	Literary Society - Washington, DC
1836:	Debating Society - Washington, DC
1836:	Adelphic Union for the Promotion of Literature and Science - Boston
1837:	Demosthenian Institute - Philadelphia
1837:	Young Men's Literary & Moral Reform Society - Pittsburgh
1841:	Gilbert Lyceum - Philadelphia
1842:	Literary Societies (two) - Albany, NY
1842:	Literary Society - Cincinnati, OH
1842:	Literary Society - Columbus, OH
1842:	Literary Society - Rochester, NY
1842:	Literary Society - Schenactady, NY
1844:	Young Men's Literary Society - Boston
1845:	Young Men's Lyceum and Debating Society - Detroit
1854:	Banneker Literary Institute - Philadelphia
1859:	Sarah M. Douglas Literary Circle - Philadelphia
1875:	Virginia Historical & Literary Society - Alexandria, VA
1877:	Negro American Society - Washington, DC
1881:	Bethel Literary & Historical Association - Washington, DC
1890:	Society for the Collection of Negro Folklore - Boston
1897:	American Negro Historical Society - Philadelphia
1897:	American Negro Academy - Washington, DC
1901:	Boston Historical and Literary Society - Boston
1910:	American Negro Monograph Company - Washington, DC
1911:	Negro Society for Historical Research - New York City

1914:   Negro Library Association - New York City
1915:   Association for the Study of Negro Life & History - Chicago:
            September 9, 1915; Incorporated Washington, DC: October 3, 1915
1916:   Negro Book Collectors Exchange - Washington, DC
1918:   First Annual Exhibition - Negro Library Association - Brooklyn,
            NY: August 7-16, 1918

APPENDIX B

African-American Social Libraries & Learned Societies
by Date of Establishment, 1828-1918

State	1828-1833	1834-1839	1840-1851	1852-1899	1900-1918	Total
Pennsylvania	4	5	1	3	1	14
New York	4	9	4	-	2	19
Massachusetts	1	3	1	1	1	7
Connecticut	-	1	-	-	-	1
Rhode Island	1	1	-	-	-	2
New Jersey	1	-	-	-	-	1
Maryland	-	2	-	-	-	2
Washington, DC	-	3	-	4	2	9
Ohio	-	-	2	-	-	2
Michigan	-	-	1	-	-	1
Illinois	-	-	-	-	1	1
TOTAL	11	24	9	8	7	59

APPENDIX C

African-American Bibliophiles Associated with Early Literary
and Historical Societies

Bibliophile Founded	Society	Role	Year
David Ruggles	Phoenix Society of New York	Member Board of Directors	1833
David Ruggles	New York Garrison Literary and Benevolent Society	Member of Executive Committee	1834
Robert Adger	Banneker Literary Institute (Philadelphia)	Member	1854

Robert Adger	American Negro Historical Society (Philadelphia)	Founding Member	1897
William Bolivar	American Negro Historical Society (Philadelphia)	Founding Member	1897
Leon Gardiner	American Negro Historical Society (Philadelphia)	Founding Member	1897
John W. Cromwell	American Negro Academy (Washington, DC)	Founding Member	1897
W.E.B. DuBois	American Negro Academy (Washington, DC)	Founding Member	1897
Henry P. Slaughter	American Negro Academy (Washington, DC)	Member	1897
John E. Bruce	American Negro Academy (Washington, DC)	Member	1897
Jesse Moorland	American Negro Academy (Washington, DC)	Member	1897
Daniel A.P. Murray	American Negro Academy (Washington, DC)	Member	1897
Arthur Schomburg	American Negro Academy (Washington, DC)	Fifth & Last President (1922-1928)	1897
Arthur Schomburg	Negro Society for Historical Research (New York City)	Founding Member	1911
John E. Bruce	Negro Society for Historical Research (New York City)	Founding Member	1911
William C. Bolivar	Negro Society for Historical Research	Corresponding Member	1911
Arthur Schomburg	Negro Library	Founding	1914

	Association (New York City)	Member	
John E. Bruce	Negro Library Association (New York City)	Founding Member	1914
Carter G. Woodson	Association for the Study of Negro Life and History (Chicago)	Founding Member	1915
Jesse Moorland	Association for the Study of Negro Life and History (Chicago)	Founding Member	1915
John W. Cromwell	Negro Book Collectors Exchange (Washington, DC)	Founding Member	1916
Arthur Schomburg	Negro Book Collectors Exchange (Washington, DC)	Founding Member	1916
Jesse Moorland	Negro Book Collectors Exchange (Washington, DC)	Founding Member	1916
Daniel A.P. Murray	Negro Book Collectors Exchange (Washington, DC)	Founding Member	1916
Henry P. Slaughter	Negro Book Collectors Exchange (Washington, DC)	Founding Member	1916
John E. Bruce	Negro Book Collectors Exchange (Washington, DC)	Founding Member	1916
Arthur Schomburg	First Annual Exhibition August 7-16, 1918 (Brooklyn, NY) Negro Library Association	Founding Member	1918

| John E. Bruce | First Annual Exhibition August 7-9, 1918 Negro Library Association (Brooklyn, NY) | Founding Member | 1918 |

Private Dominance in Black
Academic Libraries, 1916-1938

ð James E. Hooper ð

S ignificant political and economic changes influenced the development
of black academic libraries between the two World Wars. After World
War I, the reputation of big business led President Calvin Coolidge to
say with proud sincerity: "The nation's business is business." In the same
vein, Herbert Hoover extolled the virtues of rugged individualism, while other
economists predicted an unending era of prosperity based on the triumph of
private enterprise. According to business apologists, tremendous wealth at the
top of the economic pyramid, would filter down to the lowest productive class
thus creating buying power which would uphold the mighty economic edifice.
Although this philosophy held some validity, the southern black, at the lowest
level of the economic pyramid, profited little.[1]

Two northern philanthropists believed that only through liberal and advanced education could blacks hope to compete in the modern world. John D.
Rockefeller, Jr., of Standard Oil and Julius Rosenwald, of Sears, Roebuck &
Company, sought to ameliorate the lot of the southern black and were persuaded that Booker T. Washington's promise of a black artisan class was obsolete. The Phelps-Stokes Survey of 1916 reported that virtually all education for
blacks was in some way deficient. Largely as a result of the private efforts of
philanthropists, black colleges experienced remarkable growth and profound
alteration of their goals during the 1920s and 1930s.

Perhaps a shift of Fisk University's institutional values was underway in
1924 when Fisk University Librarian, Fred R. Steiner, directed a memorandum

to his president demanding the ouster of "roomers" from the library, since the aroma of bacon frying in the morning had disturbed students in the reading rooms. In less affluent times, black college librarians tended to accept greater inconveniences (Atkins, 1936, p. 40).

A more prosaic, although perhaps more accurate, measure of the revolution in black colleges involved the termination of many pre-collegiate training programs that prepared young adults for higher education. Howard University set the pace, dropping its preparatory department in 1919 (Duncan, 1955). Shortly thereafter, many prestigious schools followed suit: Fisk, Lincoln University of Pennsylvania, Wilberforce, Virginia Union, Morehouse, and Talladega. By 1930, even colleges such as Savannah, which offered no collegiate instruction in 1916, had discontinued their high schools (Regulus, 1955, p. 7). It was difficult to find even a demonstration school in black higher education by 1940, in large measure because of the successful efforts of the John F. Slater Fund, the Peabody Education Fund, the Anna T. Jeanes Fund, the General Education Board (GEB), and Julius Rosenwald, in promoting elementary and secondary education for blacks (Franklin & Moss, 1994). In summary, John Hope Franklin writes with approval that:

> The age of philanthropists contributed substantially toward bringing about a new day for education in the South. By conditional grants and aid to those institutions that had proved their worth, philanthropists did much to stimulate self-help on the part of the individual, the institution, and the states of the South. There was general approval of Northern philanthropy, when the white citizens of the South discovered that their benefactors showed little or no interest in establishing racial equality or upsetting white supremacy. (pp. 381-82)

A further indication of the improvement of black colleges would be the decline between 1916 and 1938 in the number of distinct institutions calling themselves "college" or "university." In the preceding twenty years, the number of such institutions had increased by ten (Johnson, 1938). But the most impressive proof of the transitions underway in black higher education in the 1920s is Arthur J. Klein's 1928 survey, which, unlike Thomas Jesse Jones's survey of 1916 for the Phelps-Stokes Fund, was funded by the federal government and conducted by personnel in the Bureau of Education's Division of Higher Education (1928, p. 974). Although Klein handled individual libraries in rudimentary fashion, he far surpassed Jones's survey in perception and depth.

Rather than simply appraising property, Klein (1928) offered recommendations concerning the basic financial and administrative difficulties confronting the black college:

> The government and financing of Negro higher educational institutions are acute problems. They are interrelated. The question of support rests in a large measure on methods of control. Institutions with types of government inspiring confidence have a tendency to make the most effective appeal for support. (p. 5)

Having made this statement, Klein demonstrated its validity for the seventy-nine colleges surveyed. The nine privately supported institutions, owned, governed, and controlled by independent, self-perpetuating boards of trustees, were found to have the highest average income, $261,082; the twenty-two state-owned and state-supported schools governed by appointed boards were second, with an average of $109,752; the seventeen privately supported colleges, owned and governed by black churches, averaged $66,977; the thirty-one owned and controlled by northern white denominational church boards had the lowest average income, $61,075 (Davis, 1933; Klein, 1928).[2] The total income that these figures represent, $2,283,000, was a four-fold increase over 1916, but the change Klein considered most important was the increase in black colleges' productive endowments which portended "a growing conviction that Negro higher education [would] be placed on a permanent base, through the provision of stable annual income" (p. 32).

The federal government's aid to black education, largely over-shadowed in the 1920s by private philanthropy, continued to support Howard and retained enough interest to fund the Klein survey of 1928 and his 1930 survey of land-grant institutions, which included those for blacks. By the end of the 1930s, however, federal support for black education had grown to proportions not seen since the end of the Freedmen's Bureau. This action may not have resulted from conscious policy, since President Franklin Delano Roosevelt (FDR) felt strongly the need to maintain support from the southern wing of the Democratic Party.[3] However, Eleanor Roosevelt, whose lack of constraint about opposing segregation was legendary, became the spiritual leader of a large number of "New Dealers" who administered massive recovery programs.[3] The New Dealers sympathized with the plight of the black and later, when it was politically feasible, emerged as equal rights advocates. During the 1930s, however, they found it necessary to court the southern power structure. In practical terms, this meant that the aid filtered from Washington to black college libraries was limited to amounts justifiable in general anti-depression programs and subject also to numerous state controls.

Perhaps the single most significant variety of New Deal aid which reached the black college came from the National Youth Administration's Negro Division. Southern states were generally unresponsive to the needs of black college librarianship; the Public Works Administration (PWA), however, had constructed at least two libraries in black colleges in North Carolina (South Carolina Colored Normal and Mechanical College, 1936).[4] Although the state legislature refused to appropriate money for permanent improvements, President J. Ward Seabrook saved enough from the regular budget of Fayetteville State to secure a grant from the PWA. Eventually, Governor J. C. B. Eringhouse acquiesced to this procedure, and a $36,000 building was completed in 1936 (Jones, 1969).

The library of the Alabama Agricultural & Mechanical Institute benefited from regional development planning conducted by the Tennessee Valley Authority (TVA). In 1936, the TVA, in an attempt to organize educational facilities for its employees in the Huntsville area, contracted with the State A & M Institute at Normal for job training, recreation, library service, and general adult education (Lowell, 1942). By many such small increments, federal support for black college libraries increased. An indication of the future direction of support for the ensuing sixteen years is the failure of the Office of Education in 1940 to treat black libraries separately in general reports of college and university library statistics (U.S. Office of Education, Federal Security Agency, 1940). Equally significant is the fact that the first organizational unit within the Office of Education specifically responsible for library development was established during the Roosevelt administration under Ralph McNeal Dunbar.

GOVERNING BODIES, ACCREDITING AGENCIES, & LIBRARY ASSOCIATIONS

Arthur J. Klein's 1928 survey of black higher education reflects the tremendous improvement of black college libraries between 1916 and 1927. Of the seventy-nine libraries surveyed, thirty-five held more than 5,000 volumes. In ten of the institutions, the library occupied separate buildings. On paper, Hampton Normal and Agricultural Institute had outstripped Howard University in total volumes and in average expenditures for periodicals and salaries, although in total library expenditures for books, binding, and supplies, Howard still led the field (Havlik, 1968). Eight institutions, in addition to Hampton, surpassed Fisk's 12,400 volume collection; however, Fisk ranked third in two categories by a comfortable margin: an average total library expenditure of $4,789 and an average salary expenditure of $3,169 (Klein, 1928).[5] Twenty-two institutions averaged as little as $100 in annual expenditures for periodicals, while twenty-three spent less than $500 annually on libraries, and an additional seven lacked libraries altogether.

Klein (1928) described conditions in black college libraries as dreary:

> it was found that in many cases the number of volumes reached the minimum standards for colleges or junior colleges but in these collections were found in many instances a large number of useless works, the donations for the most part of retired clergymen and others . . . the libraries contained very few public documents. . . .(p. 47)

Service provided by the library was not clearly understood in a number of schools, which had undue restrictions in the hours the library was open to students, and teachers tended to nullify their utility. Only occasionally did colleges fully appreciate that the college library should serve as a workshop for the teachers and students and that books and professional magazines were not intended merely for students.

Klein (1928) expressed optimism about the future of black libraries because the five years from 1922 to 1927 showed interest in improving service. He reported: "During this time 16 colleges had increased their expenditures from 55 to 99 percent, eight from 100 to 199 percent, ten from 200 to 299 percent, and five over 300 percent" (p. 47). Of the remaining forty institutions, twenty-one recorded less than forty-nine percent growth while nineteen did not grow at all (pp. 948-50).

Library fiscal support and collection size varied substantially according to forms of institutional governance. The collections of the nine institutions controlled by private, self-perpetuating boards all exceeded the 5,000 volume minimum recommended for senior college libraries in 1928. Funded largely by the federal government, Howard University, under the control of such a board, and having budgeted for library service for forty-two years, led black higher education in 1927 with expenditures of $11,985 (Klein, 1928).[6] The libraries of three other leading black colleges (Fisk, Atlanta, and Hampton), which had been founded by the American Missionary Association, prospered after the association relinquished control to private boards. Fisk, for example, accumulated a library endowment of $9,000. Although also under a private board, Booker T. Washington's Tuskegee was slow to direct much of its support to the library. Even so, the library employed three full-time staff, two with library training, and spent $1,000 for books and periodicals. The total expenditure for library service at Tuskegee, $3,435.41, represented 7 percent of its institutional budget. Morgan College, one of the smallest schools controlled by an independent board, claimed only 6,500 volumes, "a fairly good selection of books for collegiate work in excellent condition" and expended 3.3 percent of its total institutional income for library purposes (Klein, 1928).[7]

A second group of institutions included the thirty-one governed by northern white churches. Of the twenty-eight purporting to be senior colleges, fifteen held fewer than 5,000 volumes. The best-supported schools apparently were those controlled by the American Baptist Home Mission Board, due possibly to large Rockefeller grants to several Baptist colleges (Klein, 1928, p. 46).[8] The superiority of northern Baptist support for libraries merits reconsideration, however, in view of Klein's (1928) comment on Virginia Union:

> The library contains an extraordinarily large list of old theological books of no value to college students and of doubtful value to theology students. . . . Excessive expenditures are being made for recent theological books as compared with books of direct college usefulness. (p. 940)

A more likely candidate for top honors among white denominational organizations supporting black college libraries, the Board of Education of the Methodist Episcopal Church maintained a committee to supervise the libraries of colleges under its jurisdiction. This committee conducted two-week conferences for its librarians and periodically made "extensive purchases of books of college quality and distributed them to schools under its control" (Klein, 1928, p. 845). The committee approach benefitted libraries: when Methodist Episcopal and American Missionary Association colleges merged in Louisiana to form Dillard College in the 1930s and in Florida to form Huston-Tillotson in the early 1950s, the Methodist libraries held superior collections (O. D. Brown, personal communication, March 24, 1975; C. R. Taylor, personal communication, February 21, 1975).[9] The annual reports of the American Missionary Association (AMA) division of the Congregational Church did not mention library support, and not until the 1930s did the AMA allow $250 per annum budgets for book purchases in its institutions (Jeanetta Roach, personal communication, February 21, 1975).

Klein (1928) indicated that college libraries under black church control (thirteen of seventeen had fallen below the 5,000 volume standard) but also public institutions under black administrations did not have the same standard:

> Notwithstanding the deficiencies in the libraries of some smaller schools under northern church control, the outstanding weakness in view of size of enrollments of the institution is found in the libraries of institutions under Negro administration. (p. 46)

The plight of such institutions was typified by the African Methodist Episcopal (AME) Church's experience at Wilberforce when, in 1934, the administration applied for North Central Association accreditation. In his evaluation, Herbert S. Hirshberg, librarian of Western Reserve University, described the "book collection, . . . its organization and administration, in relation to recognized standards applied to college libraries."[10] In April 1934, Hirshberg reported that the library was 97 percent deficient and recommended:

> remodeling the building, redecorating the walls, floor covering, open shelves for all books and periodicals, an adequate budget, building up the collection on the basis of standard lists, discarding of useless gifts, and a change of personnel. (Dunlap, 1941, pp. 6-7)

Bishop R.R. Wright and successive Wilberforce presidents responded to these recommendations with the generous support of alumni and the AME Church.

Of the twenty-two publicly funded black colleges, seventeen were land-grant institutions. Four of the remaining five were teacher training schools fully dependent on state appropriations (Carnegie Commission of New York & GEB, 1941).[11] Black land-grant schools also depended on state governments because federal law limited the funding to two-thirds of an institution's total income. Of library income, Klein (1930) reported that:

> one of the principal handicaps with which the libraries are confronted is the failure of the colleges to segregate their finances from the other institutional funds. Apparently no budget is maintained. By far the best method of financing the libraries is through direct state appropriations. When funds are furnished in this way they are available only for expenditure of the library and cannot be used for other purposes. (pp. 889-90)

The case of South Carolina Colored Normal and Mechanical College proved the wisdom of Klein's recommendation for, despite library drives and student fees, the library showed no progress until 1933 when specific allocations were made by the state legislature. Until the specter of non-accreditation loomed, neither states nor most other governing bodies were seeking to correct the chronic circumstances of the black college library.

Although Howard University had been accredited by the Middle States Association in 1921, the vast majority of black colleges were under the purview of the Southern Association of Colleges and Secondary Schools. Jim Crow attitudes combined with the damning blow of the Jones survey to prohibit any southern black college from consideration for accreditation before 1929 except for state bodies or the black association formed for self-accreditation.

Arthur Klein's survey noted enough improvement in the quality of black higher education that in 1929 the Southern Association formed a committee to study accreditation for black colleges. Thereafter, other accrediting activities became meaningless. Constituted of Horace Macauley Ivy, John Henry Highsmith, and Theodore Henley Jack, the Southern Association Committee was initially funded with $35,000 from the General Education Board (GEB). For twenty years it held sway over the reputations of black colleges (Agnew, 1970, p. 28). Rather than granting equal status by accrediting the colleges, the Highsmith Committee merely "approved" them. Further, it divided those approved into the "A" rated institutions, which fully met Southern Association standards, and the "B" rated schools, which lacked only one requirement for accreditation. A. B. Beittle's impassioned speech before the conference at Houston in 1949 shows the burden felt by black college administrations since the "progressive action of twenty years ago" had become the "reactionary position" of the day (Southern Association of Colleges and Secondary Schools, 1949, pp. 214-16).

The first school to receive an A rating was Fisk in 1930, followed by Hampton, Atlanta, Morehouse, and Spelman in 1932. Fred McCuistion, executive agent of the Highsmith Committee, reported that the thirty-two A and B colleges in 1933 expended a total of $163,643 for libraries. He observed a "wide variety in the amount and quality of library service, some colleges having small but effectively operated libraries, while others have ample volumes but poor service" (Agnew, 1970, p. 28).

The great impact of accreditation on black colleges was recognized by Donald E. Riggs (1971) in his study of West Virginia's Bluefield State College:

> Perhaps the biggest boost for the library came in 1947 when the college received accreditation by the American Association of Teachers Colleges. Arbitrary standards brought forth by accrediting committees enabled the library to glean a larger share of the college's annual operating budget. (p. 11)

Although the threat of suspension could produce results, the Southern Association was less effective than it ought to have been in improving libraries.[12] According to Wallace Van Jackson, the association applied separate standards for black libraries and tended to overlook serious deficiencies (Southern Association, 1935, pp. 38-39; W. Van Jackson, personal communication, June 1974).

White library associations were less effective than any other external agency in improving black college libraries. Jim Crow laws had excluded blacks from membership in local and state library associations in the South (J. R. O'Rourke, personal communication, March 19, 1975).[13] Until such laws were ruled unconstitutional, the ALA leaders could do virtually nothing, except as individuals, for the black college library. Perhaps the most important ALA contribution involved the Board of Education for Librarianship's recommendation of Florence Rising Curtis as the director of the first library school for blacks.[14] Blacks formed library associations in North Carolina, South Carolina, and Texas, while in Virginia, black librarians met in conjunction with the Virginia Negro Education Association (M. Beal & L. R. Wilson, personal communication, 1925). Black academic librarians often assumed leadership in such associations but did not develop them widely across the South.[15]

LIBRARY EDUCATION, ORGANIZED PHILANTHROPY, & ACADEMIC LIBRARIANSHIP

Perhaps the single most important determinant in the development of black college libraries between 1916 and 1938 was the provision of relatively large numbers of trained personnel. Florence Rising Curtis (1925), prior to her work as director of the Hampton Library School, surveyed the libraries of sixteen black colleges and concluded that:

> the chief reason for a poor and inadequate library in nearly every Negro college is the fact that the library is not a separate department with a budget which would provide for salaries, books, periodicals, and binding. The alumni of some institutions are making an effort to raise money for books; in others there is a disposition to make available from general funds a fair sum for immediate needs; while in others a book shower is mainly expected to provide something of value to teachers and collegiate students. . . . A well-educated librarian could build up and care for the collection, give proper reference help to teachers and students, and guide the students' reading by suggesting books of interest and amusement. In those sixteen colleges there are but two colored librarians who [had] graduated from a library school. (p. 2)[16]

One of the librarians to whom Curtis referred, sometimes known as the dean of black college librarians, was Edward Christopher Williams. A Phi Beta Kappa student from Adelbert College of Western Reserve University, Williams became librarian of Adelbert's Hatch Library soon after his graduation. In fifteen years as head librarian at Western Reserve, he expanded the collection from 25,000 to 65,000 volumes, developed a German collection, organized a staff association, corresponded with Charles Evans, became a charter member of the Ohio Library Association, and, in one year's sabbatical, completed the two-year library course at Albany. After seven years as a high school principal in Washington, D. C., Williams assumed the position of librarian at

Howard in 1916 and retained it until his death in 1929. At Howard, Williams was unable to equal his accomplishments in Ohio although he managed to add 12,000 volumes, expanded the Moorland Collection, directed the department of romance languages, and in 1928 began work toward a Ph.D. (Josey, 1969). During his Howard years, the percentage of library expenses to total institutional expenditures slipped from the ALA-approved 3 percent to 1.5 percent (Duncan, 1955, p. 83). At the Hampton Library Conference in 1927, Williams expressed fear that the library at Howard would never develop into anything of importance (Carnegie Commission of New York and General Education Board, 1941, p. 69).

Before 1925, the corps of professionals serving black academic libraries included several whites. As late as 1939, however, when black institutions employed ninety-one black librarians, five black college libraries were still headed by whites who were more concerned with improving the libraries under their own direction than with black college libraries in general (Van Jackson, 1940, pp. 95-104). For example, Frances L. Yocom, employed at Straight College in the 1920s, concentrated on cataloging and weeding the 7,000 volume collection. Without adequate supplies or clerical help, she had little opportunity to provide other services (F. L. Yocom, personal communication, September 6, 1974, Chapel Hill, NC; Taylor, personal communication). Mabel Grace Robb at Knoxville College and Sister Bernadette at Xavier met with similar circumstances (L. N. Clark, personal communication, February 26, 1975; Curtis papers, 1939).[17]

Louis Shores's service at Fisk University may be offered as a model of academic library practice for the era. In 1929, the Fisk Library had operated under a budget for two years and employed three professional staff members. Shores directed the library, Gertrude Aiken oversaw cataloging, and Anne Rucker supervised circulation and reference. Two other staff members, Margaret Reynolds and Onilda Taylor, had received Rosenwald grants for library study. Student assistants did most of the work. Shores's tenure included the formation of an undergraduate library school, the housing of the Negro Collection, the union of the Fisk and Meharry collections, and the construction of the Erastus Milo Cravath Library (Fisk University, 1929-33; Shiflett, 1996).

Too few white librarians would serve in low-paying black colleges, and too few presidents and deans of those colleges "realized that librarians should be professional workers on a par with teachers and not be expected to act in a clerical capacity or look after the mail" (Curtis, 1926, pp. 472-474). Trained black personnel were rarely available to black colleges. The only library education available to blacks in the South before the opening of the Hampton Institute School in 1925 was the training course of the Colored Branch of the Free Public Library of Louisville, Kentucky.

James Hulbert (1943) labeled the work of the Hampton School "the greatest impetus to library development" in black higher education (pp. 623-29).

Of the products of the school and of Curtis, Edgar W. Knight (1937) had only praise:

> The record of high achievement of this school is acknowledged throughout the country. Here as at other library schools for whites and Negroes the cost of training librarians has been high, but the work at Hampton has been of the finest order and the graduates of this school have given a splendid account of themselves in so far as college and public library administrators have allowed them to operate. The Director of this school is recognized as one of the most able of all the directors of library schools in the southern states . . . [and] she has stood for more rigid limitation of students than any other director. (p. 53)[18]

Fortunately, Hampton earned a good reputation for, by 1939, when it ceased operation, the school had graduated 138 black librarians, most of whom were employed by colleges, usually as the only trained librarian in the institution (Carnegie Commission of New York and General Education Board, 1941, p. 67; *Directory of Negro Graduates of Accredited Library Schools*, 1900-1936).

Virtually every state-funded black college employed a Hampton graduate as its first professionally trained librarian. The 1930 Klein survey, implying tightened control on federal monies, provided a strong incentive for college administrations to improve library services. The devotion and quality of their first librarians varied. James R. O'Rourke notes that the library of Kentucky State at Frankfort "became an organized collection of books" under the directorship of three Hampton graduates: Olie Atkins Carpenter (1929-30), Emma Lewis (1930-34), and Anne Rucker Anderson (1934-43). From 1,000 volumes (of which 630 were discarded) in 1929, the collection began to grow to a well-cataloged 12,000 volumes by 1939. Periodicals were bound; odd furniture was replaced with Library Bureau equipment; the library was expanded and redecorated; and a course in librarianship for high school teachers was offered. O'Rourke credits library growth to President Rufus B. Atwood, clear evidence of the powerful influence of the black college presidents (J. R. O'Rourke, personal communication, March 19, 1975).

At least four Hampton graduates spent their entire professional careers in the libraries of land-grant colleges: Camille Stivers Shade at Southern, Ollie Lee Brown at Alabama State College, Martha Brown at Tennessee Agricultural and Industrial Institute, and Athelma Nix at South Carolina State. Faustina Jones writes of Ollie Lee Brown:

> [She] served the faculty, students and community unselfishly and commendably . . . she collected and preserved an appreciable amount of Black America's heritage, . . . the bulk of the Library's Collection of Afro-Americana. . . .(personal communication, March 4, 1975)

From 1931 onward, Ruby Stutts Lyells may have been the most influential Hampton graduate to serve in a publicly funded college library (G. J. Beck, personal communication, March 3, 1975).[19] She organized and built the collection at Alcorn A & M, introduced library clubs, established faculty library committees, and practiced other techniques learned under Florence Curtis. More importantly, Lyells furthered the development of black college libraries through graduate work under Louis Round Wilson in the 1940s. Her thesis on the library in black land-grant colleges provoked the association of presidents of those colleges to focus their 1944 conference on library improvement.[20]

In private institutions, too, Hampton graduates served with distinction, although seldom for such long periods (F. L. Yocom, personal communication, September 6, 1974; M. S. Grigsby, personal communication, February 18, 1975; Battle, 1960).[21,22] Several Hampton graduates and future faculty of the Atlanta University School of Library Service first served private black colleges.[23] As the practice of employing black librarians became widespread and scholarship funds became available from the GEB and the Rosenwald Fund, blacks began to attend library schools in the North and to return to black colleges to make further contributions (Carmichael, 1994, pp. 27-104).[24]

Opinions of the quality of the work of Hampton's library school graduates are divided. Virginia Lacy Jones, dean of the Atlanta University School of Library Service, stated that Curtis exerted enormous personal influence upon her, and that Hampton graduates were able to provide the essential service for black colleges of the period, building and organizing collections for the training of teachers (V. L. Jones, personal communication, May 23, 1974). Wallace Van Jackson, despite personal fondness for Curtis, felt that Hampton turned out too many "desk watchers" who did not "know books." Hampton failed to produce scholars equal to the college's professors or to teach proper methods of service for students and faculty (W. Van Jackson, personal communication, June, 1974).

The work of organized philanthropy, first felt in black college libraries during the 1920s, accelerated during the 1940s and 1950s. The great virtue of foundations like the GEB was their support only for specific purposes within realistic general policies (Jeanetta Roach, personal communication, February 21, 1975).[25] Until trained librarians became available, it was not feasible for foundations to make direct gifts for books. Therefore, in 1926, they cooperated to provide trained staff to acquire and make effective use of such gifts. The Hampton Institute Library School was established with a grant from the Carnegie Corporation; scholarships for its students were funded by the GEB; and the ALA Board of Education for Librarianship fully accredited it as a senior undergraduate library school in 1930 (Curtis, 1927, p. 378; S. C. N. Bogle, personal communication, May 10, 1930).

In 1927, when the Julius Rosenwald fund began to provide matching funds for the purchase of books for black colleges, Curtis, as a paid agent of the fund, approved lists of books sent by the colleges and forwarded them to Samuel Leonard Smith for purchase (F. R. Curtis, personal communication, November 10, 1933).[26] The benefits of the Rosenwald program were three-fold. Between 1927 and 1932, at a cost to the fund of about $60,000, nearly $350,000 flowed into forty-one black college libraries. The fund would pay one dollar for every two dollars spent by the schools for book purchases, but it required that a trained librarian be employed to organize the books and that adequate library housing be provided (Smith, 1950).

Representatives of the GEB and the Carnegie Corporation attended the first conference of black librarians held at Hampton in March, 1927. Foundations subsequently sponsored one such conference at Fisk in 1930 and three at Atlanta in the 1940s. In addition, they funded training programs for school librarians beginning in the summer of 1930 at Atlanta University and from 1936 to 1939 at Fisk, Hampton, Atlanta, and Prairie View (V. L. Jones, personal communication, May 23, 1974).

The most visible programs of organized philanthropy in black college libraries featured three attempts by the GEB to create research libraries in black universities. The GEB supported the union of the Meharry and Fisk collections in 1930 and provided funding for the $400,000 Cravath Library. In 1932, the GEB committed $600,000 to Atlanta University to endow a joint library for black colleges in the city of Atlanta (Kuhlman, 1966, p. 65).[27] The third effort for black college library cooperation followed the formation of Dillard, and it attempted to pool the libraries of Dillard, Xavier, and Southern University at New Orleans (V. L. Jones, personal communication, May 23, 1974). Louis Round Wilson, compiling "Statistics of Southern Negro University Libraries, 1938-1939" included only Fisk, Atlanta, Dillard, and Howard; the four had essentially been created by the GEB.

Although Jim Crow begot many monstrosities, it is pleasing to note that the libraries of our traditionally black colleges and universities became monuments to human hope. The dedicated work and sacrifice of individual blacks and whites overcame inadequate resources, prejudice, hatred, and the fear of one's enemies, as well as ignorance, authoritarianism, and the condescension of one's friends. Black academic libraries, thoroughly transformed in the latter part of the twentieth century, have been constructed on the foundations of scholarship, service, flexibility, and promise, honed in an earlier, more difficult era.

NOTES

[1] The crash of 1929 and the Great Depression demonstrated among other things that too little income had reached the consumer.

[2] This figure may be misleading since the 1930 *Survey of Land-Grant Colleges and Universities* indicated these state schools used only 1.9 percent of their income for library purposes.

[3] FDR's desire for the support of the southern bosses allegedly prompted the quip to Hopkins, "they may be SOBs but they are our SOBs."

[4] Athelma Nix promoted a request to the South Carolina legislature that a PWA library be considered for SC State but was refused.

[5] Lincoln, PA, 40,000; Talladega, 25,000; Tuskegee, 21,167; Atlanta University, 16,243; Virginia Union, 15,000; Johnson C. Smith, 13,500; West Virginia State, 13,078; and Wilberforce, 12,912.

[6] 1.8 percent of its fiscal 1927 budget.

[7] 69-900 passim.

[8] One of six American Baptist Home Mission Board schools was below standard, as were four of six run by the American Missionary Association division of the Congregational Church, six

of eleven by the Methodist Episcopal, one of three by the United Presbyterian, two by the United Christians, and one by the Catholic Church.

[9] Dillard was formed from New Orleans University and Straight College in 1935 and Huston-Tillotson in 1952.

[10] Klein's judgment is here brought to question since in 1927 he found that collection to be well-selected for reference and for collateral reading in support of the curriculum even lacking the Shaw list which was perhaps too generous.

[11] One president reported: "Sometime after I went to the University I had a very good friend in the state senate who followed me through a number of experiences with the governor and with legislature. Then I called on him for a grant of $10,000 for books for the library. And he called on me and said 'See here Professor, you know I have supported you for eight or ten years in your program at the university, but I just can't go with you on this program, because you know and I know and everybody knows that college students are supposed to buy their own books.'"

[12] Livingstone College was placed on probation in 1935.

[13] The librarians at Kentucky State in 1939 were apparently excepted from this general rule (Louis Round Wilson interview). Until Jim Crow laws were lifted in southern hotels, permitting blacks and whites to use the same facilities, southern cities were excluded from consideration as ALA convention sites.

[14] A telegram from Carl H. Milam to Louis Round Wilson dated 27 April 1925 reads like a secret memorandum: "Can you undertake at our expense a visit to Tuskegee and Hampton to obtain for the Board of Education for Librarianship information about library administration, standing with faculty, staff income, and presidents' probable attitude towards a school for librarianship if a few thousand dollars were given for such a school? It is important to have a report before May 1st, if possible. You are authorized to use this telegram as credentials. Avoid publicity. Wire collect."

[15] The first officers of the NC Negro Library Association were college librarians: President, Mollie Huston, Shaw; Vice President, Mollie Dunlop, Winston-Salem; Secretary, Josephine Sherrill, Livingstone; and Treasurer, Pearl Snodgrass, St. Augustine's.

[16] The report entitled "The Library of the Negro College" was based on visits in the fall of 1925 to Howard, Atlanta, Morris Brown, Spelman, Johnson C. Smith, Morehouse, Greensboro A & T, Bennett, Shaw, Winston-Salem, Allen, Benedict, Claflin, SCC N & M, and Petersburg N & I. Curtis elsewhere indicates that only one Negro held a professional degree in 1925.

[17] Perhaps the most effective white librarian who served in this period was Wilhemina E. Carothers, a graduate of the University of North Dakota and the University of Illinois, who presided over the merger of New Orleans University and Straight College libraries from 1935 through 1940.

[18] Arthur Klein recommended in 1930 that the Hampton Institute Library School be reduced to a junior undergraduate library school. Curtis's spirited defense, outlining the errors of such a course of action, prevailed (Undated letter to Arthur J. Klein).

[19] Lyell's activities did not stop with libraries for she gave bond for one of the first sit-ins, was an active supporter of the Freedom Riders, and in other less controversial ways served her community.

[20] Association of the Presidents of Negro Land-Grant Colleges *Proceedings of the Twenty-Second Annual Conference, October 24-26, 1944* (Chicago: n. p., 1944). Featured speakers included Robert Bingham Downs, Ruby Stutts Lyells, Elizabeth Atkins Gleason, and Charles Harry Brown.

[21] Yocom was not impressed for, when she replaced a Hampton graduate at Fisk in the mid-thirties, she found a large box of unprocessed books shoved in a corner. The librarian at Meharry quipped that those were probably the hard ones. Yocom reported, "They weren't."

[22] Theodus Gunn is exceptional, for he shares with Camille Shade, of Southern University, Baton Rouge, Louisiana, the record for longest continuous service to a Negro college library, forty-one years. *A History of the Carnegie Library at Johnson C. Smith University* (M. S. thesis, University of North Carolina, 1960).

[23] Eliza Atkin Gleason, Winston-Salem; Virginia Lacy Jones, Atlanta; and Wallace Van Jackson, Virginia Union.

[24] Wallace Van Jackson, Ruby Stutts Lyells, Eliza Atkins Gleason, and Arna Bontemps attended Chicago; Zenobia Coleman, O. J. Baker, and Parepa Watson Jackson attended Columbia; and Mollie E. Dunlap graduated from Michigan.

[25] Even generous benefactors could be extravagant on occasion. While in the 1940s the Woolworth Library still suffered for lack of funds at Tougaloo, Eva Hills Eastman had special library furniture flown in from California (Franklin & Moss, 1994, p. 379). Rockefeller by contrast gave the GEB $53 million to expend as it saw fit.

[26] Curtis, in a letter to Wilson dated 10 November 1933, stated that although Rosenwald monies had dried up, lists of books were still sent to her for approval. Interview with Jones and Thomas Rankin Barcus, *The Carnegie Corporation and College Libraries, 1938-1943* (New York: Carnegie Corporation of New York, 1943). Grants for library purposes begun in the 1920s by the GEB were supplemented by the Carnegie Corporation in the 1940s and by the Ford Foundation in the 1950s.

[27] Served jointly were Atlanta University, Clark, Morehouse, Morris Brown, Spelman, and Gammon Theological Center.

REFERENCES

Agnew, D. C. (1970). *Seventy-five years of educational leadership.* Atlanta, GA: Southern Association of Colleges and Schools.

Association of the Presidents of Negro Land Grant colleges. (1944). *Proceedings of the twenty-second annual conference* (October 24-26, 1944). Chicago. IL: The Association.

Atkins, E. (1936). *A history of the Fisk University Library and its standing in relation to the libraries of other comparable institutions.* Unpublished Master's thesis, University of California.

Barcus, T. R. (1943). *The Carnegie Corporation and college libraries, 1938-1943.* New York: Carnegie Corporation of New York.

Battle, M. E. (1960). *A history of the Carnegie Library at Johnson C. Smith University.* Unpublished Master's thesis, University of North Carolina.

Carnegie Commission and General Education Board. (1941). *Library Conference Held Under the Auspices of the Carnegie Commission of New York and General Education Board, March 14-15, 1941.* Atlanta, GA: Atlanta University.

Curtis, F. R. (1926). The library of the Negro college. *The Southern Workman, 55,* 472-474.

Curtis, F. R. (1927). The contribution of the library school to Negro education. *The Southern Workman, 56*(August), 373-378.

Curtis, F. R. (1925-1930). The library of the Negro college. *Papers.* Hampton, VA: Hampton Institute.

Davis, J. W. (1933). The Negro land-grant college. *Journal of Negro Education, 2*(July), 312-328.

Directory of Negro graduates of accredited library schools, 1900-1936. (1937). Washington, DC: Columbia Civic Library Association.

Duncan, A. M. (1955). *History of the Howard University Library: 1867-1929.* Rochester, NY: University of Rochester Press, ACRL.

Dunlap, M. E. (1941) Carnegie Library, Wilberforce University. *Wilberforce University Quarterly Alumni Journal, 4*(February), 6-8.

Fisk University. (1928-1945). *Annual reports, 1929-1933.* Unpublished manuscript.

Franklin, J. H., & Moss, A. A. (1994). *From slavery to freedom: A history of African Americans* (7th ed.). New York: McGraw-Hill, Inc.

Grotzinger, L. A.; Carmichael, J. V., Jr.; & Maack, M. N. (1994). *Women's work: Vision and change in librarianship: Papers in honor of the centennial of the University of Illinois Graduate School of Library and Information Science* (Occasional Papers No. 196/197 of the Graduate School of Library and Information Science at the University of Illinois). Urbana-Champaign, IL: Graduate School of Library and Information Science, University of Illinois.

Havlik, R. T. (1968). The library services branch of the U. S. Office of Education: Its creation, growth, and transformation. In M. J. Zachert (Ed.), *Library History Seminar No. 3* (Proceedings 1968). Tallahassee, FL: School of Library Science, Florida State University.

Hulbert, J. A. (1943). The Negro college library. *Journal of Negro Education, 12*(4), 623-629.

Johnson, C. S. (1938). *The Negro college graduate.* Chapel Hill, NC: University of North Carolina Press.

Jones, M. P. (1969). *History of Fayetteville State College.* Fayetteville, NC: Fayetteville State College Press.

Josey, E. J. (1969). Edward Christopher Williams: A librarian's librarian. *Journal of Library History, 6*(2), 106-112.

Klein, A. J. (1929). *Survey of Negro colleges and universities* [Bulletin, 1928, no. 7. U.S. Dept of the Interior. Bureau of Education]. Washington, DC: USGPO.

Klein, A. J. (1930). *Survey of Land-Grant colleges and universities* [Bulletin, 1930, no. 9. U.S. Dept of the Interior. Bureau of Education]. Washington, DC: USGPO.

Knight, E. W. (1937). *A study of Hampton Institute, Part 1*. Chapel Hill, NC: University of North Carolina Press.

Kuhlman, A. F. (1966). *Preliminary report on some library problems and opportunities of the Atlanta University Center*. Nashville, TN: Vanderbilt University Press.

Lowell, M. H. (1942). *College and university library consolidations*. Eugene, OR: Oregon State System of Higher Education.

Regulus, H. (1955). *An evaluation of the Savannah State College Library, Savannah, Georgia.* Unpublished Master's thesis, Atlanta University, Atlanta, GA.

Riggs, D. E. (1971). Bluefield State College Library history and development. *West Virginia Libraries, 24*(January), 10-12.

Shiflett, O. R. (1996). *Louis Shores: Defining educational librarianship.* Lanham, MD: Scarecrow Press.

Smith, S. L. (1950). *Builders of goodwill: The story of the state agents of Negro education in the South, 1910 to 1950.* Nashville, TN: Tennessee Book Company.

South Carolina Colored Normal and Mechanical College. (1936). *Annual reports of the President.* Orangeburg, SC: South Carolina Colored Normal and Mechanical College.

Southern Association of Colleges and Secondary Schools. (1935). *Annual report.* Atlanta, GA: SACS.

Southern Association of Colleges and Secondary Schools. (1949). *Annual report.* Atlanta, GA: SACS.

United States Office of Education, Federal Security Agency. (1940). *Biennial survey of education in the United States, 1938-1940.* Washington, DC: USGPO.

Van Jackson, W. (1940). Negro library workers. *Library Quarterly, 10*(1), 95-108.

Wilson, L. R. (1925). *Papers 1833-1981* (Southern Historical Collection) Chapel Hill, NC: University of North Carolina, School of Library Science Library.

A History of the Holland Public Library, Wichita Falls, Texas, 1934 -1968

❧ Andrea L. Williams ❧

S egregation of African-Americans in the United States affected all aspects of Southern Black-White relations, including activities of real or imagined intimacy. Even libraries, frequently viewed as benign institutions, reflected the prevailing social realities. The life of Libbie Fair Holland Library in Wichita Falls, Texas, is one example of a racially segregated institution.

Segregation was upheld by law. The landmark Supreme Court case, *Plessy vs. Ferguson* (1896), helped codify racial relationships providing legal justification to those whites who believed the South could handle its "Negro problem" without federal interference. Previously, the Hayes Compromise of 1877 had neutralized the likelihood of "forced intimacy." The compromise ensured victory for presidential candidate Rutherford B. Hayes, a Republican, over Democrat Samuel J. Tilden. In that election, the South did not press the issue of contested electoral votes, and a specially created Electoral Commission voted in favor of Hayes. Thus southern governments ended the hated Reconstruction rule over southern affairs, specifically important for issues affecting Black citizens (Lowery & Marszalek, 1992, p. 123).

Jim Crow laws flourished, creating an "Alice in Wonderland" world of contradictions. Every institution was forced to maneuver through barricades of racial laws and customs. White nurses could not treat Black male patients. White teachers were forbidden to teach Black students. "Negro" and "White" textbooks were kept separate. The list of restrictions was endless (Bennett, 1987, pp. 256-57).

Post-reconstruction life in the United States, especially in the South, hinged on three accepted "truths": that Slavery had been relatively benign; that Africa was the home of dark-skinned and intellectually barren peoples; and that the sciences, biological and social, could "prove" the first two assumptions. Racial etiquette during the years of segregation involved a construction of relationships, public and private, that maintained order between two racial groups that were viewed as inherently different (Newby, 1968, pp. 6-7).

The history of the Holland Public Library illustrates problems of a similar nature, in this case, how negative racial attitudes influenced an educational agency like the public library. Holland Library sprang to life in Wichita Falls, Texas, in 1934 and "officially" died in 1968. It was a branch of the Kemp Public Library, and its history parallels that of its parent. Its maintenance and operation reveal much about White and Black racial ambivalence.

Kemp was the dream of a wealthy and locally prominent White family. A successful businessman, Joseph Alexander Kemp was at various times a grocery wholesaler, land developer, and railroad investor. From 1892 to 1922 he was president of the City National Bank (Kelly, 1982, pp. 107-08). Most activities that he or his wife deemed worthy of their personal involvement received community support. During Christmas in 1916, Mrs. J. A. Kemp expressed a desire that Wichita Falls have its own library. By 1918 the grand opening had taken place (Kelly, 1982, p. 69).

Early chroniclers of racially separate libraries viewed these institutions as community centers, believing that such libraries offered an escape from poverty, ignorance, and negative racial policies (Bell, 1917, p. 170). Public libraries generally have been described as "displaying a democratic idea of being free to people of all ages, races, occupations, and beliefs. They offer recreational, informational, and educational reading. They can be used at a person's leisure" (Davis-Randall, 1943, p. 13). Some have argued that libraries are not merely places to acquire knowledge, but institutions "to prepare the individual for his or her role in society. . . . [Individuals] should be prepared for different social roles for which they are fitted" (Du Mont, 1986b, p. 505). The Kemp family's interest in libraries had grown from community ideals like these. The lack of service to Blacks put Wichita Falls in a class of cities not providing library service to this group. In 1939, a survey reported that library services in the former Confederate states matched the pattern of separate facilities for the two races with dramatic inequities in the service provided. Forty-four percent of White residents were receiving some measure of library service versus 21 percent of Black residents (Gleason, 1941, p. 93).

Holland became an important project of locally prominent Black resident, A. E. Holland. Arrie Elsworth Holland served as principal at Booker T. Washington High School from 1922 to 1946. During his tenure, the high school won accreditation, expanded its curriculum, increased enrollment, and developed a thriving sports program. A reverential obituary in the *Wichita Falls Record News* depicted a man of great achievement. Holland was prominent throughout the state, having served as president of the (Black) Teachers State Association in 1920. He almost single-handedly organized, trained, and supervised the first summer school for Negro teachers at Texas College in Tyler. For a man who marked his beginnings from a humble log cabin in Willis, Texas, to the status and respect of a principal, he had "come a long way." His wife, Libbie Fair Holland, earned much respect in her own right. She graduated from Bishop College in 1909 with a Bachelor of Science degree. From 1912 to 1918 she taught Latin and mathematics at her alma mater (*Dedication Exercises of the Libbie Fair Holland Branch of the Kemp Library*, 1934).

Although A. E. Holland's association with the library community of Wichita Falls began in the early 1930s, the question of outreach service had been raised by the Kemp Public Library Board meeting as early as 1927. Much of the city's nearly 10 percent Black population was not being served. The board mulled over a request for a proposed branch for Negroes but no decision was made at that time (Minutes of the Kemp Public Library, 11 April 1927).

A slippery economy seemed a major factor in the delay; by 1929 it was evident the economic boom was over. Oil prices had dropped dramatically (Allen, 1965, p. 40). By 1933 the library's budget had shrunk to $9,943 from a 1929 request of $15,500. The city's tax collection rate dropped alarmingly while use of the library was on the increase. Louis Round Wilson, the South's most prominent librarian, stated that "library boards hesitate to make large appropriations for Negroes while service to Whites is still inadequately financed." Such economically shaky conditions made the board's silence understandable (Allen, 1965, p. 111; Allen, 1965, p. 40; Wilson, 1938, p. 32).

Leaders interested in the Black community took the next most logical step, pushing forward to create something of their own without waiting either for economic changes or for the White community to take a more active interest. A. E. Holland and others had established the Colored Library Association (CLA) composed of the Rev. Moses Pimms; Zenobia Trimble, welfare supervisor; G. E. Denman, post office clerk; Susie E. Simms, housewife; Jacob Birk, parks laborer; Lucious Williams, pastor; Rudledge Strickland, teacher; and Annie Davis, drug store owner (Poist, 1987, p. 1B). In 1930, Kemp Library had responded to a survey on service to Blacks stating that "a Negro committee has been to the library and asked for some kind of help"; the library feels "that before long some arrangement must be made to take care of the Negroes" (Shores, 1930, p. 151).

The CLA organizers were solidly "middle class." Two individuals applied for the position of librarian: Clara Denman, wife of G. E. Denman, CLA board member; and Nina Warren (Jackson & Jackson, 1982). The board hired Warren, explaining that members at Kemp said she would "care for and issue books" at a monthly salary of $80. The parent library processed the books acquired. Holland was open daily for three hours in the afternoon with greater interest than the founders had anticipated. By June 1934, the Holland branch reported more than 100 registered borrowers (Allen, 1965, p. 63; and Minutes of the Kemp Public Library, 19 June 1934).

Other signs of success manifested a strong current of community support for the fledgling institution. The Holland Library depended in part on A. E. Holland's skill in acquiring and sustaining the interest of White patrons. Some observers have commented that Black cultural efforts often depended on interested Whites for partial financial support (Goldfield, 1990, p. 30). For example, the 1934 dedication program for the Holland Library listed prominent White citizens. Mr. Silk was described as the "initiator of the library movement for Negroes in Wichita Falls." H. D. Fillers, school superintendent, gave a greeting as did Thomas Vague from the Lions Club. Finally, Kemp Library Board President, Mrs. J. A. Kemp, gave a greeting (*Dedication Exercises of the Libbie Fair-Holland Branch*, 1934).

To help Holland Library, A. E. Holland cultivated leaders in the White community. Letters such as that of 5 January 1925 to Holland from Kemp testify to the esteem Holland met in the eyes of local power brokers: "We assure you that it was a pleasure for Mr. Kell and myself to make this small donation, in behalf of our good colored citizens." The donation was a five-acre park, Lincoln Park. On 16 March 1929, J. H. Allison, vice-president of *Wichita Daily Times* and *Record News*, solicited nine other white friends to contribute $5.00 each for Holland's $50.00 membership dues for the State Interracial Commission. Allison described "the commission [as] accomplishing a great deal in bringing about better understanding between the Negroes and White people and they [were] doing particularly important work among our Colored friends" (J. H. Allison, personal correspondence, 16 March 1929).

A strong current of community support arose for the new library. In 1935, the Booker T. Washington High School graduating class gave principal A. E. Holland a half-tone enlargement of a portrait of his late wife, Libbie Fair Holland. The portrait would eventually hang in "her" library. The Lions Club offered assistance as did the Black auxiliary of the American Legion which conducted a book drive. Efforts such as these accompanied the opening of the library in April 1934 (Jamison, 1958, p. 12; Allen, 1965, p. 63).

Collaborative efforts made the dream a reality. The local school board provided a portable building and moved it to the corner of Edison and Marconi streets (Minutes of the Kemp Public Library, 22 June 1933). James B. Marlow, former city manager, donated $10 lots to A. E. Holland as CLA trustee (County of Wichita Deed, 1936, v. 338, p. 451). Understandably, the Kemp Library Board was impressed by Holland's initiative and his stewardship of meager resources. The Policy Committee of the Southeastern Library Association hints that such efforts appealed to White library boards that were grappling with the issue of service to Negroes. Frequently, financial support was limited, more costly than originally realized, and regarded as experimental rather than permanent (Minutes of the Meeting of the Policy Committee, Southeastern Library Association 1929, in Du Mont, 1986b, p. 493).

The experimental nature of libraries for Blacks was much like Black education and the social role it implied, which became the subject of controversy. In 1910, one pundit (Odum) stated "the Negro schools taught under present conditions have not produced desired results. . . . They have been unsatisfactory." Many early twentieth-century curricula seemed to have the sole purpose of ensuring that racial roles remained intact. "Character building" with an emphasis on "humility, self-control, and satisfaction with the poorer things of life" were viewed with official favor. The society needed a population that, while ill-equipped for major technological change, would be quite suitable for a lower niche (Newby, 1968, p. 66; Goldfield 1990, pp. 56-57). With such attitudes shaping formal education, it is quite understandable that agencies such as libraries would be viewed as experimental.

Holland was considered a success at the time of its combination anniversary and memorial service in May 1935. By then the library had a used classroom that later would be enlarged with a donated building. The school district landscaped the area and provided greenery. The CLA aided in landscaping, laying walks, and planting trees. The American Legion-led book drive resulted in the acquisition of *World Book Encyclopedia* and the *Encyclopedia Americana* (Allen, 1965, p. 7; Minutes of the Kemp Public Library, 22 June 1933 and 19 June 1935).

When one considers that, by 1936, Kemp finally made new book purchases to replace its "tattered" collection, Holland and the CLA had achieved a great deal. Library service to Blacks had depended on improving attitudes toward library service in general and on a measure of racial tolerance. But the missionary-like attempts to serve Black patrons from limited funding resulted in comparatively less support for other cultural institutions (Yust, 1913, p. 165).

After the self-congratulatory period immediately following Holland's opening, the next major library development was the arrival of Jessie Freeman. The scope of her interest and experience was such that she was destined to do more than merely "take charge" of the books. She began her duties in 1945 and remained a fixture at Holland until her death in 1966. Freeman taught English for one year in Arkansas before moving to Wichita Falls and, though an occasional substitute for the Wichita Falls Independent School District, her professional career and public identity grew from her service as librarian at Holland (Interviews with Charlye Farris, August 1989 and William Freeman, 27 July 1994).

Although not formally trained in a library school, Jessie Freeman had carved a niche as an educated community-minded individual associated with service and concern for others in a genteel fashion. She was an officer in the Les Belles Lettres, a local social and service Black women's club that sponsored Negro History Week programs. She was an agent for change at the library, viewing it as a community center and using it to host club meetings. Her leadership of the library corroborated the much earlier observation of Bernice Bell (1917) who said that: "The people need the library as poverty, ignorance, and a lack of race pride have prevented friendly cooperative intercourse of the race" (p. 170).

By 1940, the population in Wichita Falls was 45,112. The work force was concentrated among males at 81.8 percent, but even women who worked outside of the home made up 30.8 percent of the population. Approximately 10 percent of non-Whites were described as "seeking work" (U.S. Bureau of the Census, 1943, v. 2, pp. 1017, 1022). Under such straitened conditions, the library might have had a role as a peoples' university, essential to a life-long learning process.

Education is frequently viewed as a means to economic self-sufficiency. A contemporary editorial on Black adult education proposed "implementation of the principle that education is a continuous process throughout life, and assumes in general that formal schooling at least to the point of functional literacy has been completed" (Thompson, 1945, p. 269). Yet southern Blacks received inferior schooling regardless of how much formal education they had. The very nature of this education brought with it uncertainty. Howard Odum, early twentieth-century sociologist, suggested that textbooks for Negroes needed modification in keeping with their lowered possibilities. "Textbooks are needed which are especially adapted to the Negro [mind] . . . and [are] graded to teach the things fundamental in their proper education" (Newby, 1968, p. 67). Attitudes such as these expressed the assumption that education must ultimately equip children to function in socially designated roles.

During the 1940s, Holland Library attempted to expand services. In 1946 the library celebrated National Book Week with a story hour, a nursery rhyme contest for children, and a book review session for adults. Florence Vaughn, a volunteer, reviewed James Street's *The Gauntlet*. Helen R. Henderson, a part-time employee, recalled that Vaughn served as a guest storyteller in which capacity she once dressed as a witch. A former librarian-educator at Prairie View A & M College, Vaughn had been one of several volunteers, children and adults, that Freeman had recruited from the community (*Wichita Falls Times*, November 10, 1946, p. 8A).

During the 1940s, the library began celebrating Negro History Week. For assistance, Freeman solicited her colleagues in the Les Belles Lettres Club. The club advanced its goal to "improve [women] intellectually, spiritually, and physically so as to live more abundant lives, and thereby benefit the lives of others," through special themes: Negro History a Foundation for Integration (1954); Negro History in an Era of Changing Human Relations (1956); and Negro History, a Factor in Nationalism and Internationalism (1958). Henderson remembered that the library staff created displays on Negro history using its own meager resources plus some materials from Kemp's collection.

Jessie Freeman was personable and friendly, "going out of her way" to make all those who came to Holland feel welcome. Childless herself, her people skills were especially noticeable with children for whom she established a summer reading club in the late 1940s. She offered the library as a meeting place for the Les Belles Lettres, the Progressive Club (another women's social group), and for Boy Scout Troop 21, which met in the library weekly for several years (Interviews with Earnestine Washington and William Freeman, August 1989).

Two disquieting notes were sounded during this period: financial short-ages and collection inadequacy. Property values required more than fifteen years to reach the 1929 pre-depression height totalling $51,913,700. Values for five-year intervals were $30,675,830 (1934); $30,722,050 (1939); $36,169,940 (1944); and $50,732,220 (1949). City taxes did not include a separate rate for library support until 1942, and then at only three cents per $100. Kemp's library income had fallen from $15,500 in 1929 to $9,225 in 1934. Limited resources resulted in few extras for a library system consisting of Kemp, Holland, and two library stations in the city (Allen, 1965, p. 111).

Eight years after its birth, Holland seemed neither "fish nor fowl," in part because its association with Kemp resulted in meager financial support. In 1942, Jessie Freeman appealed for interested clubs, organizations, and indi-viduals to donate books to the Holland Library. Holland depended on dona-tions and cheerfully accepted them, large and small, including a gift of fifty-four books from Mrs. Joe Martin along with a one-year $14 subscription to the *Christian Science Monitor.* More bountiful was the offering from Sheppard Field, an air base established in Wichita Falls during World War II. Its highly successful Red Cross Book Drive netted 4,000 books for distribution among several area libraries. Student volunteer Ruth Henderson recalled that many of these materials were outdated, but voracious young readers could quickly go through the limited juvenile offerings (*Wichita Daily Times,* February 8, 1942, p. 10B; Minutes of the Kemp Public Library, November 1946 and 16 May 1949).

Even though such donations were made, the discrepancy between the nation's professed belief in equality and democracy and its practices at home increasingly stood out during the 1930s and into World War II. An important contemporary librarian, Louis Shores, described separate branch libraries for Blacks as "poorly equipped, inexpertly staffed collections of obsolete volumes, called a 'colored branch'" (Shores, 1932, p. 377). In "Democracy Begins at Home," an article published in 1940, Francis Allen denounced recent attempts to reconsider the American Library Association's 1936 decision that confer-ence meetings would thereafter admit members "upon terms of full equality." Allen questioned librarians who "talked a lot about indoctrinating for democ-racy. . . . How can we . . . if we ourselves cling to outmoded and supremely undemocratic ideas of class and race privilege?" (Allen, 1940, pp. 56-57).

In November 1946, Holland trustees Donnell, Cline, and Robertson, along with the librarian (Barbara Chapin Jamison) met with Jessie Mae Freeman, Zenobia Trimble, and A. E. Holland. The latter two had been founding mem-bers of the Colored Library Association (CLA). Holland urged that the Hol-land branch be opened daily and, although not implemented, his proposal rep-resented an early attempt for Holland to achieve greater equality in the overall library system. While this library board meeting was apparently genteel, it was also a clear sign that the CLA questioned the Holland Library's colored branch status. World War II had marked a dividing line in Black-White relations in many parts of the country. For example, Lonnie Smith, a Black Houston dentist attempted to vote in a *de facto* Whites only Democratic Party primary. The Supreme Court in *Smith vs. Allwright* (1944) decided in the doctor's favor. Cases such as this one became numerous enough that they began to challenge racial "business as usual" (Minutes of the Kemp Public Library, November 1946; Lowery & Marszalek, 1992).

In succeeding decades, all public institutions would increasingly seek new answers to this very old question. The 1940s were characterized by a push through previous limits of what Holland's library service might become, and in Jessie Freeman, the library was led by an individual with the education and commitment to influence favorably the community she served. Still, the Kemp Public Library Board remained indifferent to the expansion of services to Blacks.

A. E. Holland and other CLA members had been lobbying for change. They promoted the celebration of Negro History Week at both Holland and Kemp. In 1950, Mrs. W. B. Bagby and Mrs. W. T. Kendall presented book reviews for both adults and children. Poster and art exhibits were mounted with the theme "Freedom with Opportunity." City merchants cosponsored an art exhibit featuring local talent. Volunteers painted the interior of the Holland Library and donated light fixtures. News accounts depicted a livelier institution than the one which had met in special meetings with the library board in 1946.

The most striking change in the Holland Library in the 1950s was its legal status. In February 1950 it began moving from a vague uncertain posture to a legally defined relationship, due to the urging of A. E. Holland and the CLA with their proposal to the Kemp Public Library Board that the city council consider receiving the Holland Library building and its lots as official city property. The CLA's intent in making this offer was to upgrade the services provided for the Black community. Board members Maer, Donnell, and Cline were appointed to inspect the Holland building. The inspectors were stunned by what they saw. Cline urged that the board unanimously report to the city council that "business as usual" was not good enough even at the Holland Library. The board agreed that improved facilities and larger collections were necessary and asked that all expenses in building repair and equipment installation be incurred by the city rather than the library's budget. The Kemp Library staff would support the effort by processing and cataloging the new books purchased (Interview with William Freeman, August 1989; Minutes of the Kemp Public Library, 12 February 1950 and 11 April 1950).

In order for the work to proceed, James B. Marlow and Joe W. Marlow, who had provided land for the CLA, forfeited their property to the city of Wichita Falls, thus the CLA gave up its claims to lots where the Holland Library had been established. In a specially called meeting, the CLA entered into an agreement with the city to spend at least $3,500 on library materials and to maintain the Holland library property. Members of the CLA present constituted a quorum: A. E. Holland, president; Jessie Mae Freeman, secretary; M. K. Curry, pastor of the Antioch Baptist Church; Ike Hayes; William A. Freeman, public school teacher; and F. D. Burnett, public school principal (County of Wichita, 1950, vol. 458, pp. 419-25).

With legal transactions completed, several months passed before a contractor began repairs. News accounts duly informed readers of Holland's renovation plans. As library board member Ernest Robertson noted in the *Wichita Falls Times* on February 13, 1950 "the quarters need renovation." This account states that Holland's problems symbolized a general financial crunch in providing library service. Holland's services had also been limited due to expanding services among various library stations and a branch. Voters were asked to raise the tax per $100 valuation from three cents to five cents. More money would have to be available than in the past according to a May 13, 1950 account in the *Times.*

By the time the newly renovated library had its grand opening in the spring of 1951, the repair costs totaled $7,700. The renovation featured a new asphalt tile floor, redecoration and painting, new shelving, new furniture, and most importantly, new books. Other changes included an increase in hours from three days a week to four hours daily, Monday through Friday afternoons, and 8:30-12:30 P.M. Saturday. Jessie Mae Freeman, successor to Nina Warren since 1945, was given a major increase in salary to $143 per month. The action of the board was a late but honorable attempt to improve Freeman's situation (Allen, 1965, p. 64).

The decade of the 1950s brought further critical questions about Holland's efforts at expansion. Could the library become a more active vehicle of informal education in the Black community? Circulation figures illustrate that between 1934 and 1954 Holland had a 58 percent increase. The library's community of possible users was always constituted of Black city residents and they never represented more than 8 to 10 percent of Wichita Falls's population during the decades the library was open. Still, such figures suggest the library had quietly earned an important niche in the local population.

Several Les Belles Club members recalled the 1950s as the decade of their most sustained use of the library's facilities. Eva Neal, a former elementary school teacher, preferred not to view Holland as a segregated institution. For her, the library had been close to home and Jessie Mae Freeman had been a close friend. Another club member, Gloria Lyday, was an active participant in the club's Negro History Week programs and viewed the Holland Library as having books that told "her story." To supplement Holland's collection, Freeman borrowed materials from Kemp, the parent institution, a practice especially important when it came to "race" books. For Lyday, the library provided materials relevant to residents interested in books about Blacks, for example, a biography of Joe Louis. When Lyday finally began using Kemp in the mid- to late-1960s, she was upset to find some of her old favorites missing (Interviews with Eva Neal and Gloria Lyday, August 1994).

Dorothy Wilson, a Holland employee from 1956 to 1957, remembered things differently. For example, a Joe Louis biography was really quite popular with adults (although written for children) because the library had such few new titles of interest to older readers. Even after the 1951 refurbishing, the Holland she remembers was never closely linked to Kemp.

> There did not appear to be a relationship. It still was two separate institu-
> tions loosely linked. For kids I feel the library was adequate because it
> was never heavily used. I remember stretches of days when there was
> little use. I'm not sure why, but maybe kids used the school library and
> saw no need to go anywhere else. Nor did ministers (who were the lead-
> ers in the black community) encourage their congregations to pursue in-
> terests that were not specifically connected to the church. (Interview with
> Dorothy Wilson, August 1994)

Holland's new physical improvements brought with them a price—the dissolution of the CLA which had labored steadily and hard through A. E. Holland's efforts. By 1950, A. E. Holland was in his 70s, and no figure would emerge during the remaining years of the library's existence to promote its interests with anything like Holland's level of energy, vision, and political skill. Librarian Jessie Freeman was beloved and viewed universally as intelligent and friendly, but she did not have a coterie of White supporters. Holland, on the other hand, had at critical points in his professional life created both public and private identities and promoted them, as opportunities arose, on behalf of ac- tivities for the Black community.

By 1950, Wichita Falls had undergone a population boom of 33.8 percent since the previous census (U.S. Bureau of the Census, 1953). Earnestine Wash- ington moved to Wichita Falls in the late 1940s and would later recall Jessie Freeman's amusement at how popular her job had suddenly become once the city took over and her salary increased. Conditions had improved radically and the library's public status had risen. The library still had a small coterie of supporters; for example, the Omega Psi Phi fraternity (of which William Free- man was a member) donated an air conditioner to complement the one the city had furnished for the newly renovated library in 1950 (Interview with Earnestine Washington, August 1989; Jones, 1976, p. 1B).

Other changes were underfoot as well. Jessie Freeman was regarded by Barbara Chapin Jamison, Kemp's librarian, as very knowledgeable about the Black community. Freeman also attended a 1954 district Texas Library Asso- ciation meeting in Mineral Wells and a state meeting in Dallas. Such continu- ing education, while haphazard, was a positive step. Public libraries, no matter how dubious their services seemed to some, certainly merited city governmen- tal support. Regardless of the financial straits Black public libraries faced, it was vital that they be led by persons with training and education for the services provided (Minutes of the Kemp Public Library, July 1954; Du Mont, 1986a, pp. 237-38).

By 1953, the Southern Regional Council reported that fifty-nine cities allowed the "full use" of main public libraries by Negroes; twenty-four communities allowed the "limited use" of facilities; and eleven, through one or more branches, allowed "full service" regardless of race. Integration was most common in large urban centers with 50,000 or more or where Blacks were few in number (Cole, 1976, pp. 61-63; Parker, 1953, p. 72).

Integration was gingerly discussed in a library board meeting in 1955 and then dropped (Minutes of the Kemp Public Library, April 1955). The matter slid into obscurity for the remainder of the decade. As other institutions grappled with this issue on a more vocal basis, the library board's silence spoke volumes. Helen Henderson worked at Holland from 1947 to 1955 as a part-time assistant to Jessie Freeman. Henderson compared the chilly atmosphere she felt in dealing with the Kemp staff with the cheerier mood she felt when she would use Kemp Library as a library patron in the mid-1960s. She did not recall visits from Kemp personnel to Holland during her tenure. Mary Gipson, an assistant from the late 1950s to the early 1960s, recalled Jamison and other staff members as cordial, cooperative, and helpful. Perhaps the difference in attitude followed a change in the general social climate as well (Interviews with Helen Henderson, August 1989; Mary Gipson, October 1989).

In the early 1950s, small concessions signaled that the racial balance of power, while still lopsided, was beginning to shift. Local news accounts were replete with random items about "Negro firsts": a respectful obituary on the head of a Black children's nursery; a Negro impaneled on a district court jury; and an editorial applauding the use of Black police officers in Black neighborhoods. While the Kemp Library may have been silent, other voices were being heard, yet as strife involving civil rights increased nationally, racial changes and improvements in Wichita Falls were achieved calmly and without any sense of grand drama.

In the decade of the 1960s, many social-political issues reached a combustible point. Even public libraries, frequently lampooned as bastions of ultra-conservatism, were affected by the civil rights movement among Black Americans. In Danville, Virginia, the public library was desegregated due to sit-ins and legal action. Formerly, library cards for Black patrons were only valid at black branches. Following demonstrations, the library reacted by closing its doors (Mendelson, 1962, p. 62).

Library journals were beginning to examine the necessity of such actions as Black Americans made effective use of direct confrontation. Reporters described sit-ins designed to force racial integration of public libraries. Eric Moon discussed integration in an editorial now recognized as a classic, "The Silent Subject." He urged the ALA to encourage Southern trustees who had peacefully desegregated to aid others just beginning the process in their librar-

ies. He also called for moral support for all librarians and organizations engaged in the fight for library users' rights (Moon, 1960, pp. 4436-37).

The passage of the Civil Rights Act of 1964 made the continued segregation of public accommodations in hotels, restaurants, theaters, parks, and other
public places illegal. Even a Gallup poll taken in January 1961 showed that 76
percent of White Southerners believed the desegregation of public facilities was
inevitable although the means by which the social revolution would come varied from the vocal to the placid (Goldfield, 1990, p. 146).

Library services for Blacks remained stagnant in Wichita Falls. In 1963,
the city had the dubious distinction of having the second smallest collection
among five Texas municipalities of comparable size. Two years later, Wichita
Falls was the sixth in library income of six libraries surveyed (Allen, 1965, p.
112). The 1960 census showed a population of 101,724 of which 8,223 were
black. While the median school years completed was 11.8 for Whites, the figure was 8.9 for Blacks (U.S. Bureau of the Census, 1963).

Dorothy Allen (1965), historian of Kemp Public Library, commented on
the low number of registered library card holders in the non-White sections of
Wichita Falls. Residents were described as low-income, less-educated, and
"consequently with less motivation for reading" (p. 93). Such an appraisal,
without further analysis of the community, failed to address the needs of nearly
10 percent of the community's residents. A lack of motivation should never be
viewed as even partial response to inadequate library services. Available circulation figures show a small decrease of 4 percent from 1954 to 1959 but a major
increase of 39 percent from 1959 to 1963. The popularity of the collection was
remarkable given the indifference of city government to Holland's staff, collection, and services.

Library users from the Black community on the east side seemed to have
taken the situation as a given. After graduating from Howard University's law
school in the 1950s, Charlye Farris returned to her hometown. She recognized
the library's shortcomings but also viewed it as "our library to be loved and
cherished. In the midst of its faults it seemed okay because we saw it as an
intellectual center in the Black community, a place that was not a joint" (Interview with Charlye Farris, August 1989).

Earnestine Washington recalled that most people who used the library
were children who came because Jessie Freeman made them especially welcome. Freeman went out of her way to involve them in what she was able to
offer; occasionally she took them on field trips. Equilla Luke remembered that
as a child growing up she could visit the library, one of the few places (outside
of church) that her grandparents entrusted her to go without their immediate
supervision. The Jessie Freeman she remembers did not overly monitor or
attempt to curtail her reading interests, but allowed her interests to roam as
widely as Holland's eclectic collection would take them. From the age of eight
up to her late teens, her reading fare varied from *An American Tragedy* to
works by Willa Cather. Apparently, the respect garnered for Jessie Freeman

precluded any serious scrutiny of either limits or the unmet potential of Holland Library (Interviews with Earnestine Washington, August 1989 and Equilla Luke, August 1994).

In 1962, the Kemp Library Board issued a statement that service would be open to all users regardless of race who wished to use the main library or any branch (Allen, 1965, p. 93). Yet, most Holland Library users did not regard this policy with enthusiasm. Many residents such as Earnestine Washington still preferred the familiarity of Holland. Except for a small Black middle class, many Black residents did not have cars. Residents felt that with Holland in the midst of the Black community, they had little need to change.

Additional observations from the Holland staff explain the reluctance of Blacks to use the Kemp Library or the branches. Freeman maintained her Black clientele due to her love and respect for, and her pride in, Black history and culture. Such was the recollection of Mary Phillips, a high school student hired in 1960. Freeman paid Mary and her twin sister, Martha, from her own resources until 1962 when the city began to consider them as official employees. Although she left Wichita Falls to attend North Texas State University from 1964 to 1966, Mary returned to the city and the library. When Freeman died in 1966, Mary Phillips was selected as the new librarian and, like her predecessor, was someone who took a special interest in working with children.

Others with a more jaundiced view held that the library was in dire need of reexamination. In November 1967, Barbara Jamison reported that Mary Gipson had requested an assistant. Jamison felt that the relatively low circulation at Holland did not justify the added expense. While Mary Gipson charitably recalled the board as agreeable to work with, she believed that it held a limited vision of what Holland could become. The level of services and hours of opening had not changed substantially since 1950, when the building had been remodeled. Thus the library became a part-time institution with minimal services for children and no programs for families. The library badly needed more space, expanded reference services, an improved building, and new equipment. If the Holland Library were to attract more people, major improvements were needed; otherwise the library would have to be closed (Minutes of the Kemp Public Library, 16 November 1967; Allen, 1965, p. 94).

By mid-1966 Jessie Freeman had died and A. E. Holland was 90 years of age; he would live only three years longer. Those who recall both with a combination of awe, respect, and admiration admitted that there was no corps of actively involved supporters who could fill the vacuum left by Freeman and Holland. After the Holland Library was transferred to the city in 1950, its fortunes lay in the hands of forces outside the Black community. The library was allowed to rise or fall on its own perceived merits, but in reality it was ensnared in a dead-end. With only token financial support from the city and quiet praise from the Black community, its limited services were able to attract only the very young.

By early 1968, city administrators began to discuss the relocation or discontinuance of the Holland branch since the building stood in the way of a proposed Edison Street extension. These talks proved to be the final nail in the coffin. Jack Davis, city manager, contended that Holland had been the product of a segregated era, always inadequate in books and facilities. After the building was gone, library users would be served by Kemp (Minutes of the Kemp Public Library, 12 June 1968; City of Wichita Falls Inter-office Memorandum, 1968).

Bob Hughey, assistant city manager, and Barbara Jamison, city librarian, described the library closing as the most reasonable response to heavy expenses, minimal usage, and increasing maintenance requirements. Jamison cited studies suggesting where branches should be located. While the arguments they offered were reasonable, they were made in the context of recent attempts by Holland personnel to improve services by proposing additional staff and increased hours. Intransigence on the board meant that Holland was destined to be second rate. The decision to close the library was simply one more in a larger pattern of benign neglect (Minutes of the Kemp Public Library, 12 June 1968). Although sharp controversy arose over the court-ordered closing of the segregated Booker T. Washington high school, little controversy arose when the Holland Library closed on August 1, 1968.

In April 1968, Mary Phillips married and moved away. The only remaining staff member at Holland was custodian William Freeman, husband of the late Jessie Freeman. He accepted the city's offer to transfer to Kemp Public Library, and he served as clerk-page until his retirement. The property's appraised value of $6,800 was transferred to the city's library's fund (Interview with Mary Phillips, 1989; City of Wichita Falls Inter-office Memorandum, 1969; Parker, 1979, p. 1B).

Eva Neal felt that the better educated population was saddened, but that most residents were likely indifferent to Holland's closing; the library had not touched their lives in the same way that the old dual school system had. At its demise, Holland was a reminder of the past rather than part of the bright path to a future that involved integration ("Board Recommends Library Closing," 1968, p. 24A; "School Board Reveals," 1968, p. 1A).

After usable volumes from the collection were transferred to Kemp, the Holland Library building itself served variously as a storage facility, a home in Petrolia, Texas, a Greek restaurant, and today it is a Chinese restaurant. In looking back at why the library died with barely a murmur, Charlye Farris says concisely:

> We saw it as inevitable and necessary for it to close; it was a remnant of a
> separate but unequal age, that no one ever pretended was o.k. Keeping it
> open with all its inadequacies would be extending another remnant of a
> part of our history we were trying to dismantle. (Poist, 1987; interview
> with Charlye Farris, August 1989)

REFERENCES

Allen, D. L. (1965). *Kemp Public Library: a history, 1896-1963.* Unpublished master's thesis, University of Texas at Austin.

Allen, F. (1940). Democracy begins at home. *Junior Librarian, 1*(2), 56-57.

Bell, B. W. (1917). The colored branches of the Louisville Free Public Library. *Bulletin of the American Library Association, 11,* 70.

Bennett, L. (1987). *Before the Mayflower: A history of black America.* Chicago, IL: Johnson Publishing Company.

Board recommends library closing. (1968). *Wichita Falls Times,* July 11, p. A24.

City of Wichita Falls inter-office memo: Administration. (1968). Minutes of the board of aldermen (July 29). City Clerk's Office, City of Wichita Falls, 1300 Street, Wichita Falls, TX 76301.

City of Wichita Falls inter-office memo: Department of public works. (1969). Transfer of right-of-way bond funds to library funds (May 29) City Clerk's Office, City of Wichita Falls, 1300 Street, Wichita Falls, TX 76301.

Cole, E. D. H. (1976). *A history of public library service to blacks in the south, 1900-1975.* Unpublished Master's thesis, Texas Woman's University, Denton, Texas.

County of Wichita deed record. (1936, January 29). *Vol. 451:* p. 19389.

County of Wichita deed record. (1950, October 20) *Vol. 458:* pp. 419-425.

Davis-Randall, B. (1943). Public library service for negroes. *News Notes: Bulletin of the Texas Library Association, 19*(April), 13-14.

Dedication exercises of the Libbie Fair-Holland Branch of the Kemp Library. (1934). Unpublished manuscript, April 29.

Dumont, R. R. (1986a). The educating of black librarians: An historical perspective. *Journal of Education for Library and Information Science, 26*(Spring), 233-249.

Dumont, R. R. (1986b). Race in American librarianship: Attitudes of the library profession. *Journal of Library History, 21,* (Summer), 488-509.

Gleason, E. (1941). *The southern Negro and the public library: A study of the government and administration of public library service to negroes in the South.* Chicago, IL: University of Chicago Press.

Goldfield, D. (1990). *Black, white, and southern: Race relations and southern culture, 1940 to the present.* Baton Rouge, LA: Louisiana State University Press.

Jackson, C. E., & Jackson, G. M. (1982). *The history of the Negro in Wichita Falls, Texas: 1880-1982.* Unpublished manuscript, including J. H. Allen correspondence of March 16, 1929.

Jamison, B. (1958). Kemp Public Library in Wichita Falls. *Texas Libraries, 20*(1), 11-13.

Jones, C. (1976). Library buildings odyssey comes to an end. *Wichita Falls Times,* August 14, p. 1B.

Kelly, L. (1982). *Wichita County Beginnings.* Burnet, TX: Eakin Press.

Lowery, C. D., & Marszalek, J. F. (1992). *Encyclopedia of African-American Civil Rights.* New York: Greenwood Press.

Mendelson, W. (1962). *Discrimination. Based on the report of the United States Commission on Civil Rights.* Englewood Cliffs, NJ: Prentice Hall.

Minutes of the Kemp Public Library. (1927-1968). Wichita Falls, TX: Kemp Public Library Board.

Moon, E. (1960). The silent subject. *Library Journal, 85*(22), 4436-4437.

Newby, I. A. (Ed.). (1968). *The development of segregationist thought.* Homewood, IL: The Dorsey Press.

Parker, L. J. (1953). *A study of integration in public library services in thirteen southern states.* Unpublished Master's thesis, Atlanta University.

Parker, M. (1979). Library work soothing claims former educator. *Wichita Falls Times,* 15 January, p. 1B.

Plessy versus Ferguson. (1896). 163 *U.S. Reports* 537 (May 18).

Poist, P. (1987). Educator started library in wife's memory. *Wichita Falls Times,* February 25, p. 1A.

School board reveals sweeping change. (1968). *Wichita Falls Times,* July 12, p. 1B.

Shores, L. (1930). Public library service to Negroes. *Library Journal, 55*(February), 150-154.

Shores, L. (1932). Library service and the Negro. *Journal of Negro Education, 1*(3-4), 374-380.

Thompson, C. H. (1945). Editorial note: Adult education for negroes in the United States. *Journal of Negro Education, 14*(3), 269.

U.S. Bureau of the Census. (1933). *15th census of the United States, Vol. 2.* Washington, DC: USGPO.

U.S. Bureau of the Census. (1943). *16th census of the United States, Vol. 2.* Washington, DC: USGPO.

U.S. Bureau of the Census. (1953). *17th census of the United States, Vol. 2.* Washington, DC: USGPO.

U.S. Bureau of the Census. (1963). *18th census of the United States, Vol. 2.* Washington, DC: USGPO.

Wilson, L. R. (1938). *The geography of reading: A study of the distribution and status of libraries in the United States.* Chicago, IL: American Library Association and the University of Chicago Press.

Wichita Falls Times. (1942). February 8, p. 10B

Wichita Falls Times. (1946). November 10, p. 8A.

Yust, W. F. (1913). What of the black and yellow races? *American Library Association Bulletin,* (Spring), 159-167.

The Ugly Side of Librarianship

Segregation in Library Services from 1900 to 1950

ε❧ Klaus Musmann ❧ε

> I pity the man who cannot read, who, like the man without natural sight, cannot see and understand the beauties of the boundless universe of God; and I pity, too, the man who, though he can read, has not learned to love books and does not enjoy through them the companionship of great intellects and great hearts. (Cansler, 1929, p. 401)

Few contemporary accounts exist that have treated the topic of segregation in libraries in a comprehensive and systematic way. Donnarae MacCann (1989) stated that the literature on library service to minorities is less developed than the publications on libraries and immigrants (p. 103). A few doctoral dissertations explored very limited aspects of this topic (both in terms of time and service orientation) or were biographical in nature. A large number of articles, essays, and masters' theses have examined this subject from a local perspective, but no truly exhaustive study on libraries and segregation has ever been published. This essay on segregation in libraries represents a preliminary sketch on the services provided by libraries to African Americans during a period of strict segregation. The eventual aim is to gather sufficient information to write a comprehensive historical narrative of this period.

The period under review covers two landmark U.S. Supreme Court decisions. In 1896, the court ruled in *Plessy v. Ferguson* that the provision of separate but equal public accommodations and facilities for white and "colored" persons was within the confines of a state's rights. This decision provided the legal basis for all subsequent segregation (Plessy v. Ferguson, 1896).

It was not until 1954 that this decision was overturned when the court ruled in *Brown v. Board of Education* (1954) that separate but equal educational facilities were inherently unequal and therefore unconstitutional.

After this historic decision, a great number of studies on libraries and African Americans appeared, but nearly all of them excluded the period prior to 1954. Many of the publications dealt with continuing discrimination in employment for African-American librarians although a few accounts depicted the problems of coming of age in a segregated society. Among the several perceptive essays covering this subject rather well and objectively is Du Mont's (1986) "Race in American Librarianship: Attitudes of the Library Profession." Clack's (1979) contribution in the *Encyclopedia of Library and Information Science*, "Segregation and the Library," likewise deserves attention. Also of interest is the previously cited article by MacCann (1989) comparing library services to immigrants and minorities in her book, *Social Responsibility in Librarianship*. Another worthwhile collection of essays was selected for *Educating Black Librarians* (Speller, 1991). Some of these are essential reading for anyone interested in this topic, and they are particularly recommended for the history of library education at a predominantly African-American institution, North Carolina Central University.

In "A Study in Contrasts," MacCann (1989) compared the substantial efforts public libraries expended on service to immigrants beginning in the 1880s and contrasted these efforts to the minimal services provided to African Americans. In 1916, the American Library Association (ALA) instituted a committee designed to coordinate library services to immigrants, the Round Table on Work with the Foreign Born. Active for some thirty years, this committee spanned a period marked by widespread hostility toward immigrants. Immigration restrictions were instituted during the 1920s, but ALA continued to provide extensive services and assistance to immigrants. Yet, the same individuals within the American Library Association considered the problem of delivering library services to African Americans as a regional one and, therefore, not worthy of the attention of the national organization of librarians. MacCann (1989) expressed it rather well when she stated that many of the same arguments used in support of service to immigrants could have been applied to assistance to African Americans. "Like immigrants, Black Americans were a large percentage of the population only in certain regions, yet a profession mobilized itself for the sake of advancing immigrant, but not African American, interests" (p. 103).

Beginning in 1913, the Louisville public library offered a highly successful training program for black library assistants, but access to higher education was severely limited for African Americans. Edward C. Williams, the first African American to receive a library degree, graduated from the New York State Library School in Albany in 1900 (Jackson, 1939, p. 215). Few other African Americans were able to join him in becoming librarians. By 1925, only six African Americans were known to have graduated from accredited library schools and to have served actively in their chosen profession. Between 1925 and 1939 the Hampton Institute in Virginia was the only library school available to African Americans. The school was closed in 1939. In 1941, the School of Library Science at North Carolina College for Negroes and the Atlanta University School of Library Service were founded. Accredited in 1943, Atlanta was the only predominantly African-American school to receive ALA's seal of approval until 1975. During that year, North Carolina Central University was also accredited. Atlanta's dean, Eliza Atkins Gleason, was the first African American to receive a doctorate in librarianship (Stevenson, 1991, p. 116).

In 1903, library service for African Americans was established in Memphis, Tennessee, apparently as a cooperative arrangement between the Lemoyne Institute, a private school, and the public library of Memphis. During the same year, according to Casper Jordan and E. J. Josey (1977), the Charlotte Public Library in North Carolina created a separate library for African Americans. Evidently, it was the first such institution with its own independent board (p. 16). A year later, similar library services were provided in Galveston, Texas, through a black high school. In 1905, the first separate branch library building for African Americans was constructed in Louisville, Kentucky. Over the next few years, branches of public libraries serving the African-American population were established in a number of states. At least sixteen such segregated facilities had been established by 1918 (Reason, 1975, p. 23).

One such facility was built in Knoxville, Tennessee, with the aid of the Carnegie Corporation. During the opening ceremony, Charles Cansler (1929), the principal of a black high school, praised the construction of the building:

> These people know, as all of us know, that a little more than 50 years ago the printed page was sealed to Negroes. They did not possess the key that unlocks the storehouse of the treasures of the world. They had eyes, but they could not see. They had ears, but they could not hear. They had intellects, but they could not think.
>
> To those who have lived in that other world, who walked the streets of Knoxville when the statutes of our state provided a penalty for Negroes being found with books in their possession, how great must seem the transformation as they view our beautiful new Carnegie library, with its ample and splendid equipment for the members of their race. (p. 400)

It may be difficult for a contemporary reader to grasp fully the meaning of this speech. Cansler did not present some colorful abstractions merely to illustrate a point. African Americans in many southern states had not been permitted to acquire their own books; they were punished for attempting to read or write. Legislation in many states expressly prohibited the African-American population from learning how to read. When Charles Cansler spoke of statutes prohibiting the ownership of books, many individuals in his audience understood his remarks from personal experience. For example, legislation enacted in Virginia in 1831 read as follows:

All meetings of free Negroes or mulattoes at any school house, church, meeting house or other place for teaching them reading or writing, either in the day or the night shall be considered an unlawful assembly. Warrants shall direct any sworn officer to enter and disperse such Negroes and inflict corporal punishment on the offenders at the discretion of the justice, not exceeding twenty lashes. Any white person assembling to instruct free Negroes to read or write shall be fined not over $50.00, also be imprisoned not exceeding two months. (Guild, 1936, pp. 175-76)

At the turn of the century, a relatively high percentage of African Americans continued to dwell "in that other world" Cansler had mentioned. Although African Americans had made tremendous strides in the intervening years, they had not eradicated entirely one of the most pernicious legacies of slavery: the inability to read or write. Census figures for 1870 showed that only 20 percent of African Americans had been classified as being literate during that year. This percentage had risen to 70 percent by 1910 and to almost 80 percent by 1920 (U. S. Dept. of Commerce, 1975, p. 382).

Libraries cannot thrive in an environment where a large number of individuals are prevented from reading or are prohibited from owning books. "Libraries can not flourish in illiteracy as trees can not grow in a desert," stated William F. Yust (1913), librarian of the Rochester Public Library, in an address to the ALA conference in 1913. Yust asserted that the establishment of libraries for African Americans was a relatively unimportant objective for the majority of either the black or the white population. He blamed the small number of libraries which served the African-American population upon the fact that educational facilities were of very recent origin. However, he also singled out the attitudes of white people who thought that educating African Americans was not a desirable goal since it would "spoil a good plow hand." Without education, Yust continued, libraries could not exist. Education must precede the establishment of libraries.

He chastised librarians for enforcing segregation in Southern libraries and for providing library collections "of dubious value, so unsuitable as to be almost worthless....the discarded refuse of garrets and overcrowded store rooms, which should have gone to the paper mill, but was sent to these poor children through mistaken kindness" (Yust, 1913, pp. 159-64). Throughout the southern United States, Yust stated, segregation functioned in all educational and religious institutions including libraries. He cited four possible methods for providing library services to the largely unserved population of African Americans in the southern states: (1) African Americans could be admitted to the same building on an equal basis although such a policy would be unacceptable to the white majority. Yust quoted an unnamed source who described the objections as follows: "There are white people who are deterred from using the library because in so doing they must touch elbows with colored folks....We could do better service to both races if there could be a separation, for we must take the people with their prejudices, especially in the use of the library, which is a purely voluntary matter." (2) African Americans could be admitted to the same building, but a separate room would be provided for library services to this group. One unnamed librarian stated that educated African Americans would not come to the library under such conditions. "Many of the educated and cultured negroes (for there are some even in the South) will not come unless they can do so on the same social equality and use the same apartments as the white patrons." (3) African Americans could establish their own library under their own boards, but Yust ruled this out assuming "inferior results on account of [African American] inexperience and lack of knowledge regarding every phase of the work." (4) The most acceptable solution in the view of Yust, a white librarian, was to establish "a separate branch in charge of colored assistants who are under the direction and supervision of a white board and a white librarian." Yust offered no apologies for such an arrangement, insisting that such segregated facilities would improve library services to African Americans. He proposed such arrangements for northern cities in order to reach a larger number of African Americans living in the segregated neighborhoods of large urban areas.

In 1922, the *Library Journal* featured a brief excerpt claiming that the first branch library for African Americans had been founded in Galveston, Texas, in 1905. "So far as we know this was the first branch library for colored people to be established anywhere in the country. The plan has proved a decided success with us" ("Galveston," 1922, p. 206). This "branch" was located in an addition of a segregated high school building with the principal of the school responsible for the library. The work was performed "by a colored girl who has had at least a high school education." This library subscribed to 21 periodicals and contained 1,100 volumes which, by 1918, had grown to approximately 3,000 volumes. "Conditions in Galveston required that the use of library privileges by the colored citizens should be separate and distinct from their use by the white people." As these conditions were never elucidated, one must assume that the white population did not tolerate the presence of African-American readers in their libraries.

A few descriptions of these early segregated branch libraries for African Americans can be found in contemporary literature. Rachel Harris (1915), an assistant in the Eastern Colored Branch of the Louisville Free Public Library, described her experiences in this particular branch, defended the establishment of segregated branches, and employed arguments used by W.E.B. DuBois to defend her own position. She quoted DuBois as follows:

> Every argument which can be adduced to show the need of libraries for whites applies with redoubled force to Negroes. More than any other part of our population they need instruction, inspiration, and proper diversion; they need to be lured from the temptations of the streets and saved from evil influences, and they need a growing acquaintance with what the best of the world's souls have thought and done. It seems hardly necessary in the twentieth century to argue the necessity and propriety of placing the best means of human uplifting into the hands of the poorest and lowliest of our citizens. (p. 385)

Harris argued that such facilities benefitted African Americans greatly by providing free access to books. In her view, a segregated facility was preferable to none at all:

> All of us felt the sting of segregation, but there were those among us who decided to make the best of it, as we knew there were some on the Library Board who felt that they were doing what would prove of more benefit to our race than if the branch were not established. (p. 390)

Moreover, Harris regarded her own people as better acquainted with the needs of African Americans and therefore of greater assistance to them. She stated that the African-American staff of her branch knew its patrons well and provided them with superior service.

> Those of another race cannot know our wants, our habits, our likes and dislikes as we do. They are not thrown among us in the various walks of life and are therefore really not as competent to deal with us as we ourselves are—*if we are prepared.* However much they might try, it would be impossible for them to give us the service that our own race can give in an atmosphere where welcome and freedom are the predominant elements; and this is surely the condition in the colored branch libraries in Louisville. (Harris, 1915, p. 390)

Due to the small number of readers among African-American adults, this particular branch reached out to the young, offered story hours, organized a literary club for boys as well as girls, offered instruction in French, and started a debating society for high school students, the Douglass Debating Club. Thomas Blue, librarian in charge of the two African-American branch libraries, founded the clubs to promote the use of the library (*American Library Annual 1915-1916*, 1916, p. 79). Harris proudly stated that many of the boys, who had participated in these activities only a few years earlier, were now college students, had become teachers or university professors, or attended medical schools. The library staff, Harris modestly noted, deserved some of the credit for this success. The staff had encouraged the boys to continue with their education and had helped them to select only the best of available reading materials. The unexpected success of this branch library made it possible to convince authorities to build another branch on the east side of Louisville in 1914.

Harris praised the help she received from the white staff of the main library although she probably could not or would not have criticized her administration in print. Instead, she commended the librarian and several department heads for their cooperative attitude and "wise supervision." As previously mentioned, this branch also served as a training center for African-American library workers. The library conducted an apprentice class for high school graduates and trained all of its own library assistants. Harris stated that a local residency requirement was waived for African Americans who wished to enter the program.

Some six months later, the editors of the *Library Journal* published much of the same information that Harris had presented in her article. However, the information which appeared in the professional journal had been quoted from an official pamphlet issued by the Louisville library on the occasion of the tenth anniversary of the "first branch for colored people" ("Colored Branches of Louisville Public Library," 1915, pp. 872-74). Much of the information presented was similar although quite a different spin had been put on the material. An appearance of scientific objectivity was introduced by the presentation of many facts and figures. In typical library fashion, circulation figures and building measurements were presented, volumes and users had been counted, and the number of meetings of the organizations that met at the library were duly enumerated. Some of the figures were truly impressive, others were merely useless, such as a listing of the external dimensions of the two branch libraries. Nearly 9,000 individuals were registered as borrowers during the ten years of branch services, and nearly 600,000 volumes had been checked out over the same time period. At the time of publication, nearly 5,000 borrowers were registered. The circulation had grown from almost 18,000 volumes to 105,000 volumes a year.

These impressive figures were presented without context. Omitted were an analysis of the readers' background, information on their social and economic status, and general demographic data. What percentage of the Louisville population consisted of African Americans? How far did readers live from the branch libraries? Were public transportation facilities available for the users of these two branches? Such elementary background information was never presented. Also missing from this report was any description of the organizational structure of these branches and their relationship to the main library. No explanation was included concerning the difficulties the staff had overcome in order to make these branches successful. The staff was never even mentioned; one might assume that this omission was because the staff consisted solely of African Americans or others without library degrees. Any mention of segregation was omitted or was conveniently turned upside down by characterizing it as exclusivity. Platitudes about library services abounded. "This was the first free public library in America exclusively for colored readers and it marked an epoch in the development of the race." This epochal service was accomplished with total holdings of a mere 14,000 books and 137 periodical subscriptions.

Neither Harris nor the *Library Journal* mentioned the longtime director of the "Colored Department" of the Louisville Public Library, Thomas F. Blue. Blue had graduated from Hampton Institute and the Richmond Theological Seminary. He was brought in to work for the Louisville library when its Western branch was opened in 1905. The success of these two branches was in no small part due to the leadership exercised by Thomas Blue (Jackson, 1939, p. 216).

A brief summary of round table discussions "for workers among colored people" at ALA's Swampscott conference was published in the *ALA Bulletin* in 1921 (pp. 200-01). Ernestine Rose, branch librarian of the 135th Street branch in New York City, served as temporary chair of this first discussion group. She wrote that these discussions "brought out different points of view, differing methods, and widely divergent conditions." By reading her notes, one quickly becomes aware of the dismal state of library service to African Americans in many parts of the country. Some of the difficulties discussed by the participants were inadequate representation on governing boards, poor relationships between white and African-American staff members, segregated facilities, and the lack of availability of suitable reading materials. Also prominently mentioned was the role played by the NAACP among African Americans. In New York, the organization was perceived as benign, cooperative, and even beneficial, but in the Southern states, the NAACP was distrusted and was considered to be a radical group. The participants in this first round table voted unanimously to establish a permanent round table in order to further explore library work with African Americans.

The first formal round table was held a year later during ALA's Detroit conference in 1922. The space devoted to the reporting of this meeting in the *ALA Bulletin* was much more extensive than a year earlier, but the problems of racism in library service to African Americans had remained the same ("Work with Negroes Round Table," 1922). The published report of this meeting was primarily a summary of the responses to a questionnaire prepared by Ernestine Rose. Respondents were from 98 of 122 institutions. Analysis of the collected data was anecdotal, nevertheless, some interesting facts can be gleaned. African Americans were universally excluded from the governance of libraries. One library stated that no "particular factions" were represented on its board. One must assume that African Americans were excluded from serving on the board because of their "factionalism." Apparently, only white nondescript business men could qualify for such a peculiar "no particular faction" group. The Atlanta public library responded to the survey with a candor that expressed the contempt the librarian held for black citizens: "We tried having an advisory committee from the colored people, but as they did not confine their activities to advice, we disposed of them" ("Work with Negroes Round Table," 1922, p. 363).

Two segregated libraries were exceptions to the norm. African Americans elected their own boards for the branches they operated. From Charlotte, North Carolina, the white librarian stated that "I have nothing to do with their library in an official way, but always assist them in any way possible." The Savannah, Georgia, librarian stated that "their library has a board entirely composed of Negroes. The situation is all wrong, but conditions make it inadvisable to bring about a change at this time" ("Work with Negroes Round Table," 1922, p. 363).

None of the surveyed libraries employed African Americans educated in a library school. Libraries with segregated facilities employed only black library assistants at such facilities. The Cleveland Public Library did not have a single African American on its staff, relying instead on assistants who were thought to be "sympathetic" toward African Americans "and interested in their welfare." Apparently, only the New York Public Library was sufficiently courageous to "experiment" with the employment of an integrated staff at one of its branches, the 135th Street branch, which later became the Schomburg Center for Research in Black Culture.

Libraries employed three different training models to educate its black employees. Six libraries relied on assistants trained at the Louisville Public Library. Another model, reported by seven libraries, involved employees "trained by the white head librarian or by heads of departments also white." Six other libraries planned to send African-American assistants to library schools although none had actually done so at the time of the survey.

One paper on the training of African-American library assistants stated that such training was still in "the pioneer stage." The writer, Ethel McCollough (1922) of Evansville, Indiana, appeared convinced that the training of African Americans was "much more difficult than among whites, because of their sensitiveness and lack of mental training" (p. 365). A Miss Rice of Chicago asserted that there were no problems in the libraries of Chicago. She claimed that there had been some staff discomfort when two African-American assistants were added to the staff of one branch library, but that the feeling of uneasiness had disappeared. She added that "colored children do not seem to prefer the colored assistants above the white."

Another author stated that racial integrity should be kept intact by training leaders to develop "co-operation with white people." She described librarianship as in the rear guard of the professions. "While other professions have growing numbers of Negroes, only a few librarians have been trained" ("Work with Negroes Round Table," 1922, p. 365). She also predicted a bright future for African-American librarians. "The trained Negro librarian has a virgin field to work among his own race. He is much needed to supplement the work of schools, which are often open only a few months in the year." Thomas Blue of the Louisville library presented a paper on the training of African-American librarians, but his paper was not summarized in this round table report. He was the only participant identified as an African American. The editor of the *ALA Bulletin* had inserted "colored" behind his last name.

Service to African-American readers was likewise unsatisfactory. Only two southern libraries provided "unrestricted" access to African Americans. A library in Kentucky stated that African Americans had the "privilege to draw books from [the] library, but [were] not allowed access to shelves or reading room" ("Work with Negroes Round Table," 1922, p. 362). The public library of Jacksonville, Florida, occupied a very small building, but stated that one of the library's largest rooms was set aside "for colored people." Sixteen southern libraries were not accessible to African Americans at all but had established segregated branches. Several other libraries provided book deposits in schools for the use of students and one library admitted adults in the evening to such a facility.

Some libraries in the East and Midwest provided not only access to libraries but also gave special services to African Americans. On closer examination, these special services turned out to be merely the establishment of additional school deposits or the location of an extra branch in an African-American residential section while allowing black readers full access to other libraries within the same system.

The survey elicited interesting responses about collection development for an African-American readership. Several of the large city systems reported large collections of books on what were termed "Negroid" subjects, topics that were never really defined. Many of these libraries reported that African Americans were able to suggest books for inclusion into the collections. One library stated that it bought everything "on the Negro unless too radical." Another library practiced the same philosophy by buying everything "in print on the Negro question that is not too old or too rabid." This type of book selection indicated the prevailing practice among some public libraries. The cherished ideal of freedom from censorship appeared to have been conveniently ignored.

On a more general observation, Ernestine Rose spoke of the potential for an increase in segregation in the northern states. She thought that it was spreading, but that no one else seemed to share her concern. "Legally, colored and white are on the same ground, but in many cases there is not a real feeling of equality in the library." In the end, the round table for workers with colored people decided that these problems "were too sectional in character to be regularly organized as an A.L.A. section." Rose, the chair of the round table, wanted it to be a permanent one within the American Library Association, but her proposal was watered down and she was instructed "to ask the president of ALA for a round table next year, if thought necessary by her."

A year earlier, Rose had written about her experiences of working in Harlem. In a lengthy exposition of community life in Harlem, she explained the rewards and the problems of a white person working in such an environment. She was much in favor of integration at all levels. She seemed convinced that the major problem was segregation, the "separate life with distinct beliefs and aims which separates all colored people from all whites at the present time" (Rose, 1921, pp. 255-58). In her opinion, segregation was the major obstacle in making the library an integral part of the community. She opposed changing her branch library into a "colored" one, that is, operating it with only African-American assistants. She believed that African Americans were "standing together in a steadfast belief in their own destiny to be worked out within and by themselves." In her opinion, the library had an important role to play in this awakening of a great people.

In 1990, Betty Jenkins wrote a tribute to Ernestine Rose, noting that a white librarian in a black neighborhood constituted a potentially precarious situation. However, Rose's enthusiasm and her belief in the public library, helped to transform this rather undistinguished branch library into a vital community center for African Americans. She organized committees to encourage community organizations to meet at the library, to sponsor exhibits of black artists, and to form a "Division of Negro Literature." She transformed the library into a clearinghouse of information on black culture and received the hearty endorsement of many African-American writers and editors.

The second officially sanctioned round table, "Work with Negroes," took place in Hot Springs, Arkansas, in 1923. Ernestine Rose did not attend this meeting, but she had prepared a paper which was read by Harry Lydenberg of the New York Public Library. Rose's report focused upon the admittance of an African-American applicant to New York's library school; the student had been admitted "on precisely the same terms as the white, and . . . all facilities offered by the school had been at her command" ("Work with Negroes Round Table," 1923, p. 275). She added that a second African-American library school student was attending the Carnegie Library School in Pittsburgh during the same year. But the intervening year had not seen any other improvements in the restrictions imposed on African Americans. Most of the public libraries in the southern states did not permit access to their collections. Only the libraries of Fort Worth, Texas, and Covington, Kentucky, provided admittance to the main libraries although visits to the reference area and the reading rooms were not permitted in Fort Worth.

Henry Gill of the New Orleans Public Library read a paper on books for African Americans. He stated that no statistics existed on this subject and that "even the little defective information that we have" has not been analyzed. "No serious effort has been made to study the psychology of the negro and determine the existence or non-existence of a biological or ethnological distinctiveness that would make the mental attitude of the negro in the selection of books different from that of our Caucasian American people" ("Work with Negroes Round Table," 1923, p. 277). Gill continued by stating that no investigations had been made to find "negro racial traits and characteristics that would disclose themselves in the choice of books and that would be essentially or even superficially different from the selection of other races." He claimed that it had been "plainly established" that in "'the so-called higher capacities, such as constructive imagination, the apprehension of meaning or relationship, reasoning power,' they are decidedly less efficient than the whites" ("Work with Negroes Round Table," 1923, p. 277). He felt that Southerners knew African Americans much better than people in the north, and he "objected to the idea that sentimentality colored the South's relations with the negro." He stated that "there is real affection for household servants, especially the nurse, but there was no sentimentality over it." He claimed that black and white relations would soon take a turn for the worse in the northern states. Gill predicted that this relationship "would rival the extreme bitterness" that existed "on the Pacific coast against the Hindu and Japanese." In Gill's opinion, racial differences created racial irritation. However, he continued, no laws prohibited the ownership of land by African Americans in the southern states unlike those of the western states. In an argument intended to discredit Ernestine

Rose, Charles Johnston of the Cossitt Library in Memphis stated that there were no problems in libraries as long as there was only a small number of African Americans among the general population. But what was there to do, he asked rhetorically, "when the population was forty, fifty, or sixty per cent negro?" ("Work with Negroes Round Table," 1923, p. 278).

In 1930, Louis Shores published a survey on public library services to African Americans in 80 cities with a large number of African-American residents (Shores, 1930). Shores prefaced his article by stating that Fisk University had been approached repeatedly to establish a library school. Survey results were intended to provide the basis for such a decision. In analyzing responses, Shores divided the cities into five categories.

His first category included some eighteen cities which did not provide library services of any kind to African Americans. Among the larger cities in this category were Dallas, Miami, and Shreveport, Louisiana. Shores's second category included libraries which permitted limited use of their facilities by African Americans. Lawton, Oklahoma, permitted its black citizens to come and check out books but did not permit them to stay at the library. Similar arrangements were in effect in Fort Worth, Texas. Other cities, primarily larger ones, permitted African Americans brief visits to the main libraries for materials not available in segregated branches, a practice remaining as long as such visits were not publicized.

Shores's third category included all public libraries which provided segregated public library services. New Orleans, Memphis, and Atlanta were among the largest cities in this category. Interestingly, only Louisville provided somewhat generous support for its segregated facilities. The city employed nine librarians, circulated nearly 157,000 volumes, and appropriated almost $19,000 annually for its segregated branches. No other cities employed more than two librarians or spent more than $6,000 annually on library services to African Americans. Also at the Louisville library "the head of the colored department and his eight assistants [had] the same responsibilities and salaries as workers in the white branches." Libraries in the fourth category were classified by Shores as operating segregated branches or branch libraries which were used largely by African Americans "but with free use of all libraries." Baltimore fell into this category as did Chicago, Detroit, Los Angeles, and New York. The respondent in Baltimore declared that no "distinction in service should ever be made in service to the public." However, when it came to admitting African Americans for library training, equality did not exist in Baltimore. No African American had ever been admitted to its training program. "It does not seem probable that during the near future there will be need of Negro librarians in our public library system." According to Shores, the same was true for Pittsburgh. The hiring of an African-American librarian had "never been considered, and I doubt seriously if any move to do so will be made in the near future." Kansas City permitted African Americans to use all of its library facilities but would not admit any blacks into its training programs since the Kansas City schools were segregated. The librarian at the African-American branch was white since the library has "never found an efficient colored one." The respondent added that an African American could never work at either the main library or at any of the white branches.

In Shores's last and fifth category, he grouped libraries which granted full use of all of their facilities to everyone. Boston, Brooklyn, and Cleveland were included among these. No African Americans were among the staff at the Boston Public Library but, previously, a few women had been employed. The training facilities were open to all although no qualified African American had been admitted during the three years prior to the survey. The same held for Cleveland. In principle, Western Reserve's library school was open to all qualified candidates, but no African-American student had ever been admitted to the school.

In 1936, the American Library Association held its annual convention in Richmond, Virginia. Prior to the meetings, the association had made the following arrangements for its African-American members:

> The American Library Association has obtained the promise from the John Marshall and Jefferson Hotels that Negro delegates to the conference may use the same entrance as the white delegates and will be received and housed in the same manner during the conference meetings. *This does not mean that Negro delegates may obtain rooms and meals at these hotels* as this is forbidden by Virginia laws.
>
> *Those meetings which are a part of breakfasts, luncheons or dinners are not open to Negroes,* who may, however, attend sessions which are followed by meals provided they do not participate in the meals. ("The Spectre at Richmond," 1936, p. 592)

A number of letters responding to these conditions imposed on African-American librarians appeared in professional journals. The writers urged the American Library Association to boycott southern states as sites for future conventions. Yet, during the association's conventions in 1937 in New Orleans, in 1938 in Kansas City, and in 1939 in Milwaukee, African Americans were still not permitted to stay in the convention hotels selected by ALA. One southern librarian voiced his approval of the segregated hotel facilities and stated that such a treatment of African Americans was justified because of long-standing customs and was also practiced in the "federal establishment":

> Few Negroes have attended Westpoint [sic]. Annapolis has never graduated a Negro. A Negro is welcome in the Navy only as a mess boy or a cook. No Negro has sat on the bench of the Federal Judiciary. In the capital city of the U.S., right under the gilded dome of the Capitol, Negroes are excluded from dining in the Senate-Restaurant but they are welcome as waiters. (Cunningham, 1936, p. 515)

In 1943, the first African American was elected to the governing council of the American Library Association. No other action was taken by the organization on behalf of African Americans until after the Supreme Court decision of 1954. Du Mont stated that it was not until the 1950s that the integration of library services was even discussed in professional literature as a viable alternative to the prevalence of segregated service. Following the Supreme Court decision, and especially after the passage of the Civil Rights Act in 1964, some of the traditional obstacles against African Americans started to disappear. In an ironic twist of fate, the years since the enactment of the civil rights legislation even saw the beginnings of a reversal in the employment patterns for African-American librarians. The dean of one African-American library school commented sarcastically on the many urgent telephone calls she had received "to recommend the 'instant' Negro" for a position of responsibility (Jones, 1970, p. 41).

However, many libraries in the South remained segregated institutions until well into the 1960s, and many of the southern state library associations refused to admit African-American librarians as members. As can be seen from the foregoing, the American Library Association made few attempts to enforce equal treatments for its African-American members nor did the association make any collective efforts to assist in improving library services to such a large group of unserved individuals. As MacCann (1989) stated so eloquently, African Americans "were to be treated as a permanent American underclass and library history shows the library profession's culpability in sustaining that status" (p. 103).

REFERENCES

American library annual 1915-1916. (1916). New York: Bowker.

Brown versus The Board of Education of Topeka, Shawnee County, Kansas. (1954). 347 *U. S. Reports*, 483, pp. 483-500.

Cansler, C. W. (1929). A library milestone. In J. S. McNiece (Ed.), *Library and its workers: Reports of articles and addresses* (pp. 399-404). New York: Wilson.

Clack, D. H. (1979). Segregation and the library. In A. Kent (Ed.), *Encyclopedia of library and information science* (Vol. 27, pp. 185-204). New York: Marcel Dekker.

Colored branches of the Louisville Public Library. (1915). *Library Journal, 40*(12), 872-874.

Cunningham, J. (1936). Negro segregation. *Library Journal, 61*(7), 515.

Du Mont, R. R. (1986). Race in American librarianship: Attitudes of the library professions. *Journal of Library History, 21*(Summer), 488-509.

Galveston. (1922). *Library Journal, 47*(5), 206.

Guild, J. P. (1936). *Black laws of Virginia: A summary of the legislative acts of Virginia concerning Negroes from earliest to present.* Richmond, VA: Whittet & Shepperson.

Harris, R. D. (1915). The advantages of colored branch libraries. *Southern Workman, 44*(July), 385-391.

Jackson, W. V. (1939). Some pioneer negro library workers. *Library Journal, 64*(6), 215-217.

Jenkins, B. L. (1990). A white librarian in black Harlem. *Library Quarterly, 60*(3), 216-231.

Jones, V. L. (1970). A dean's career. In E. J. Josey (Ed.), *The black librarian in America* (pp. 19-42). Metuchen, NJ: Scarecrow Press.

Jordan, C. L., & Josey, E. J. (1977). A chronology of events in black librarianship. In E. J. Josey & A. A. Shockley (Comps. & Eds.), *Handbook of black librarianship* (pp. 15-23). Littleton, CO: Libraries Unlimited.

MacCann, D. (1989). Libraries for immigrants and "minorities": A study in contrasts. In D. MacCann (Ed.), *Social responsibility in librarianship: Essays on equality* (pp. 97-116). Jefferson, NC: McFarland.

Plessy versus Ferguson. (1896). 163 *U. S. Reports*, 537(May 18).

Reason, J. H. (1975). Library and segregation. In A. Kent, H. Lancour, & J. Daily (Eds.). *Encyclopedia of library and information science* (Vol. 16, pp. 23-26). New York: Marcel Dekker.

Rose, E. (1921). Serving New York's black city. *Library Journal, 46*(6), 255-258.

Rose, E. (1921).   Work with negroes round table. *ALA Bulletin, 15*(4) 200-201.

Rose, E. (1922).   Work with negroes round table. *ALA Bulletin, 16*(4), 361-366.

Shores, L. (1930). Public library service to negroes. *Library Journal, 55*(4), 150-154.

Spectre at Richmond. (1936). *Wilson Bulletin for Librarians, 10*(9), 592-593.

Speller, B. F. (Ed.). (1991). *Educating black librarians* (Papers from the 50th anniversary celebration of the school of library and information sciences, North Carolina Central University). Jefferson, NC: McFarland.

Stevenson, K. C. (1991). Annette Lewis Phinazee and the North Carolina Central University School of Library and Information Sciences, 1970-1983.   In B. F. Speller (Ed.), *Educating black librarians* (Papers from the 50th anniversary celebration of the school of library and information sciences, North Carolina Central University) (pp. 113-140). Jefferson, NC: McFarland.

U. S. Department of Commerce. Bureau of the Census. (1989). *Historical statistics of the United States: Colonial times to 1970* (Part I, Chapts. A-M, p. 382). White Plains, NY: Kraus International.

Work with negroes round table. (1923). *ALA Bulletin, 17*(4), 274-275.

Yust, W. F. (1913). What of the black and yellow races? *ALA Bulletin, 7*(4), 159-167.

From Segregation to Integration

Library Services for Blacks
in South Carolina, 1923-1962

ი Dan R. Lee ი

I n 1932, Charlotte Templeton, librarian in Greenville County, South Carolina, wrote to Louis Round Wilson, stating that, in her opinion, "Negro
extension work will have to be done (at least in S.C., Georgia, and Mississippi) with no great publicity or it will create antagonism" (Charlotte Templeton
to Louis Round Wilson, Chapel Hill, N. C., 1929, Louis Round Wilson Papers).
Caution and apprehension on the part of officials in providing library services for
blacks would persist for the next thirty years. Native black South Carolinian Rice
Estes (1960), a librarian at Pratt Institute, wrote that the South's "own librarians,
the majority of whom would be overjoyed to see the present situation improve,
cannot easily speak out because of fear of reprisals and political retaliation" (p.
4419).

The political atmosphere and general public sentiment of this era proved
sufficient to intimidate those organizations and individuals involved with library
development. Quite often the advances made for blacks were brought about
through the efforts of non-governmental agencies or concerned citizens with
state and local agencies offering minimal support.

Like most other states in the region, South Carolina in the first half of the
century suffered from slow economic growth, a small tax base, and an inadequate
educational system. In 1930, the state had the highest illiteracy rate in the country (U. S. Bureau of the Census, 1933, Table 142, p. 281). For the large population
of transient sharecropper families, many of whom were black, regular school
attendance was not an option. Educational opportunities for the black popula-

tion were limited in facilities, funding, and school schedules. The school year for blacks in 1932 was comprised of only 114 days, compared to 169 days for whites (U. S. Dept. of the Interior, 1933, p. 95).

While library services in general were slow to develop, services for blacks, who comprised 45.6 percent of the state's population in 1930, were markedly lacking (U. S. Bureau of the Census, 1933, p. 84). The southern states suffered from poor educational systems and slow library development. In 1931, only 11 percent of blacks in the Southern states were reported to have public library service (Franklin, 1980, p. 217). A 1935 study found that, of 565 Southern public libraries, only 83 (14.7 percent) provided service to blacks (Joeckel, 1938, p. 15).

EARLY RESISTANCE TO LIBRARY SERVICE FOR BLACKS

Determined efforts to keep blacks from gaining access to libraries in the state have been documented in library charters and in the correspondence of library officials. One of the most striking examples involves the activities of the Charleston Library Society. The society turned down an offer for assistance from Andrew Carnegie in 1905, out of fear that acceptance of such funding would commit the staff to serving the general public, and therefore blacks. After a personal meeting with Carnegie, William Courtney, president of the Charleston Library Society, responded in a letter dated 4 February 1905:

> Underlying this tax situation is a contingency which should be avoided: in a mixed community such as Charleston, it is believed that however small a tax might be levied for the library, the smallest colored tax payer would have legal rights of admission, which could hardly be avoided. As this is undesirable in every way, taxation could not well be resorted to.... (Carnegie Library Correspondence, 1905, microfilm reel 5)

Courtney's successor, Robert Wilson, echoed this view, continuing dialog with Carnegie but resisting the concept of a free public library (Carnegie Library Correspondence, 1911).

At least two public libraries in the state produced documents explicitly stating racial restrictions. In 1925, the charter of the Florence Public Library restricted access to "all white persons of good repute" (Hux, 1986, p. B1). Use of the Carnegie Public Library in Sumter was limited to "all white citizens of Sumter County" (*Code of Laws of South Carolina*, 1942, vol. 3, § 5560). Libraries in the state were established with an unwritten understanding that blacks would not be given access to white facilities, since the social mores of the time were generally sufficient to prevent mixing of the races in public institutions.

As county library systems were established, provisions for black branches or deposit stations were often included. Prior to county support, black libraries resulted from cooperative efforts among black public schools, concerned individuals, philanthropic organizations, and WPA (Works Progress Administration) demonstrations.

EARLY LIBRARIES

Among the earliest libraries for South Carolina's blacks during this century were the Greenville County Library's Negro Branch and the Dart Hall branch of the Charleston Free Library. In Greenville, a wealthy textile mill owner advanced the cause of library service by funding a demonstration which soon gained public tax support. Thomas F. Parker's plan for library development included provisions for services to blacks in the county, and in 1923 South Carolina's first tax-supported black library was established in the Phyllis Wheatley Association's headquarters. In a speech in 1926, Parker proclaimed "the library opened the first Negro public library in South Carolina, with the largest budget for a Negro public library in the Carolinas, and with progressive methods and aims which are attracting outside attention" (Perry, 1973, p. 15).

An attempt in 1921 to secure a Carnegie library for blacks in Charleston proved unsuccessful. G. D. Brock, of the Charleston Young Men's Christian Association, contacted the Carnegie Corporation requesting financial support, with the association offering to provide housing and staff. The corporation responded that no new projects were being undertaken (Carnegie Library Correspondence, 1921). Six years later, Susan Dart Butler, the daughter of a black minister of the city, utilized the family's Dart Hall and her late father's personal library to provide a reading room for the black community. Butler supplemented her father's collection with books donated and purchased with monies from fund-raising projects, such as community dances held at Dart Hall. Hours of operation in 1927 were 5 p.m. to 8 p.m., three days a week (Bolden, 1959, p. 14). Butler, who served as librarian until 1957, provided this service at her own expense until the library was made a branch of the Charleston County Free Library in 1931. Butler continued to provide the use of Dart Hall for a token amount of one dollar per year until 1952, at which time the county purchased the building ("Charleston County Buys Dart Hall...," 1952, p. A14).

One of the individuals who provided books for the Dart Hall Library was Cecelia P. McGowan, chairperson of the South Carolina Committee of the Inter-Racial Commission. A 1926 article in *Library Journal* reported on McGowan's efforts to "work out a plan for sending small traveling libraries into the rural Negro schools in South Carolina" ("Traveling Libraries for Negroes," 1926, p. 1121). The work of McGowan and Butler, both members of the Inter-Racial Commission, became instrumental in securing Rosenwald funding for the county in 1930 (Walker, 1980, pp. 91-92).

JULIUS ROSENWALD FUND

The Julius Rosenwald Fund served South Carolina by providing funding for both public schools and library services. Sears, Roebuck & Company chairman Julius Rosenwald was strongly influenced by the work of Booker T. Washington. As a result, the philanthropist became heavily involved in furthering educational opportunities for blacks in the United States and especially in the rural South. The fund assisted in the construction of public schools for blacks, with funds matched by state and local communities. As of 1925, this agency had assisted in the construction of 190 schools in South Carolina, representing an investment of over $1 million ("The Rosenwald Rural Schools for Negroes," 1925, p. 677).

In the early 1930s, the Rosenwald Fund provided grants for the establishment of county libraries in seven southern states. The financial arrangements resembled those for school construction, based on matching funds. The community provided a progressively larger percentage over the course of five years at the end of which the community was to provide full support. The agreement stipulated that both Rosenwald funds and local matching funds support reading materials, salaries, and other service-related costs but not rent or purchase of buildings (Embree, 1949, p. 66).

In 1930, Richland and Charleston counties became sites for Rosenwald library demonstrations. The Richland County Library received a grant of $75,000 and Charleston received $80,000, distributed over a five-year period ("Progress and Needs," 1931, p. 235).

Although the Rosenwald Foundation stipulated that, as a condition for funding, library service was to be provided for blacks on a basis equal to that for whites, it appears that the two counties did not actually offer equal service for the two races. Lucy Hampton Bostick, librarian at the Richland County Library, reported in 1936 that "there is a branch for Negroes which serves the city while the rural Negroes are reached through the schools and deposits throughout the county" ("Richland County," 1936, p. 10). Bostick went on to state that "thirty-four Negro schools with 2,585 pupils had deposits which are operated on the same system as the white schools..." (Richland County, 1936, p. 12). The following figures for books deposited for student use were provided by the librarian: for 3,406 white students, 7,709 books; for 2,585 black students, 1,515 books ("Richland County," 1936, p. 12). This breakdown amounts to 2.3 books per white student, and only .58 books per black student, figures indicating that the services for the two races, reportedly offered "on the same system" were far from proportionate.

In addition to the main library, for the exclusive use of whites, four branches for whites were established in Charleston County during the Rosenwald Demonstration era. With a population of over 50 percent black, the only black branch for the city or county was Dart Hall, although a second black branch was opened in the city for a brief time. County service was provided through deposits in black schools. Although a book truck served rural areas, apparently no direct service was offered to blacks. Louis Round Wilson reported in 1935 that "the book truck is used for direct service to white rural schools and for delivering boxes of books to all rural Negro schools" (Wilson & Wight, 1935, p. 40).

The WPA & Library Development

During the late 1930s and early 1940s, in the absence of an active state library board in South Carolina, the WPA performed the functions of such an agency. Assuming the responsibility for public and school library development, the WPA established regional libraries, deposit stations, bookmobile service, and even book repair units. Separate library services were provided for blacks in some, but not all, areas where service for the white population was established.

The WPA approached the need for library service to blacks with caution, and at times deferred from offering such service. Edward Barrett Stanford (1944), whose *Library Extension Under the WPA* focused heavily on South Carolina, made the following report concerning the handling of a tri-county regional library demonstration for the counties of Horry, Georgetown, and Marion:

> Service to the 46,000 Negroes, who comprise 42 per cent of the region's population, has been deliberately postponed by those in charge of the demonstration. Since such service as these folks receive throughout the state is characteristically extended from agencies which were established to serve the white population, it was deemed expedient to concentrate first on developing a strong and permanent regional system, without forcing the racial issue. (p. 176)

Thus, library service for blacks was perceived as a sensitive issue in the state, even when provided on a segregated basis and on a scale markedly inferior to that for whites.

The number of black units and black workers varied throughout the period of WPA library demonstration. A 1940 report in the *Southern Frontier* found thirty WPA library units for blacks in the state, with a total book stock of 32,238 volumes. Blacks operated twenty-five of these (Frayser, 1940, p. 2). According to Stanford (1944), in 1941 the WPA operated twenty-five units for blacks, compared with 392 units for whites. Of 688 WPA workers employed in library service in 1941, twenty-eight were blacks working with black units (p. 176).

Prior to WPA involvement, twenty-one of the state's forty-six counties were without publicly supported libraries (Walker, 1981, p. 2). By 1941, all forty-six counties had received WPA assistance, but only twelve of these were offering services for blacks through WPA demonstrations (Stanford, 1944, p. 158). Overall, the WPA made great strides in establishing interest in library development in the state, with demonstrations paving the way for permanent publicly supported systems. As with WPA demonstrations, these libraries would also offer services for blacks on a limited and segregated basis.

COMMUNITY LIBRARY SERVICE FROM SCHOOLS

Public library services worked closely with public school systems during the first half of this century. The state's library legislation of 1928, which allowed for "the issuance of bonds by school districts for the erection, equipment, and maintenance of libraries as well as schools" set the stage for involving local school boards in library operations (Frayser, 1933, p. 20). Beginning in 1931, the Chester School District provided funding for public library support, with the local black school, Finley High School, receiving a portion of the funding for serving the black community (Walker, 1981, p. 18). The Barr Street Library for

Negroes, a branch of the Lancaster County Library, served under the authority of the Lancaster County Board of Education from 1936 to 1960 (Floyd, 1961, pp. 15-16). A number of other libraries throughout the state, including the Florence Public Library, operated under local school control, funded through taxes raised by local school districts.

With the close association between public school systems and libraries, it is not surprising that a large number of rural communities were served by school libraries. In her 1933 report, "The Libraries of South Carolina," Mary Frayser found this to be a common practice in rural areas for whites as well as for blacks, with teachers generally serving as librarians for the school and community (Frayser, 1933, p. 32). Frayser reported that only forty-four out of 215 black high schools (20.5 percent) held collections of library books at this time. The figures for black elementary schools were considerably lower (Frayser, 1933, p. 29). In a 1938 survey, Frayser found more evidence of community service through schools. Among the black schools offering such service that responded to the survey were Colleton Training School, Marion County Training School, Abbeville County Training School, Allendale County Training School, Bell Street School (Clinton), Alston High (Summerville), Lancaster County Training School, Drayton High School (Newberry), and Finley High School (Chester) (Mary Frayser Papers, 1938).

Emily America Copeland, director of the Library Science Department at South Carolina State College, in a 1947 report to the Negro Advisory Committee of the Southern States Cooperative Library Survey Committee, provided additional evidence of the widespread practice of community library service operating out of black schools for that decade. Copeland's (1946-47) survey found that "of the 27 counties served by county and regional libraries, 123 stations [were] maintained in Negro schools, which [served] both school and adult populations" (p. 5). Schools extending library service to the community rarely received additional funding to provide such service.

Although school-based community library service emerged in both white and black communities, the latter depended on this and other inadequate library services for a longer period, without access to main city or county libraries. Copeland recognized the need for better services under the existing system of separate facilities. In her report, she stated "in spite of the fact that Negro public libraries are branches, they are the main libraries for the Negro population and should provide service as complete as a main library does." In a prophetic tone, Copeland (1946-47) went on to advocate public library involvement in adult literacy programs (p. 5).

The school setting provided a convenient, if not always effective, means of community library service, operating with a minimal amount of additional funding, materials, and personnel. Several disadvantages are evident with such an arrangement. The school setting would seem to have deterred extensive use by adults. Also, many of the libraries were open only during school terms and had limited hours of operation during the school year.

Among the public schools offering service to the public was the Laing School at Mt. Pleasant, a branch of the Charleston Free Library. A report in the *South Carolina Library Bulletin* in 1948 described the limited hours of service: "It is designed primarily for the use of colored adults and is housed in the student library of the school. Library hours are from 4 to 7 on Thursdays" ("Growth of Library Service to Negroes," 1948, p. 2). A privately supported school on St. Helena Island also provided community library service to blacks. The Penn Normal, Industrial, and Agricultural School began in 1862 as an effort by Northern abolitionists to educate former slaves. In addition to offering service to adults in the community, the Penn library also provided extension service to the island's public schools from 1916 to the 1930s (Copp, 1987-1988).

Although teachers generally served as librarians for these community libraries operating out of school buildings, in some locations the principal performed this function. The principal of the Laing School in Mt. Pleasant also served as librarian. Euriah Simpkins, principal and teacher at the Plum Branch Rosenwald School in Saluda County, directed the first Faith Cabin Library, which opened in 1932 (Carr, 1958, p. 15).

BOOK SOURCES

With little if any public funding for library services, many communities relied upon donations of used books. Occasionally, special new collections were also provided. The Julius Rosenwald Fund, in addition to supporting school construction and library operations in the South, made available sets of books considered of interest to blacks. These book sets, offered between 1928 and 1948, consisted of fourteen to fifty books, a substantial collection for many small rural schools at the time. Similar to supporting library demonstrations and school construction, the fund provided book sets to libraries on a matching basis. The fund provided one-third of the cost and the State Department of Education and the local community divided the remainder of the cost (Embree, 1949, p. 263).

Collections of books had been provided earlier in the century by James H. Gregory of Marblehead, Massachusetts. Gregory donated collections of approximately fifty books each to a number of black libraries in the South, with the Library School of Atlanta University acting as distributor. Gregory planned for each set to be made available to the community and to be exchanged among the participating libraries on a yearly basis to provide some diversity in reading ("Marblehead Libraries," 1910, p. 498). That the Laing School, in Mt. Pleasant, Massachusetts, was listed as a recipient of a Marblehead collection suggests that this facility served the public as early as 1910.

Black philanthropist Harvey Kelsey, a native of Chester County residing in Washington, D.C., helped establish the book collection for the WPA regional library for Colleton and Dorchester counties. In 1939, 5,000 volumes were donated (Frayser, 1933, p. 2. See also, Stanford, 1944, p. 168). Lancaster County also received Kelsey collections; Kelsey donated more than 6,000 volumes to the black branch, later named the Kelsey Library (Walker, 1981, p. 34).

One of the most unique movements which provided book collections and inspired community members to build libraries was directed by Willie Lee Buffington of Saluda, South Carolina. Buffington, a white mill worker, led a campaign for donations of "unused used books" which eventually provided collections for over one hundred communities in South Carolina and Georgia.

FAITH CABIN LIBRARIES

Inspired by black schoolteacher Euriah Simpkins, Buffington sent out five letters in 1931 requesting used books for the newly erected Plum Branch Rosenwald school where Simpkins taught. One of the individuals receiving a letter, a minister in Harlem, New York, responded with 1,000 volumes collected by his congregation. This initial donation resulted in the first Faith Cabin Library, formally opened in 1932. Residents of the Plum Branch community pooled their resources and labor to construct an 18-by-24-foot log cabin library near Simpkins's school. Thirty-one other communities in South Carolina and approximately seventy-five communities in Georgia received Faith Cabin collections as news of Buffington's efforts spread through the national press, radio broadcasts, and public appearances by Buffington (Carr's 1958 thesis provides a detailed study of the Faith Cabin Library movement and biographical information on Buffington. See also, Lee, 1991).

As with the first Faith Cabin library, separate buildings, usually constructed near school buildings, resulted from community labor, although collections were also placed in classroom buildings when separate facilities could not be secured. With limited financial support for these libraries, teachers and principals provided free staffing. Buffington promoted the idea of service to adults in school settings with Faith Cabin libraries.

As a condition of receiving Faith Cabin Library book grants, the sponsoring institution had to agree to allow all residents of a community access to the collections. In a letter to a high school principal in 1948, Buffington wrote:

> You should know that we are interested in a community program, not just a school program. The library should be housed in a separate building from the school and while it serves the students of the school should also be open to the adults of the community. (Buffington to King, personal communication, 1947)

Buffington joined the faculty of Paine College, a Methodist-supported black institution in Augusta, Georgia, in 1944. From this date until the early 1960s, most of the new Faith Cabin libraries were established in Georgia. The Faith Cabin locations in South Carolina continued to receive support from Buffington, who visited the sites and supplemented the collections, while establishing at least one new library in the state (in 1949, a book grant of 4,000 volumes was made to St. Matthews, S.C. [W. L. Buffington, 1950]. Reports of visits to various South Carolina and Georgia library sites appear in Buffington's reports to the

Student-Faculty Assembly, Paine College, and reports to the Board of Trustees, Paine College [Buffington, 1950]).

JEANES TEACHERS & HOME DEMONSTRATION AGENTS

Groups not specifically designated to provide library services also played important roles. Jeanes teachers and county home demonstration agents constituted non-library personnel who assisted with basic library services in addition to their regularly assigned duties. Programs such as the Jeanes Program and the Slater Fund, which merged in 1939 with the Peabody and Randolph funds to become the Southern Educational Foundation, helped to provide some privately financed assistance toward educational opportunities for blacks in the southern states region. The Jeanes Program, from the beginning of the century, provided small rural black schools with trained teachers. These individuals offered a variety of services to the schools and communities, assisting local teachers as well as students and actively distributing reading materials for both students and adults in the community. Stanford (1944) noted the work of Jeanes teachers in South Carolina during the WPA era:

> Owing to the lack of separate bookmobile facilities for Negroes, these teachers have helped the WPA project materially in many counties by personally assisting in the distribution of deposit collections of books to rural Negro schools not otherwise reached by county library demonstrations. (p. 183)

In Aiken, the county library began offering service to blacks in the community out of Schofield Normal and Industrial School, the local black training school, in 1946. In this community, a Jeanes teacher also functioned as librarian, overseeing the collection and distribution of books to other schools in the county ("County and Regional Libraries," 1946, p. 5). Louis Round Wilson, in *County Library Service in the South*, reported on the work of a Jeanes teacher in Charleston County in the 1930s:

> Many of the schools which were not served by the Free Library received packages of books from the Jeanes supervisor, who had rendered this service for a number of years. Her collection of books is kept in her home and has been built up largely by gifts from local residents and friends in the North. (Wilson & Wight, 1935, pp. 40-41)

Alice LaSaine, Jeanes supervisor for Charleston County, and probably the teacher referred to by Wilson, distributed books to county residents in the late 1920s. Her activities attracted the attention of officials from the Julius Rosenwald Fund, who visited Charleston to study the situation there prior to funding the county's Rosenwald library demonstration (Walker, 1976, p. 92). LaSaine is listed in the "Roll Call of Workers" section of *The Jeanes Story: A Chapter in the History of American Education, 1908-1968* (Williams et al., 1979) as having served in Charleston County from 1931 to 1957.

The Jeanes teacher for Sumter County, Annie E. Sanders, reported in 1937 "we have bought four sets of books from the Rosenwald Foundation and now have a project to start a circulating library, which we hope will soon be realized" ("Sumter County," 1937, p. 8). Ulysses S. Gallman, Jeanes teacher for Newberry County, worked to secure a Faith Cabin library for his school in 1933. Gallman offered the following report on the varied activities of this library in 1937: "The Faith Cabin library is used as a reading center for all the teachers in the schools of Newberry County; it also sends out books and magazines to those schools that have started libraries" ("Newberry County," 1937, p. 13).

Negro Home Demonstration Agents, in addition to their regular duties, were recruited into library service in the 1940s. Distributing materials loaned by the State Library Board, these individuals provided book delivery to rural readers. The *South Carolina Library Bulletin* reported:

> The agents in 9 counties where countywide service is not available to Negroes have received collections of books from the State Library Board.... The books are housed in the offices of the agents and are circulated through their clubs, and in some instances from their offices on the days they are open to the public. ("Books for Rural Negroes," 1949, pp. 2-3)

By 1950, fourteen counties were utilizing home demonstration agents to distribute books in black communities (*7th Annual Report...*, 1950).

COUNTY LIBRARY DEVELOPMENT

With the end of WPA assistance in 1943, an era of concentrated federal support came to a close and responsibility for library funding shifted to state and local government. The State Library Board, formed in 1929 without funding, began assuming a more important role in state library development. In 1943 the state legislature began offering limited funding for the agency, which promoted county-wide service. This agency administered State Aid Grants to public libraries and, beginning in 1956, became responsible for administering funds under the Library Services Act (Walker, 1981, pp. 2-3).

In 1948, the State Library Board began book deposit service to blacks. The plan called for the "loan of collections of books to communities where no library service is available to Negroes, or to small public libraries serving Negroes with inadequate bookstock" ("State Library Board Inaugurates...," 1948, p. 2). Black librarians were assisted with the selection of materials for these collections. These deposits, ranging from 100 to 200 books, were distributed with assistance from home demonstration agents. By 1953, the board had increased its aid with book grants of 250 to 500 volumes (Walker to Holden, personal communication, NLSF, 1953).

Branch libraries and bookmobile service increased significantly during the late 1940s and the 1950s. In 1947, Estellene Walker, state librarian, reported:

> At present county-wide service is given the negroes in Anderson, Pickens, Greenville, Cherokee, Lancaster, Darlington, Richland, and Orangeburg counties. City libraries serve the Negro population in York, Spartanburg, Green-

wood, Aiken, Kershaw, and Florence counties. Charleston has perhaps the
outstanding service for the entire Negro population of the county. (Walker
to Buffington, personal communication, 1947)

A South Carolina State Library survey in 1952 found twenty-six county or city
libraries with black branches. Charleston County had the highest number of
branches, with four, and Dillon, Spartanburg, and Laurens counties reported
having two branches each ("Public Libraries Serving Negroes...," *Negro Library
Service Files*, 1951-52).

The State Library Board played a limited role in the development of library
services for blacks. This might be attributed in part to the attitude of the agency's
director, Estellene Walker. In contrast to Emily America Copeland, who pointed
out the inadequacies in library and educational services for blacks, Walker at
times chose to blame blacks for conditions in the state. In a July 1955 letter to
Library Journal's Junior Libraries Editor Gertrude Wolff, Walker expressed her
opinion that "the slow development of library service for Negroes is due to the
Negro's lack of interest in library service. Where a request has been made for the
service, it has usually been extended" (Walker to Wolff, personal communication, NLSF, 1955).

As late as 1954, it was reported that approximated 479,716 South Carolinians
were without public library access, the majority of whom were rural blacks (*Eleventh Annual Report of the South Carolina State Library Board...*, 1954, p. 6). In
1955, Estellene Walker declared that "progress is being made quietly to provide
books and library service for the Negro population" (Walker to Wolff, personal
communication, NLSF, 1955). Like Charlotte Templeton in 1932, Walker perceived a need for unpublicized, almost covert, library services for the black population. Reporting in January 1964 on the status of services for blacks in the state
in 1955, Walker commented that "nine libraries give duplicate service, that is,
equal service is maintained for both races, but it [was] separate" (Walker to
Wolff, personal communication, NLSF, 1955). As was common for those espous-
ing the "separate but equal" doctrine, the provision of some degree of services
was automatically validated as being equal to services offered to whites.

BEGINNINGS OF INTEGRATION

In a 1964 letter to *Library Journal* Editor Eric Moon, Estellene Walker wrote:

> The Richland County Library which serves Columbia, described in the
> [*Library Journal*] article as one of three Southern cities which have made no
> attempt to desegregate any of their public facilities, was completely inte-
> grated in 1952. This library was the first in South Carolina and one of the
> first in the Southeast to take this step. (Walker to Moon, personal commu-
> nication, NLSF, 1964)

The extent to which the Richland County Public Library was used by blacks
is unknown, and the knowledge of its availability to the black community is
questionable. Attempts by Lucretia Jeannett Parker in 1953 and by Bernice
Lloyd Bell in the early 1960s to determine the library's policy and extent of service

to blacks were unsuccessful, as no response to either questionnaire was received from the librarian (Parker, 1953, p. 53. See also, Bell, 1963, p. 70). Prevalent social mores of the time would seem to have prevented much in the way of extensive integrated use of the facility in a state with laws still prohibiting mixed dining. In fact, the long-standing traditions of the region were sufficient means of segregation even without specific legislation.

As late as 1960, a demonstration was held by blacks in Columbia against segregation in the city's public facilities, including the main library. A group of Allen University and Benedict College students, requesting to register as borrowers at the Richland County Public Library, were directed to the Waverly Library. In response to the incident, Lucy Hampton Bostick, the Richland County librarian, remarked: "Negroes have used this library for 30 years. Their demonstration is pointless and completely stupid" (Cox, 1960, p. B1). This statement implied that the facility had been integrated since 1930, the first year of Rosenwald funding, but in reality blacks were expected to use the Waverly Branch. The requirement that blacks be registered at the black branch would seem to do little to encourage integrated use of the main library.

The student lunch counter sit-ins in Greensboro, North Carolina, in February 1960 served as a catalyst for anti-segregation protests throughout the region. Libraries were not exempted from demonstrations, as was witnessed by integration attempts in South Carolina, Virginia, and Tennessee during 1960, and other southern states in subsequent years. Between 1960 and 1962, library demonstrations occurred in the South Carolina cities of Greenville, Sumter, and Florence.

The demonstrations in Greenville were especially controversial and met with much resistance by local officials. From March to July 1960, the Greenville Public Library was the scene of repeated peaceful efforts by blacks to integrate the facility. On March 1, 1960, a group of approximately twenty blacks, constituted primarily of high school students, attempted to use the main library. As a result, the individuals were asked to leave, and the library was closed for the remainder of the day. The March 16 sit-in resulted in the arrest of seven black students, ages 16 to 18. Although the students were charged with disorderly conduct, both police officers and library officials commented on the quiet and peaceful nature of the group ("Negroes Face Trials in Library Incident," 1960, p. 1). Two separate sit-ins on July 16 resulted in the arrests of eight black high school and college students, including Greenville native Jesse Jackson, on trespassing charges (Timms, 1960, p. A1). On July 28, a lawsuit was filed against the library, stating that the plaintiffs were "denied the use of these tax supported facilities solely because of their race and color" ("Public Library Closes: Integration Suit Brings Action," 1960, p. B1). Two weeks prior to the trial, the library board, at the request of the mayor and city council, closed both the main library and the black branch to avoid integration at all costs. Mayor Cass issued the statement that "these same groups, if allowed to continue their self-centered purposes, may conceivably bring about a closing of all schools, parks, swimming pools, and other facilities" (Walker, 1960, p. 1).

The closing of the library proved successful in preventing immediate court action, as the judge in the case ruled that there was no operational library to rule against (Crocker, 1960, p. A1). The door was left open for court ordered integration, however, and officials agreed to reopen on a segregated basis seventeen days after the closing "for all persons who have proper reasons for using the facilities, but demonstrations will not be tolerated" ("Library Opens at Greenville as Integrated," 1960, p. 1). Even at this point, another method of segregation was implemented. Separate tables designated "male" and "female" were briefly set up in order to prevent mixing of blacks and whites of the opposite sex ("Sexes Divided at City Library," 1960, p. 8).

In Sumter, attempts at integration of the Carnegie Public Library ended in the arrest of twenty-three blacks, most of whom were students at nearby Morris College. Three separate groups of students entered the library on February 21, 1961, and through a group spokesman, requested use of a library book. When directed to the black branch in the local black high school, each group refused to leave the building. Police were then called in, and the individuals were charged with breach of peace. Nineteen of the twenty-three arrested were convicted and fined $100 or thirty days in jail ("19 Negro Students are Convicted Here," 1961, p. 1).

In 1962, the Florence Public Library was also the scene of sit-ins by black students. In this case, the action prompted the library board to quietly allow integration of the main library (Hux, 1986, p. B1).

Integration of most libraries in the state occurred with less resistance than the Greenville and Sumter libraries. In May 1960, a group of fourteen black students successfully registered for library cards at the Darlington Public Library ("14 Negroes Given Cards to Darlington Library," 1960, p. 3). The Spartanburg Library Board had already decided to allow blacks to use the previously whites-only libraries in the county in the late 1950s (Prior, 1960, p. 10).

In 1961, Rice Estes, a South Carolina native and librarian at Pratt Institute, wrote a letter to the state library director urging support of library integration. Estellene Walker, formerly librarian for the U. S. Army, replied in language reflective of her earlier post:

> You may be surprised to find that the battle you are urging us to fight has already been won. The exhortation to combat of a warrior who has sought refuge above the Mason-Dixon line has a hollow sound in the ears of veterans whose battle scars are proof of front line fighting. (Walker to Estes, personal communication, NLSF, 1961)

Walker was, of course, exaggerating a barely begun trend. Integration of South Carolina's library facilities was in its early stages in 1961, although the integration of the Greenville County Library had prompted other libraries to take action. In a memorandum to Walker in mid-1963, the State Library Board's field service librarian wrote:

> Pickens, Laurens, and Greenwood are all giving service to Negroes in the main libraries now. Pickens voted to do so more than a year ago following the disturbance in Greenville.... None of these libraries have attempted to serve Negro patrons on the bookmobiles, since the issue has not yet arisen. (Callaham to Walker, personal communication, NLSF, 1963)

Black branches continued to operate in most communities after integration, but most ceased to be functional by the early 1970s. In Pickens, the Carver Branch Library operated out of the Pickens County Training School until 1966, when the library building was destroyed by fire (Aiken, n.d.). The Bowler Library in Florence served as the black branch until 1970 (Hux, 1986, p. B1). In Greenwood, the Benjamin Mays Branch Library remained open until 1971 ("Benjamin Mays Branch Library," n.d.).

Conclusion

The slow development of library services for blacks in South Carolina was not unique to the state. Most states in the South suffered from the same economic and educational problems and from blatant segregation. Provision of library services for whites took precedence over those for blacks, and those services for blacks were generally inferior in quality and in size of collections, library hours, staff, and facilities.

The decade of the 1930s was witness to significant steps toward providing the beginnings of services to blacks. These were often the result of cooperative efforts among several groups or agencies, most of them with roots outside the state. The Rosenwald Fund established library demonstrations in two of the more urbanized counties of the state, with funding matched by local governments. Black philanthropist Harvey Kelsey's book donations were utilized by the WPA library projects in Colleton, Dorchester, and Lancaster counties. Faith Cabin libraries, founded by Willie Lee Buffington, received book donations from individuals and organizations across the country and benefited from the assistance of Jeanes teachers, FERA (Federal Emergency Relief Agency), and WPA workers.

The collaborative efforts of this era are exemplified by the second Faith Cabin Library, which was built in Ridge Springs in 1933. This library came into existence through the efforts of founder Willie Lee Buffington, the federal government, the local board of education, a Jeanes teacher, local residents, and citizens from across the nation. T. F. Hammond, the Jeanes supervisor for Saluda County, cooperated with Buffington in securing a Faith Cabin Library collection for the Ridge Hill Rosenwald School. An article about Buffington's work, published in the Hampton Institute publication, *Southern Workman*, resulted in a surge of book donations from around the country. The FERA, the predecessor to the WPA, provided laborers for the construction of a log cabin library, with the Saluda County Board of Education and local residents providing the lumber (Carr, 1958, pp. 17-18).

Federal efforts through the WPA had a significant impact on library development in general, but no attempt was made to establish equal service for the large black population in the late 1930s and early 1940s. The increase in city and county library systems in the 1940s and 1950s led to the establishment of numerous black branches. As with other services, this tradition of separate libraries favored the white population, with better facilities, collections, and hours. Not until the mid-to-late 1960s were blacks in most areas of the state finally allowed the same access to libraries as the white majority.

Ernest Lander (1962), professor of history at Clemson College, at the Fortieth Annual Meeting of the South Carolina Library Association in 1961, commented that "once the Negro had secured his freedom the South was unwilling to grant further concessions except when forced to" (p. 8). Unfortunately, this was true for public libraries in the state, holding back for as long as most other institutions in the granting of equal access and services. As witnessed in Greenville and Sumter, integration of public libraries was not an easy transition, with resistance by local governments and library boards. Prompted by challenges from blacks, the "separate but equal" phase of public services would give way to the long-delayed process of integration, advancing a more practical and effective form of service without racial restrictions.

REFERENCES

Aiken, M. (n.d.). *Carver Branch Library*. Unpublished typescript, Pickens County Library.
Bell, B. L. (1963). *Integration in public library service in thirteen Southern States, 1954-1962*. Unpublished Master's thesis, Atlanta University.
Benjamin Mays Branch Library. (n.d.). Unpublished typescript, Greenwood County Library, Greenwood, SC.
Bolden, E. E. (1959). *Susan Dart Butler: Pioneer librarian*. Unpublished Master's thesis, Atlanta University.
Books for rural negroes. (1949). *South Carolina Library Bulletin*, 5(1), 2-3.
Buffington, W. L. (1950). *Report of Faith Cabin Library, May 25th, 1950*. Collection of W. L. Buffington, Jr., Spartanburg, SC.
Carnegie Library Correspondence. (1905, 1911, 1921). Carnegie Corporation. New York: Microfilm reel 5.
Carr, L. D. (1958). *The Reverend Willie Lee Buffington's life and contributions to the development of rural libraries in the South*. Unpublished Master's thesis, Atlanta University.
Charleston County buys Dart Hall, plans to continue negro library branch there. (1952). *Charleston News and Courier*, 17 December, p. A14.
Code of Laws of South Carolina. (1942). vol. 3, §5560.
Copeland, E. A. (1946-47). *Library service for negroes in South Carolina: A report to the Negro Advisory Committee of the Southern States' Cooperative Library Survey Committee*. Unpublished Negro Library Service Files, South Carolina State Library, Columbia, SC.
Copp, R. V. (1987-88). The library at Penn Center: One hundred twenty-five years of library tradition on St. Helena's Island. *South Carolina Librarian, 31(2)/32(1)*, 14-20.
County and regional libraries. (1946). *South Carolina Library Bulletin, 2(3)*, 5.
Crocker, J. W. (1960). Judge dismisses library suit here. *The News* (Greenville, SC), 14 September, p. A1.
Demonstration is stupid—librarian. (1960). *The Observer* (Charlotte), 29 April.
Eleventh Annual Report of the South Carolina State Library Board, July 1, 1953-June 30, 1954. (1954). Columbia, SC: South Carolina State Library Board.

Embree, E. (1949). *Investment in people: The story of the Julius Rosenwald Fund.* New York: Harper.

Estes, R. (1960). Segregated libraries. *Library Journal, 85*(22), 4419.

Floyd, V. C. (1961). History of Lancaster County Library. *South Carolina Librarian, 6*(1), 15-16.

14 negroes given cards to Darlington Library. (1960). *The News,* 7 May, p. 3.

Franklin, H. R. (1980). The black public libraries in the Southeast. In A. L. Phinanzee (Ed.), *The black librarian in the Southeast.* Durham, NC: North Carolina Central University.

Frayser, M. E. (1933). *The libraries of South Carolina* (Bulletin 292, October). Clemson, SC: South Carolina Agricultural Experiment State of Clemson Agricultural College.

Frayser, M. E. (1940). Negroes use libraries. *Southern frontier, 1*(4), 2.

Growth of library service to negroes. (1948). *South Carolina Library Bulletin, 4*(4), 2.

Hux, R. (1986). The Bowler Library: A forgotten heritage for many years. *Florence Morning News,* 19 May, p. B1.

Joeckel, C. (1938). *Library Service* (Staff Study no. 11, prepared for Adv. Comm. on Education). Washington, DC: USGPO.

Lander, E. (1962). Quoted in *South Carolina Librarian, 6*(2), 7-10.

Lee, D. R. (1991). Faith Cabin Libraries: A study of an alternative library service in the segregated South, 1932-1960. *Libraries & Culture, 26*(1), 169-182.

Library opens at Greenville as integrated. (1960). *The State* (Columbia, SC), 20 September, p. 1.

Marblehead Libraries. (1910). *Southern Workman, 39*(9), 498.

Mary Frayser Papers, Winthrop College Archives and Special Collections, Box 32-290, Subject Matter File: Questionnaires, 1938.

Negro Library Service Files (NLSF), South Carolina State Library, Columbia, SC.

Negroes face trials in library incident. (1960). *The Piedmont* (Greenville, SC), 17 March, p. 1.

Newberry County. (1937). *Jeanes Teacher, 2*(April), 13.

19 negro students are convicted here. (1961). *Daily Item* (Sumter, SC), 10 March, p. 1.

Parker, L. J. (1953). *A study of integration in public library service in thirteen Southern States.* Unpublished Master's thesis, Atlanta University.

Perry, E. (1973). *Free reading for everybody: The story of the Greenville Library.* Greenville, SC: n.p.

Prior, J. H. (1960). Spartanburg faces library race issue. *The Piedmont,* 15 September, p. 10.

Progress and needs in library extension. (1931). *Bulletin of the American Library Association, 25*(5), 235.

Public library closes: Integration suit brings action. (1960). *The Observer* (Charlotte, NC), 3 September, p. B1.

Public libraries serving negroes, with types of service, 1951-52. Unpublished typescript, Negro Library Service Files, South Carolina State Library, Columbia, SC.

Richland County. (1936). *Intercounty Library News, 1*(February), 10.

Richland County. (1936). *Intercounty Library News, 1*(August), 12.

Roll call of workers. (1979). In *The Jeanes Story: A chapter in the history of American education.* Jackson, MS: Jackson State University.

The Rosenwald rural schools for negroes. (1925). *School and Society, 21*(6 June), 676-677.

7th Annual Report, South Carolina State Library Board, July 1, 1949-June 30, 1950. Columbia, SC: South Carolina State Library.

Sexes divided in city library. (1960). *The News* (Greenville, SC), 22 September, p. 8.

Stanford, E. B. (1944). *Library extension under the WPA: An appraisal of an experiment in federal aid.* Chicago, IL: University of Chicago Press.

State Library Board inaugurates book deposit service for negroes. (1948). *South Carolina Library Bulletin, 4*(2), 2.

Sumter County. (1937). *Jeanes Teacher, 2*(April), 8.

Timms, L. (1960). 8 negroes sit-in at library here. *The News* (Greenville, SC), 17 July, p. A1.

Traveling libraries for Negroes. (1926). *Library Journal, 51*(22), 1121.

U.S. Bureau of the Census. (1933). *Abstract of the fifteenth census of the United States.* Washington, DC: USGPO.

U.S. Department of the Interior. (1933). *Office of Education Bulletin*, no. 2, 95.

Walker, E. P. (1981). *So good and necessary a work: The public library in South Carolina, 1698-1980*. Columbia, SC: South Carolina State Library.

Walker, L. S. (1980). Black librarians in South Carolina. In A. L. Phinanzee (Ed.). *The black librarian in the Southeast*. Durham, NC: North Carolina Central University.

Walker, R. (1960). White and negro libraries closed. *The News* (Greenville, SC), 3 September, p. 1.

Williams, M. M., & Jackson, K. V. (1979). *The Jeanes Story: A chapter in the history of American education, 1908-1968*. Jackson, MS: Jackson State University.

Wilson, L. R. *Louis Round Wilson Papers* (No. 3274, Series V, Southern Historical Collection, University of North Carolina).

Wilson, L. R., & Wight, E. A. (1935). *County library service in the South: A study of the Rosenwald Library demonstration*. Chicago, IL: University of Chicago Press.

Reading for Liberation

The Role of Libraries in the 1964 Mississippi Freedom Summer Project

❧ Donald G. Davis, Jr. & Cheryl Knott Malone ❧

"We gathered to start work and my library learning began with a thud," wrote Virginia Steele, a Mississippi Freedom Summer volunteer who had just graduated from the University of California at Berkeley library school. In recounting her experience of 1964, Steele described finding a jumbled heap of some 20,000 books in the Greenville, Mississippi, apartment rented for the Freedom Summer project. Volunteers hauling donated books from the northern United States had been harassed along the way (hostile whites had slashed the truck's tires). The volunteers had broken many of the boxes filled with books in their haste to deliver their cargo and get out of town. In the heat and humidity of a Deep South summer, local African-American residents and white volunteers sorted and shelved the spilled books, working for three days before they could even get close enough to a window to open it. "By the end of the first week," Virginia Steele (1965a) remembered, "there could have been no doubt in the minds of either volunteers or Negro or white community that the project was, indeed, concerned with books" (pp. 78-79).

But that concern with books, so palpable that summer, has been largely ignored by historians. The Mississippi Freedom Summer Project has received much study in the context of the political and social climate of the period, especially because it was marred by violence and it took place in a presidential election year.[1] "Freedom Summer" brought several hundred college students and other volunteers from the most prestigious institutions in the United States to Mississippi for ten weeks of extensive involvement and intensive work to promote and implement voter registration, alternative schools, and community centers. Though as many as fifteen or twenty of the more than forty such centers had libraries, the story of library planning, establishment, maintenance, and legacy has not been told. This paper presents in preliminary form the story of these community center libraries, drawn from a variety of sources including archival records of the participating organizations, personal letters and reminiscences, oral histories, and newspaper accounts.

FREEDOM SUMMER BACKGROUND

Freedom Summer was one of the most important and pivotal projects of the civil rights movement of the 1960s. Organizers intended to infiltrate Mississippi, the most recalcitrant of the Southern States, with white visitors who would work side-by-side with black residents for a few months. The white college students would be mostly "elite," with well-connected parents from northern states. Freedom Summer organizers knew that the presence of whites would not lessen the violence that white Mississippians would aim at civil rights workers, but they guessed, rightly, that the news media would be more inclined to cover white-on-white attacks and so bring national attention to their local efforts (Mendy Samstein quoted in McAdam, 1988, p. 38).

The Freedom Summer idea, rooted in the civil rights movement of the 1950s, grew more directly out of the student-inspired activism that began in 1960 when four black college freshmen staged a sit-in at Woolworth's whites-only lunch counter in Greensboro, North Carolina. Within a year, the Student Nonviolent Coordinating Committee (SNCC) had been formed and had begun cooperating with the Southern Christian Leadership Conference (SCLC) and the Congress of Racial Equality (CORE), in addition to the older National Association for the Advancement of Colored People (NAACP). As a direct-action strategy, SNCC's Robert Moses, a 26-year-old New Yorker, organized a voter registration campaign in McComb, Mississippi, in 1961. He conducted classes explaining how to register voters, and then he accompanied volunteer registrants to the courthouse where their attempts often were rebuffed with jailings and beatings. One farmer who allied with Moses was murdered, indicating the extent of racial oppression in Mississippi. The leadership of SNCC, CORE, SCLC, the NAACP, and other civil-rights organizations decided to avoid competing with each other by banding together in a coalition, the Council of Federated Organizations (COFO). Under Moses's direction, COFO conducted a mock election in 1963 to prove that blacks did want political participation and to protest the presence of segregationist candidates on the Republican and Democratic slates. Moses received help from liberal white lawyer Allard Lowenstein who organized white students at Stanford and Yale to go south to help register blacks for the Freedom Vote. The establishment of the Mississippi Freedom Democratic Party and its work during the 1964 national election resulted from this initiative (for recent scholarly treatments of these events, see Dittmer, 1994; Burner, 1994; Rothschild, 1982).

BOOKS BECOME BASIC

Soon after the successfully integrated Freedom Vote project, Bob Moses presented his plan for Freedom Summer, convincing reluctant members of SNCC, CORE, and SCLC of the advantages of white participation in the movement for black civil rights. The group agreed that the three components of Freedom Summer would be voter registration, freedom schools, and community centers. Voting was the goal, and the schools and community centers functioned to further that goal (Sitton [1964] announced the Freedom Summer Project to the public). Freedom Summer libraries provided the information that underlay the accelerating voting effort; they also supported the combined recreational and educational functions of the community centers. CORE's Benjamin A. Brown had run that organization's Books for Mississippi Project, collecting 25,000 volumes in Fall 1963 and shipping them to CORE offices in Meridian and Canton (CORE Papers, Letter from Benjamin A. Brown to the Brotherhood Council, October 7, 1963; see also CORE Papers, "CORE Southern Education Project Report, February 29, 1964" and "CORE Books for Mississippi Project Presents 'Volume II,'" n.d.). Michael (Mickey) and Rita Schwerner, a white couple from New York working for Moses, had demonstrated the need for libraries. In January 1964, they had moved to Meridian, the state's second largest town, to establish a community center. The Schwerners knew that, in addition to all the other deprivations black Mississippians faced, in "low-income areas there [were] insufficient library facilities for the young, and [that] Negroes [were] denied access to many of the existing facilities" (Mickey Schwerner quoted in Huie, 1965, p. 49).

Within days of their arrival in Meridian, the Schwerners had established a library of several hundred volumes from Tougaloo College and from the COFO headquarters in Jackson. Ten books went out on loan almost immediately. With donations from bookstores, churches, publishers, organizations, and individuals, channeled through CORE's Southern Education Project (formerly known as Books for Mississippi), they had accumulated 10,000 books by the end of their first month, but many remained stored due to a lack of shelving space. At the request of the NAACP Youth Council, they designated a room next to the library as a quiet area for reading (Rita Schwerner quoted in Huie, 1965, pp. 45-46).

Based largely on the experience of the Schwerners in early 1964, COFO's leaders issued a "Prospectus for the Summer" outlining the proposed programs of the Freedom Schools, the voter registration drive, and the community centers. With health promotion activities, film showings, job training, organized sports, and library services, the community centers were intended to provide "basic services" long denied black residents of the state (SNCC Papers, 1982).

To the young college-educated organizers who understood the revolutionary potential of books and reading, libraries were integral to the project's success. Even though they were not mentioned in early promotional materials about the project, by late spring the following line appeared in virtually all descriptions: "Each center would have a well-rounded library—to which Negroes in many communities now have no access" (Lowenstein Papers, "Mississippi: Structure of the Movement, Present Operations, and Prospectus for this Summer" [1964]; "Civil Rights Movement, 1963-1964"). COFO's Emmie Schrader began planning the Freedom Libraries from her office in Jackson. Hearing of CORE's Southern Education Project and its book drive for materials on black culture and life, Schrader wrote to CORE asking for donations (CORE Papers. Letter from Emmie Schrader to Benjamin A. Brown, June 2, 1964).

Graduating library school student Virginia Steele at Berkeley heard about Freedom Summer and applied. The COFO staff in Jackson knew just where to place her. On May 17, 1964, Schrader wrote to Steele: "We were very glad to find that a professional librarian is joining the Mississippi Summer Project. . . . Would you be in charge of one of these Freedom Libraries for the summer? Your job would be to recruit some local students or whomever you can to help you catalogue the books, fix up the library room, set up some kind of workable sign-out system, and in general publicize and run the library."[2]   Steele agreed, although she had never organized a library.[3] But even before she had a chance to tackle that new experience, her duties expanded.

At a week-long orientation in Oxford, Ohio, for volunteers in schools and community centers, a COFO staff member asked Steele to coordinate all of the project's libraries. In that role, she addressed the library volunteers during the week explaining the basics. Drawing from knowledge hastily gained from librarians at Berkeley and the local public library in Oxford, she did what she could. For example, she suggested they fashion book pockets out of halves of old envelopes, that they sort 3x5 cards into alphabetical order by author, paste paper inside books with the date due, and that they keep a register listing by number, the name, parents' name(s), address, and phone number of borrowers. She also told the volunteers to prepare library membership applications and to issue borrowers' cards as a method of building self-esteem. For guidance, Steele recommended Susan Grey Akers's (1927) *Simple Library Cataloging*, Mary Peacock Douglas's (1941) *The Teacher-Librarian's Handbook*, and Ruth Sawyer's (1957) *How to Tell a Story*. She stressed the importance of keeping books in good reading order, and she told her listeners about Bro-Dart's (1955) *Modern-Simplified Book Repair* and about Demco Library Supplies and Gaylord Brothers (Sally Belfrage Papers, "Orientation Notes," 1965). During that week of orientation, word came of the disappearance of black Mississippian James Chaney, white volunteer Andrew Goodman, and civil rights veteran Mickey Schwerner on their way back from investigating a church burning. Although their bodies would not be found until August, the young people at orientation suddenly understood the gravity of their position. Several consulted two psychiatrists at the orientation sessions in order to sort out feelings of apprehension and anxiety before heading south (Nancy Ellin to Cheryl Knott Malone, personal communication, January 12, 1994).

Feeling her lack of concrete experience, Steele wrote a letter a month later recalling, "I wanted to cry 'HELP' in a number of ways. . . ."[4] Her help would come from the volunteers' families and churches outside the South who conducted book drives to stock the libraries, from the other women volunteers (since the men were assigned to the more dangerous task of voter registration), and to courageous local residents who appeared at her door to shelve as well as borrow books.

LIBRARIES & LIBRARIANS

Virginia Steele apparently was the only trained librarian who volunteered for the Freedom Summer Project. Since libraries in community centers already existed in Meridian and Greenwood, COFO assigned her to Greenville, one of the more tolerant towns in Mississippi, notable for the moderate editorial voice of its newspaper, the *Delta Democrat-Times*.[5] She expressed often her gratitude for the moderation and cooperation shown by the police chief, the town librarians (white and black), and others.[6] Volunteers from other parts of the state came to Greenville for rest and relaxation (Waldron, 1993, p. 310). In short, the small Delta city was a good place for establishing library relationships. Steele's personal story appeared in several articles in local newspapers and in the publications of regional library associations.[7]

Over the course of the summer, COFO volunteers and staff members established community centers in a number of localities (Lowenstein Papers, "Development of the Mississippi Project," [Fall 1964?]). Depending on how one defines and counts libraries, we estimate that approximately twenty-five existed in the some forty-five project sites at the end of Freedom Summer—perhaps as many as fifteen in community centers (eight with as many as 10,000 volumes each) and the rest in Freedom Schools.[8] Although Steele tried to exercise some oversight for all the libraries, she was most concerned with those in the community centers in which volunteers were more likely to have full-time responsibility for library development.[9] While a complete accounting of the center libraries is not yet possible, the list in Table 1 provides some information about the place and the personnel involved. Each center and library surely had its unique anecdotes and special good and bad memories for those who participated in them.

Canton

Karol Nelson (now McMahan, 1994), a public school teacher from California, spent her first couple of days in Mississippi too dazed by "culture shock" to do anything more than unload and dust books for Virginia Steele in Greenville. Nelson and two college students then boarded a bus to a rural area outside Canton (the location of the community center library) where they set up a Freedom School in a one-room frame church. When they arrived at the building, they

TABLE 1

LIBRARIES AND LIBRARIANS IN COMMUNITY CENTERS

Batesville	
Biloxi	
Canton	[Karol Nelson, at a rural Freedom School nearby]
Clarksdale	
Cleveland	
Greenville	Virginia Steele
Greenwood	Barbara Johnson and Sally Belfrage
Harmony	
Hattiesburg	Nancy Ellin
Holly Springs	
Meridian	Rita Schwerner (before June)
Mileston	Gene Nelson
Ruleville	Linda Davis and Heidi Dole
Shaw	Judy York
Vicksburg	Bryan Dunlap

found boxes of donated books waiting for them, along with new shelving that the men of the church had built in the foyer (Karol Nelson McMahan to Cheryl Knott Malone, personal communication, June 1, 1994).

Greenville

Notwithstanding her more congenial social environment in Greenville, Virginia Steele's account of her initial experience (that began this essay) conveys the heat, humidity, and exhaustion that she and others felt. Steele was generally delighted with the quality of the donated books:

> People had taken the trouble to search out books by and about Negroes, the most valuable to us and the most eagerly sought by local students and adults, about civil and human rights, and a surprising quantity of children's books, of which we couldn't have gotten enough, particularly picture books. ... I learned that it was important not to label or separate children's books and elementary readers as such, but to put them where they could be easily and naturally accessible to everyone. Adults or young people who are

unable to read more difficult things are extremely shy about reaching for them—just the opposite to the highly educated volunteers who avidly looked through them at any opportunity. (Steele, 1965a, pp. 78-79)

Greenwood

In Greenwood, the noted activist and writer Sally Belfrage, who died in April 1994, told of her first encounter with the library at which she tried to restore order. Her engaging account of the summer chronicles the situation.

> There was no one conspicuously in charge of anything, so we wandered upstairs and waited with the rest. The library, my future domain, spread over most of the second floor—a large, light, square room with windows on three sides, divided by waist-high partitions. Big pegboards blocked off other sections of the room, and books spilled off shelves, out of boxes, and around the floor. In operation since spring, the library had been compacted into half its original allotment to make room for extra desks. (Belfrage, 1965, p. 35)[10]

People were sleeping in the library when she arrived. Belfrage continued:

> Other bodies still lay huddled up in sleeping bags, trying to drown out the day, but if someone on an urgent errand didn't jar them awake, curious neighborhood children kept stepping on them. I got going on the books. The remnants of a cataloguing system were falling out of various cigar boxes, but it looked as if [the system] would have to be abandoned. The fiction shelves, where I began, were stocked with antiques, scores of Horatio Algers, nineteenth-century ladies' books, some valuable-looking first editions, numbered sets of Thackeray, Dickens, and Conan Doyle, eleven copies of *The Vicar of Wakefield*, a lot of esoteric modern fiction, and a very few novels which might conceivably generate some interest if they could be got at. Everything had been donated by Northerners whose good intentions were not so much in doubt as their grip on certain realities. Boxes kept arriving full of people's charitable throwouts, instead of anything new or imaginative, but now and then came a useful carton of new children's books; American, Southern, or Negro histories; how-to books—good things. (Belfrage, 1965, p. 47)[11]

Hattiesburg

Nancy Ellin labored in the Hattiesburg library alongside her husband Joseph who taught in the Freedom School. A letter from Joseph to his parents described conditions:

> Nancy is now a full-time librarian, which she enjoys very much. She keeps the library open 8 hours a day (9-12, 3-6, 7:30-9:30) and it's very heavily used. She already has a thick file of names of borrowers. We have about 6,000 books in the library, main branch, and are opening new branches in several places in town and at Palmer's. (The Negro library supplied by the city has about 2,000 books or so. Negroes can also use books in the main library downtown but can't get a card or take anything out). What will happen to these libraries after we leave, heaven knows; finding people to continue the program is [the] number one problem now. (Sutherland, 1965, p. 112)

Nancy Ellin herself described the facility as:

> a very narrow room with bookshelves on each wall and double shelves
> down the middle. . . . Lots of books came from the New York City teachers
> union [that] had an officer in Hattiesburg. . . . There were some great
> donations. Someone sent ten copies of the *Ebony* history of blacks in the
> United States. I did not know too much—just unpacked and put books on
> the shelves. I went to Greenville and heard someone—it must have been
> Virginia Steele—give a talk about putting mini-libraries in homes and other
> ideas. I also heard that a librarian somewhere took all the junky books (and
> there were plenty of those given) and sold them for recycling and bought
> encyclopedias with the money. I've always felt—I know people did a lot
> of important things in schools and libraries—but I felt the main reason we
> were there was as witnesses or hostages. So I don't feel bad about being so
> ineffectual [as a librarian]. (Ellin to Cheryl Knott Malone, personal commu-
> nication, January 12, 1994. See also Ellin, 1964)

Ruleville

Illustrator Tracy Sugarman witnessed a day-long effort to establish a library
in a dilapidated house in Ruleville. Volunteers fresh from orientation had dropped
off boxes of books in the backyard, and those assigned to Ruleville began clean-
ing the house as others sorted the books by subject. Wrote Sugarman (1966):

> They tore open the corrugated boxes, yelling delightedly as they would
> discover a treasured book from their childhood or a reference volume that
> had saved their life on a college thesis. These were people who knew and
> loved books, and their happiness shone as they tore with relish into the
> mountains of pulp. (p. 108)

As they sorted the books by subject, they threw many into a pile they labeled
"crud." The "crud" books eventually served as supports for the library's shelving, fashioned from boards harvested off the old outhouse in the backyard.
Children from the black neighborhood surrounding the house showed up and
began looking at the books even before the students could get them on the
shelves (Sugarman, 1966, pp. 109, 111). On the day Ruleville's Freedom School
opened, a volunteer named Heidi Dole showed twelve 4-through-7-year-olds
around the library, then held her first story hour while another volunteer, Linda
Davis, offered her first literacy class for a group of seven older women (Sugarman,
1966, pp. 122-23).

Shaw

Judy York reported at the end of July to the Project Library Co-ordinator,
Virginia Steele, by answering a questionnaire. She described her library as consisting of one very crowded room in the community center. About half of the
donated books were usable; some had been received from other centers and sent
on to still others. There were thirty-eight boxes of semi-sorted textbooks. About
fifty adults had borrowed from two to ten books each, and about 100 children had
borrowed about ten books each. A continuing problem was how "to get people

to either move books or build shelves" (Steele Papers, Memorandum to Mississippi Summer Project Librarians from Library Co-ordinator Virginia Steele, July 28, 1964).

Vicksburg

By the end of the summer, Bryan Dunlap had supervised one of the best community center libraries in the state. Unfortunately, this facility was bombed in the early fall, and the 8,000-volume collection was almost totally destroyed. Rebuilding began immediately, however (SNCC Papers, Ellen Maslow to Lawrence Minear, personal communication, October 14, 1964).

Most of the volunteers that Virginia Steele tried to coordinate were so busy coping with the heat, putting their collections in order, and helping new readers (not to speak of other duties, such as helping with the schools, voter registration drives, and other various demands), that they had little time to respond to what supervision there was or to get together for mutual encouragement. Nevertheless, the questionnaire that she distributed to the project librarians, dated July 28, 1964, helped to focus their attention on the library's physical characteristics, the collection of materials, methods of acquisition, services provided, and use and participation by patrons, as well as recurring problems and plans for the future (Steele Papers).

One general meeting for project librarians convened at the Greenville community center on Saturday, August 15, at the suggestion of COFO Community Center Coordinator Annell Ponder. This was planned so that the participants could join in "a roof raising" of the new community center in Mileston and see the library the next day. Steele asked travelers to visit as many libraries as possible on their route "to help size up your own, get ideas, and maybe some sense of relief if you've felt guilty about your own difficulties and disorganization" (Steele Papers. Memorandum to Library Workers from Steele, August 7, 1964). She encouraged her librarians to be prepared to brainstorm about several problems, of which the principal ones were:

1. Who will keep the library going? How can the care and use be self-perpetuating?
2. What are the best plans for dispersing the mass of books available?
3. Ways of involving young people in the use and concern about libraries.
4. Novel ways of interesting people in taking out books.
5. Simple, perhaps self-help systems for check-out and return and for arranging books.
6. Useful supplies, "gadgets," methods of marking, etc.
7. Problems of weeding, clutter, labeling shelves clearly, and orderly, sensible storage.
8. How to get books we need: Negro Life books, children's books, particularly with integrated pictures, etc.
9. What should go on a simple instruction sheet for setting up a little library from scratch?

These queries concluded with nine innovative ideas that the volunteers had already submitted (Steele papers, pp. 2-3). Within a week, a duplicated document that incorporated the discussions of the previous weekend was completed. Entitled "Setting Up a New Library," it may still stand as the best two-page guide for a basic library in primitive conditions (Steele Papers, COFO Freedom Libraries, August 18, 1964). Steele left Mississippi in the late summer after most of the volunteers had gone back to their colleges and universities feeling that she had not done all that could be done. The lack of visibility for the libraries, compared with other phases of the project, might have supported her self-assessment. However, Bryan Dunlap from Vicksburg responded to one of her letters of self deprecation by saying:

> I considered you—and do—the most valuable person the Freedom Libraries had going for them. My idea for professional help in the FLs came not out of nothing, but out of my observation of the things you were trying to put over last summer. When I've thought about improving libraries here, which has been frequently, I've felt your absence very acutely—you having been the only person to date in my acquaintance who has really cared about their existence. (Steele Papers. Bryan R. Dunlap to Virginia Steele, personal communication, May 15, 1965)

One can imagine that other library volunteers had similar feelings.

IMPACT OF FREEDOM LIBRARIES

Few organized records remain about the continuation or disposition of the Freedom Libraries. COFO intended for community centers, complete with libraries, to become permanent, but by the fall of 1964 it had become obvious that the organization did not have sufficient resources to maintain them and so, when possible, turned them over to local volunteers (CORE Papers, "Mississippi Field Report," January 19, 1965). Some centers shut down at the end of the summer when the northern summer volunteers left, although about 300 of the 800 or so volunteers remained for part of the next year. Several Freedom Libraries, including one in Indianola and one outside Canton, were deliberately destroyed by fire (Bernice M. White to Cheryl Knott Malone, personal communication, August 17, 1993; Karol Nelson McMahan to Cheryl Knott Malone, personal communication, June 1, 1994). But some were dispersed to local individuals and groups, stored for future centers, or merged with local integrated public libraries (Jo Ann Ooiman Robinson Papers, "Madison County Freedom Schools, Summer Project, 1964" [August 25, 1965], "Moss Point-Pascagoula" [November 19, 1964]). About fifteen community centers and several school sites remained open with staffing arranged by the National Council of Churches and/or local residents or COFO staff (Steele, 1965a, p. 80; Steele, 1965b, p. 150; Lowenstein Papers, "Books," 1965; Findlay, 1993, pp. 76-110).[12]

In spring 1965, a group of librarians generally affiliated with the American Library Association (ALA) became interested in continuing the libraries in Mississippi and formed the Friends of Freedom Libraries. In June, the group sent

Miriam Braverman, a young-adult specialist from the Brooklyn Public Library, to tour Mississippi. She visited eight sites in nine days, finding that "each civil rights headquarters houses a library, which is used by students, parents, and teachers" (Braverman, 1965, p. 5045). She described the great variety of physical conditions and collections and pleaded for contributions to bring appropriate books to the libraries. The final portion of her report treated the relationship of the Freedom Libraries to the public library movement in Mississippi.

The relationship of the project libraries and the public libraries was varied, reflecting the ambivalence of professional librarianship in the state. Since the adoption by the ALA of a policy condemning racial prejudice in its "Statement on Individual Membership, Chapter Status, and Institutional Membership" (ALA, 1962, p. 637) at the Miami Beach annual conference in 1962, tensions had arisen between southern state library associations (ALA chapters) and institutional members and the national association. The Mississippi Library Association (MLA) delayed the response (that would have indicated compliance with the national association's integration objectives) due to internal dissension and a reluctance either to upset its constituents or to oppose ALA. Finally, in December 1963, MLA informed ALA that it could not comply. Three months later, ALA Executive Secretary David W. Clift notified MLA that it had forfeited its chapter status until such time as it could certify compliance (ALA Archives, Letter from David H. Clift to Maria F. Person, March 18, 1964. See also Hunter, 1992, p. 70). At the initiative of E. J. Josey, ALA further strengthened its pro-integration position by resolving at the 1964 St. Louis conference that "all ALA officers and ALA staff members should refrain from attending in official capacity or at the expense of ALA the meetings of any state associations which are unable to meet fully the requirements of chapter status in ALA" (ALA Archives, "Civil Rights, 1963-1970." See also, Josey, 1994).

Some Mississippi library leaders claimed that, while they were personally and professionally against segregation, they were bound by state law and needed ALA support while they tried to resist and change that law. Lura G. Currier, spokesperson for this group and for the Mississippi Library Commission, acknowledged in fall 1963 that she could not affirm compliance of her agency with ALA policy and would allow the ALA membership to lapse. She needed no further reminders that "just when [Mississippi librarians] most needed professional help the only group to which [they] could turn felt it necessary to cleanse itself of [them] because of conditions which were not created by librarians and which cannot possibly be solved by them" (ALA Archives, Letter from Lura G. Currier to ALA, September 11, 1963). Currier covertly supported the Freedom Summer Project efforts and eloquently appealed to publishers for simplified texts for adults (Steele Papers, draft of essay of reminiscences by Virginia Steele [1965]). In the main, however, the library community in the state tended to ignore the inequities of service and the efforts of the Freedom Libraries (Peebles & Howell, 1975).[13]

Braverman documented the variety of tactics used to inhibit library service to blacks before, during, and after the coming of the Freedom Libraries. With very few exceptional examples of integrated service, the picture was not a pretty one. Unfortunately, the quality of service differed little from that in many white communities. In 1965, the process of integration was just getting underway. Braverman (1965) closed thus:

> I spoke to many as they were released from jail, still in a state of shock from the brutalities they had experienced or witnessed. It is not surprising, then, that many boys and girls should prefer to use the Freedom Library. They work after school, do their homework at night and are afraid to risk walking in the white section at night. . . . The Freedom Libraries, therefore, play a role in making available to the local Negro population books they cannot get anywhere else. Until the social system of Mississippi becomes less repressive for the Negro, the Freedom Libraries will continue to be needed. (p. 5047)

The effect of this unique experiment was both immediate and lasting. During the hot eventful summer of 1964, Freedom Libraries served civil rights goals in at least two ways: (1) by delivering books to the people who had no other access to them, and (2) by instilling an appreciation of information in people who then demanded service at their local public libraries. Access to books was important because of the information available in them. Freedom Summer organizers and volunteers wanted Mississippi blacks to learn about the political system they were to become a part of and about their own proud history. But beyond this, activists wanted books to offer recreation to people who labored, as the saying went, "from cain't to cain't" (Sugarman, 1966, p. 64).[14] Once local residents had been exposed to the information and entertainment value of books, they might be moved to sit in at the local public library—which is exactly what happened in Hattiesburg toward the end of the summer, in a case that eventually made it to the U.S. Supreme Court (*Adickes v. S. H. Kress & Co.,* 1970. See also Cresswell, 1996).[15] By mid-September, blacks in Indianola were regularly trying to use the whites-only Seymour Public Library. That winter they would meet at the still-functioning Freedom School and march to the library to stage a sit-in or picket (SNCC Papers, "Segregation and Brutality in the Mississippi Delta—Sunflower County," [Fall 1964]). Such activity eventually forced public libraries in Mississippi to comply with the Civil Rights Act of 1964.

Freedom Libraries offered hope to the next generation. Sally Belfrage wrote of the frustration and exhaustion that haunted her as she daily tried to interest downtrodden and intimidated people in registering to vote, faced police harassment and brutality, and told the hungry that the donated food had run out. "By . . . three o'clock on any afternoon, you are tired," she reported, "but, at three, the children come . . . thirty children waiting in line for books . . . especially about rockets and jets and other children" (CORE Papers, "Special Report—Community Centers," [n.d.]). There was a hunger for learning that dispelled fear, that seemed to compensate for the negative aspects of the summer's work. As Karol Nelson McMahan said of the "faith-in-books" attitude apparent at the Freedom

School and Library outside Canton: "Students would tell us they wanted to learn French, or black history . . . and we said, 'Oh, you want to learn this? We'll find some books and learn it.' We had confidence . . . there was an air of possibility." (Karol Nelson McMahan to Cheryl Knott Malone, personal communication, June 1, 1994). That air of possibility permeating the project, frightened and enraged white Mississippi.

Had there been no other gauge for measuring the importance of books to blacks, the reaction of whites would serve as an indicator. For example, three white and three black SNCC volunteers were stopped at 2:30 a.m. on May 6, in Oxford, Mississippi, as they hauled a trailer-load of 3,500 to 4,000 books. They told Oxford officials that they were on the way to Rust College in Holly Springs where they were to deliver the books for use during Freedom Summer. Armed with a search warrant, the sheriff forced the men to unload the contents of the car and trailer, totaling about 9,000 pounds of material. The sheriff called an investigator with the Mississippi State Sovereignty Commission, who arrived on the scene to question the men. Finally, after paying a $19.50 fine, the men were released to continue their trip around 4:30 that afternoon. Another sheriff, in an unmarked car, immediately began following them, cited them for reckless driving, and escorted them to Holly Springs, where they were held in the county jail for investigation. The men eventually paid fines of about $300 before receiving a sheriff's escort to Rust College (*FBI File, the Student Nonviolent Coordinating Committee,* 1991. See also Paul Burney Johnson Family Papers, report by Tom Scarbrough [May 19, 1964]).[16] Despite such efforts to thwart Freedom Libraries, tens of thousands of books infiltrated Mississippi, much to the delight of some local residents. When a volunteer, speaking at a mass meeting in Meridian that summer, mentioned the library that the Schwerners had organized, a standing ovation erupted (CORE Papers, letter from Bob Gore to Benjamin A. Brown [n.d.]).

In his book on the Mississippi Freedom Project, sociologist Doug McAdam (1988) wrote that: "There is an ignorance about Freedom Summer in contemporary America that bears no relationship to the impact the project had at the time" (p. 116). The same may be said of Freedom Libraries with respect to the library profession. While evaluating the significance of the Summer Project and the impact of the libraries was, and continues to be, difficult, the question is an important one. It has engaged the minds of the planners, the participants, the professional library community, and now, library historians (for a helpful assessment, see Lowenstein Papers, "A Unitarian Universalist Presence in Mississippi [Report and Record of Denominational Team Visit]," January 1-9, 1965, especially the section "The Dynamics of Mississippi Today").

Freedom Libraries alone did not change attitudes, but they enabled the project to liberate African Americans in Mississippi from white domination.[17] In the end, the establishment of Freedom Libraries constituted a form of direct action, an attack on what James W. Silver (1964) described as "The Closed

Society" where ideas and information represented a genuine threat to vested interests of the status quo (see also Jencks, 1964).[18] Freedom Summer Libraries simply did what libraries are supposed to do—with their typically immeasurable, but nevertheless real, impact on the individual human mind.

NOTES

1. The project is covered in cursory fashion in many of the standard treatments of the Civil Rights Movement of the 1950s and 1960s. One of a number of journalistic accounts is by Atwater (1964, 15 ff). Among the published volumes of eyewitness accounts are by Belfrage (1965), Von Hoffman (1964), Holt (1965), Sugarman (1966), Sutherland (1965), and Tucker (1965). The two main histories of the project itself are by Rothschild (1982) and McAdam (1988) and include some information on the libraries.

2. The letter from Emmie Schrader is in a collection of papers related to the project in the possession of Virginia Steele, Santa Rosa, California, hereafter cited in text as the Steele Papers. An interview with Virginia Steele, Santa Rosa, California, November 5, 1993, by Donald G. Davis, Jr., provided general information on the Freedom Libraries. The three-page student application for the Mississippi Summer Project asked for numbered choices for participation in various phases of the project—including community centers, freedom schools, and voter registration—and subjects one could teach. It also asked for six skills, one of which was in library science.

3. Though she had listed teaching as a first choice, Steele wrote: "Yes, I would like to set up the library. I will try to come prepared as best I can to do either. You all decide. I think the library work is probably what I ought to do since I've just gone through a perfectly ghastly year getting a library degree. . . . There are too many others already there who know as much as I do. But I'll be boning up on setting up a small library. And I'll talk authoritatively if you want me to" (Steele Papers, Letter from Virginia Steele to Emmie Schrader, May 25, 1964).

4. Letter from Virginia Steele to "Fellow Students and Classmates" at the School of Library Science, University of California, Berkeley, July 1, 1964 (Steele Papers). "I was overwhelmed at the idea of setting up a library all by myself. I had memorized the history of printing last summer session for the final exam . . . yet I did not know what the basic steps were for setting up a library and what the minimum essentials were."

5. One example related to the *Delta Democrat-Times* in which "One of [Hodding Carter, Jr.'s] reporters led me . . . the last 35 miles I had to drive into Mississippi, so I wouldn't be driving alone. This on a bright, hot Sunday afternoon in June in the USA in 1964." Letter from Virginia Steele to "Fellow Students and Classmates," July 1, 1964 (Steele Papers). Scanning the *Delta Democrat-Times* from May through August 1964 reveals generally full reporting of COFO activities in Greenville, surrounding counties, and the entire state. The paper dealt with a variety of issues related to the project, including reporting itself (June 24), new laws passed to deal with the project initiatives (May 15 and June 22), and the involvement of the National Council of Churches (June 14, Sept. 3).

6. Steele wrote that she "felt that the Project workers in Greenville were being given genuine protection. . . . I never heard anything from any [of her colleagues] except a solidly expressed belief that [Police] Chief Burnley was a man of integrity dedicated to law, order, and *justice*." Letter from Virginia Steele to David A. McCandless, September 10, 1964 (Steele Papers).

7. Besides the articles in *California Librarian* and *Southeastern Librarian*, cited above, several newspaper accounts appeared, among them "Freedom Worker Reports," *Morgantown Post* (Morgantown, WV), September 15, 1964; "Rights Worker Says Mississippi in Web," *Morning News* (Wilmington, DE), February 4, 1965; and "Mississippi Snared in 'Web,' Ex-Rights' Aide Says," *Evening Journal* (Wilmington, DE), February 4, 1965.

8. Evidence for the viable centers with libraries is conflicting. (1) McAdam (1988) lists some 25 known community centers in Appendix C, "Accounting of All Projects at Summer's End," pp. 255-256. (2) The "July 10 [1964] Report on Summer Community Centers," produced by COFO (Sally Belfrage Papers), states that there were 13 community center projects, including rural Mileston (Holmes County) about which little was known. (3) "Special Re-

port—Community Centers—September 1964," produced by COFO (Steele Papers), states that there were "23 community centers that are now operating in Mississippi." (4) Holt (1965) describes briefly 25 sites under the heading, "Freedom Centers—What's Happening: September 1964," pp. 123-125. This list apparently includes both schools and community centers. (5) A document from winter 1964-1965 projects that for summer 1965 there would be 15 community centers in 15 communities with 61 full-time workers. "Development of the Mississippi Project" (Lowenstein Papers).

9. For an example of a library run in conjunction with a Freedom School, refer to the experiences of Karol Nelson (now McMahan [1994]) in Canton and rural Madison County; and Sutherland (1965), pp. 161-163.

10. The Greenwood library's activities were greatly curtailed in the later part of the summer as its space was preempted for other project needs.

11. An obituary by Ben Sonnenberg appears as "Sally Belfrage," *The Nation*, April 4, 1994.

12. One illustrative note about the Mileston library indicates that it was overflowing with more than 10,000 high-quality volumes and that proffered donations were actually being turned away.

13. Peebles and Howell (1975) do not mention anything after 1954 in their slightly more than one page devoted to "Library Service to Negroes." In a telephone conversation with Donald G. Davis, Jr. in spring 1994, Jeannine Lackey Laughlin (1983) maintained that the Freedom Libraries had no impact whatsoever on public library development in Mississippi.

14. Charles McLaurin explained, "Cain't see in the mornin' cause it's too early, and cain't see at night 'cause it's too late" (Sugarman, p. 64).

15. Cresswell (1996) documents an inconclusive "read-in" protest by Tougaloo College students at the Jackson Public Library in 1961, as well as successful, though sporadic, library sit-ins elsewhere in the South.

16. Special thanks to Reid S. Derr for supplying a copy of the Scarbrough document (Paul Burney Johnson Family Papers).

17. In its fuller dimensions, of course, the project was conceived to be an effort in the liberation of all Mississippians, white and black, as well as the American public, especially those with influence to effect change.

18. Silver's (1964) often cited paper was a seminal analysis of the Mississippi mind and quickly became required reading for the project staff and volunteers. Jencks's (1964) late summer piece provided an interpretive framework for the project.

REFERENCES

Adickes v. S.H. Kress & Co., 398 *U.S. Reports* 144 (1970).

Akers, S.G. (1927). *Simple library cataloging.* Chicago, IL: American Library Association.

Allard Kenneth Lowenstein Papers 1940-1980. Southern Collection, University of North Carolina at Chapel Hill.

American Library Association. (1962). Statement on individual membership, chapter status, and institutional membership. *ALA Bulletin, 56*(7), 637.

American Library Association Archives, University of Illinois at Urbana-Champaign. [Cited in text as ALA Archives.]

Atwater, J. (1964). If we can crack Mississippi . . . . *Saturday Evening Post*, July 25-August 1, 1964, 15 ff.

Belfrage, S. (1965). *Freedom summer.* New York: Viking Press

Braverman, M. (1965). Mississippi summer. *Library Journal, 90*(2), 5045-5047.

Bro-Dart Industries. (1955). *Modern-simplified book repair: A "how-to-do-it" booklet on easy, inexpensive book repair the Bro-Dart way.* Newark, NJ: Bro-Dart Industries.

Burner, E. (1994). *And gently he shall lead them: Robert Parris Moses and civil rights in Mississippi.* New York: New York University Press.

Cresswell, S. The last days of Jim Crow in American libraries. *Libraries & Culture, 31*(3-4), 557-573.

Dittmer, J. (1994). *Local people: The struggle for civil rights in Mississippi.* Urbana-Champaign, IL: University of Illinois Press.

Douglas, M. P. (1941). *The teacher-librarian's handbook.* Chicago, IL: American Library Association.

Ellin, J. (1964). WMU [Western Michigan University] faculty member describes freedom schools' effort in south. *Kalamazoo Gazette*, July 18.

FBI File, the Student Nonviolent Coordinating Committee. Characterization and Membership. (1991). Wilmington, DE: Scholarly Resources.

Findlay, J. F., Jr. (1993). *Church people in the struggle: The national council of churches and the black freedom movement, 1950-1970*. New York: Oxford University Press.

Holt, L. (1965). *The summer that didn't end*. New York: William Morrow.

Huie, W. B. (1965). *Three lives for Mississippi*. New York: Signet.

Hunter, C. W. (1992). The integration of the Mississippi Library Association. *Mississippi Libraries, 56*(3), 68-71.

Jencks, C. (1964). Mississippi: From conversion to coercion. *New Republic, 151*(August 22), 17-21.

Jo Ann Ooiman Robinson Papers 1960-1966. State Historical Society of Wisconsin, Madison, Wisconsin. [Cited in text as Jo Ann Ooiman Robinson Papers.] Special thanks to Louise Robbins for her assistance with the Robinson papers.

Josey, E. J. (1994). Race issues in [American] library history. In W. A. Wiegand & D. G. Davis, Jr. (Eds.), *Encyclopedia of library history* (pp. 534-535). New York: Garland Publishing.

Laughlin, J. L. (1983). The Mississippi library commission: A force for library development Unpublished doctoral dissertation, Indiana University, 1983. *Dissertation Abstracts International, 44-03A,*602.

McAdam, D. (1988). *Freedom summer*. New York: Oxford University Press.

McMahan, K. (1994). Mississippi revisited: Musings. *West Austin News* (Austin, TX), January 13.

Mendy Samstein Papers. "Notes on Mississippi," State Historical Society of Wisconsin, Madison, Wisconsin.

Papers of the Congress of Racial Equality, 1941-1967. (1980). Sanford, NC: Microfilming Corporation of America. [Cited in text as CORE Papers.]

Paul Burney Johnson Family Papers. Report by Tom Scarbrough, May 19, 1964. McCoin Library and Archives, University of Southern Mississippi, Hattiesburg, Mississippi.

Peebles, M., & Howell, J. B. (1975). *A history of Mississippi libraries*. Montgomery, AL: Mississippi Library Association.

Rothschild, M. A. (1982). *A case of black and white: Northern volunteers and the Southern Freedom Summers, 1964-1965*. Westport, CT: Greenwood Press.

Sally Belfrage Papers (1962-[1963-1964]-1966). State Historical Society of Wisconsin, Madison.

Sawyer, R. (1957). *How to tell a story*. Chicago, IL: Compton.

Silver, J. W. (1964). Mississippi: The closed society. *Journal of Southern History, 30*(1), 3-34.

Sitton, C. (1964). Negroes to spur Mississippi drive. *New York Times*, March 16.

Steele, V. (1965a). "Freedom Libraries" of the Mississippi Summer Project. *Southeastern Librarian, 15*(2), 76-81.

Steele, V. (1965b). A new librarian on the Mississippi summer project—1964. *California Librarian, 26*(3), 145-150, 178.

Student Nonviolent Coordinating Committee Papers, 1959-1972. (1982). Sanford, NC: Microfilming Corporation of America. [Cited in text as SNCC Papers.]

Sugarman, T. (1966). *Stranger at the gates: A summer in Mississippi*. New York: Hill and Wang.

Sutherland, E. (Ed.). (1965). *Letters from Mississippi*. New York: McGraw-Hill.

Tucker, S. (1965). *Mississippi from within*. New York: Arco Publishing.

Virginia Steele Papers. Private collection of the author, Santa Rosa, California.

Von Hoffman, N. (1964). *Mississippi notebook*. New York: David White Company.

Waldron, A. (1993). *Hodding Carter: The reconstruction of a racist*. Chapel Hill, NC: Algonquin Books.

Racial Integration at the University of Houston

A Personal Perspective, I

❤ Edward G. Holley ❤

Our profession has too little in the way of oral history about libraries and librarianship, thus grateful appreciation is extended to Mark Tucker and others who planned this book. We certainly would have benefited in the past if we had done more. As with all remembrance of things past, mine will consist of personal perspectives on what occurred during the 1960s at the University of Houston (UH). The remarks are based on personal reminiscences as well as on calendars from those days plus printed annual reports and a few conversations with others at Houston during the period of my directorship from September 1962 to December 1971. These are subject to the normal biases characteristic of such reminiscences.

To set the stage, I begin with a section from my final annual report, summing up my years as Director of Libraries, which was completed in the fall of 1971:

> In the sixties, when librarians were in scarce supply, the University of Houston was fortunate to have a corps of dedicated professionals. They had been trained by Mrs. Ruth S. Wikoff, who held a variety of titles during her long tenure and retired as Associate Director of Libraries [and Professor] in 1967. [The staff's] initial skepticism at an inexperienced young man [me] was warranted, but [its members] let him prove himself and all of us learned a great deal in the process. Our numbers expanded over the years so that there are as many professional librarians as there were total full-time staff in the fall of 1962. Among the more notable aspects of their profes-

sionalism has been an unwillingness to parrot the answers they thought the director wanted to hear. Few have been bashful about letting their complete professional views be known. Yet no director has ever had . . . more competent or more loyal staff [members]. Their productivity and professional growth have been out of all proportion to the size of the staff, which was, and remains, small for the size of the University. We owe much also to the clerical and technical staff who assume responsibilities here that would horrify our colleagues in some libraries. They deserve more attention, and more thanks, than they have received in recent years.

Perhaps nowhere was the progressiveness of the staff more apparent than in its conscious decision to be the first unit on campus to add a black person [Myra Allen] to its clerical staff [paraprofessional in today's terms] (1964) and its faculty (1967). [I meant *entire* university faculty, not just the library faculty; Ruth Wikoff had won faculty status for librarians long before I came on the scene]. We look back in amazement that the first event occurred only seven years ago and with equal surprise that in September, 1969, E. J. Josey could still write in the *Wilson Library Bulletin* that "the only associate directorship of a university library in the entire country to be held by a black librarian is filled by a very able person in the State of Texas at the University of Houston."

Our decision to invite Dr. Charles D. Churchwell to join us as Assistant Director for Public Services and Associate Professor was fortunate for the University of Houston and for him. When he left us in 1969 to become Director of Libraries at Miami University in Ohio, he had earned respect and stature throughout the community for his professional competence as well as for his personal warmth and charm. Though we have much yet to do, especially in integrating the professional staff, we can take some satisfaction that representation of ethnic minorities on the full-time staff now amounts to 28 percent.

It should be added that the libraries also employed one of the first Hispanic paraprofessionals, Mary Lee Flores Barrossa, in Cataloging, also in 1964; but its first Hispanic professional, Robert Rodriguez, did not come as an Assistant Catalog Librarian until 1969. Our first paraprofessionals, both African-American and Hispanic, remained on the UH Library staff and advanced up our five step promotion ladder, for fourteen and fifteen years, respectively. Although I have not made a study of minority employment in libraries for this period, I would hazard a guess that this record might be one of the better ones for the 1960s.

How did all this come about, especially in a library staff consisting mostly of white southern women librarians? Let me repeat a phrase I quoted above: "[they] were dedicated professionals;" and they had served under Ruth Wikoff, whose dedication to the profession and to faculty status were articles of faith. Several were also "liberal democrats" in the context of those times.

However, one should not overlook the fact that Houston, then the sixth largest city in the country and still growing, was very much a segregated city, and the university was situated in an area rapidly changing from an all-white student body to one with significant numbers of African-American students, despite the presence four blocks away of a state-supported historically black university, Texas Southern University.

The story of the first African-American employee is easily told. Because the university had become a state institution in September 1963 and immediately experienced increases in enrollment (that first year the number of new students was 3,765 added to a previous enrollment of 13,665), there was an immediate need for new faculty, new librarians, additional staff, and new buildings. For example, in two years (1965-67), we added thirty-one new paraprofessional staff members. Searching for paraprofessional staff was no easy task, but it was certainly helped by the very competent people in the personnel department who went out of their way to secure the best people available. The problems of integrating large numbers of people into our departments was made easier by the competent department heads such as Mary Louise Vance in Acquisitions, Mary Jane Treichler in Serials, and Ruth Morton in Cataloging. They all had high professional standards and sensitivity to the needs of the persons who worked with and for them. The same was true of the reference division heads—Sara Aull in Science, Virginia Murphy in Humanities, and Julian Brandes in Social Science—though they had fewer paraprofessionals than did the technical services librarians. All the librarians worked closely with new employees and encouraged them to seek advancement but, as occasionally happened, also summoned the courage to terminate the few who did not measure up.

Fortunately for the university, both the state and federal governments greatly increased their support for education at all levels during the administrations of Governor John Connally and President Lyndon Johnson. From a reasonably good college-level library, the University of Houston needed to move to acquire research materials to support graduate study and research.

Relevant to this discussion was the passage of the Civil Rights Act in 1964, which empowered the U.S. Attorney General to bring lawsuits on behalf of black plaintiffs and, under Title VI of the Higher Education Act of 1965, prohibited spending federal funds in segregated schools and colleges. So the University of Houston, with substantial federal funds becoming available from the Great Society legislation, made plans to begin integrating its student body, staff, and faculty. As was true of most universities, integration proceeded slowly at Houston.

As director, I had frequent contact with the director and assistant director of personnel. Charles Stranger, assistant director, and a dedicated UH alumnus, asked me if the library would be willing to employ a black person among the rapidly expanding technical services staff. I responded positively after consulting our department heads, one of whom, Ruth Morton, was emphatic that we should. I believe her exact words were: "If we don't give those people a chance they never will get anywhere." Thus the first African American, Myra Allen [later Cormier], became a paraprofessional in the Catalog Department, and she was soon followed by others in Acquisitions and other library units. She was actually preceded by the aforementioned Hispanic by four months. Almost without exception, the new paraprofessional staff members learned quickly, performed their duties competently, and advanced along the five step ladder we created for paraprofessional staff with the help of the personnel department. We even had one assistant in the director's office who did not perform adequately, and she was terminated. I might add that the paraprofessional staff outnumbered the professional staff by two or three to one during that period, and that was unusual for many university libraries. Indeed, we never could have accomplished so much without them and, as I noted in the report above, the clerical and technical staff "assume responsibilities here that would horrify our colleagues in some libraries."

I should also add that, in keeping the staff small, we made a determined effort to see that their salaries were adjusted upward on a regular basis. That was easier to do in those heady days of the 1960s, a period which historian Roger Geiger calls "The Golden Age on Campus" (*Research and Relevant Knowledge: American Research Universities Since World War II*, 1993). There was money for staff, for books and journals, and for buildings. The University of Houston received its share and maybe a little more because appropriations were tied to enrollment and type of program. We never thought there was enough money to keep pace with expanding enrollments and new programs, but in the words of the old phrase, "I been rich (relatively) and I been poor," and being relatively rich is surely better when it comes to libraries. By the time of my departure in December 1971, budgeted positions in the libraries included thirty-five professionals and eighty support staff, plus large numbers of student assistants.

When Ruth Wikoff announced her decision to retire in 1967 after thirty-four years at the university (she had been the second librarian hired when the University of Houston was still a junior college in 1933), we decided that she was irreplaceable as associate director. We needed to readjust the administrative structure with three assistant directors: public services, technical services, and collection development, the last position reflecting the heavy emphasis upon expanding the collections. If we could have found someone who could be associate director, I am sure that I would have gone that route. Indeed, I believe I asked Charlie if he would like that title, but he declined because he thought that was more responsibility than was warranted at that time in his career. So we were looking for two persons for the public and technical assistant directors. We had already "bombed out" in searching for the technical services slot, subsequently filled by Larry Besant in 1968. I remind you that this was a period when professional librarians with some experience were in short supply. That situation undoubtedly played a role in Houston's willingness to take a chance on me in 1962. I learned, near the end of my tour there, that the professional librarians had voted 9 to 3 against my appointment, not, as Ruth Wikoff told me, because they had any questions about my qualifications but because of my lack of administrative experience. The administration and Wikoff thought differently, to my good fortune, but that is a story for another time.

Well, the search for the two positions had not gone well. We had looked at a couple of people, one of whom we did not want and another who decided to go elsewhere. In January 1967, I went to ALA Midwinter in New Orleans and had asked around about possible candidates with no results. Then I ran into Charlie

Churchwell, whom I had known at Illinois. We were both rushing to meetings but paused in the hallway of the Roosevelt Hotel long enough for me to ask what he was doing. He said he was Assistant Circulation Librarian in charge of the large bookstack operation at Illinois and had just completed his doctoral dissertation subsequently published as an ACRL Monograph, *The Shaping of American Library Education,* in 1975. I asked him about his plans. He said he could go into library education (he had taught at Prairie View A & M in Texas during the early 1950s), but he really thought he wanted to go into administration. The Dean of Libraries at Illinois, Robert B. Downs, had been helping him, just as he had given Charlie additional opportunities at Illinois. Immediately wheels began turning in my head. Here might be the solution to my problem, though I didn't mention that to Charlie. As we were both pressed for time, we had to part and I asked him to keep in touch.

When I returned to Houston I said to Ruth Wikoff, "I believe I have found a solution to our problem." I told her about my meeting with Charlie, his background, and his experience. I also noted that he was black. Her response was, "I don't care what color he is. Is he qualified?" As an Illinois native, she had enormous respect for the University of Illinois and especially for Robert B. Downs. I'm sure his recommendation for my own appointment had weighed heavily with her. So I told her I would like to ask the department heads how they would feel about bringing Charlie down for an interview. This was long before search and affirmative action committees had become a fact of life, but I would never have appointed a professional librarian without consulting with the department heads. Again, the department heads were willing, especially after I detailed Churchwell's credentials. Our catalog librarian responded the same way she did about the earlier integration. Others said: "Well it will be different, but we should try." Then I went to see my boss, John Allred, vice president for Academic Affairs, who was aware of my unsuccessful attempts to find a replacement for Wikoff. I said, "John, you know we have had a hard time finding a replacement for Mrs. Wikoff. What would you think if I were to bring a well-qualified black librarian to campus for an interview?" He responded: "Ed, you know we don't discriminate!" Since we had not employed any black faculty member up to that time, I knew no such thing. Anyway, I immediately called Charlie, invited him down to talk with us, and he came for a visit on February 7-9, 1967. As I knew he would, he impressed everybody: paraprofessionals, the library faculty, and the University Library Committee members, who were surprised but expressed admiration that the library was willing to take this step. He also impressed the vice president and president. My guess is that they were greatly relieved; we had not yet employed a black faculty member, and Charles Churchwell would be an excellent beginning. A little later that year, the School of Education also made an offer to an African American at the assistant professor level in the School of Education. However, Churchwell came as the first faculty member and as an Associate Professor. He assumed his duties a month before the education professor. Let me not mislead you about my motives. I did not go looking for a minority assistant director. I sought a competent assistant director and, having located him, determined that he had the qualifications by which he would succeed.

Success was almost immediate. Charlie settled into the position as assistant director for public services and made so many friends so quickly that we really didn't consider how unusual this was. He was and is an excellent administrator. His contacts with faculty and students as well as library staff were, for the most part, well received. He was also helpful to the university administration, especially to the dean of students, doing much on campus quietly and often behind the scenes. African-American students visited him. I know that a few of the younger ones regarded him as an "Oreo"—i.e., black on the outside and white on the inside, but as my wife, Bobbie Lee, noted, they did seek his advice when they got into trouble. White faculty consulted him on library problems. Racial unrest and anti-Vietnam protests would soon cloud this picture, one in which Charlie's assistance would be invaluable not just to the library but to the entire campus.

I'm not suggesting that there were not some faculty who didn't make snide remarks. An example was reported to me by our library faculty. One disgruntled, recently retired faculty member paused at their luncheon table in the Faculty Club and asked them how they were getting along with the "Nigger in the Library." One of our southern women librarians stiffened and responded promptly, "*Dr.* Churchwell is doing an excellent job" and indicated that the conversation was terminated. Our library faculty were not about to let anyone get away with such remarks. They knew that most such prejudiced individuals were leftovers from an earlier period, and their own credentials couldn't stand much scrutiny. I'm sure there must have been others. We never shared these incidents with Charlie. I don't recall anyone ever making such comments to me, and I am sure I would have remembered. I do remember numerous comments from different faculty members on what a great job Dr. Churchwell was doing and how helpful he had been to them and their students. I was pleased but hardly surprised.

In preparing for this paper, I asked several former staff members how they remembered Charlie. Similar phrases came up several times: "We never thought of him as a black person or as a person of different color," "he was respected for what he was," his respect for every person, "a dear friend," wonderful sense of humor, charming, dignified. One person reminded me of a Christmas party in the library lobby. In a nativity scene, Charlie played Joseph and one of our paraprofessional white staff members, Beulah Sealock, was Mary. Later, that staff member told her supervisor, Sara Aull, that she had been a little nervous beforehand but hadn't mentioned it to Sara. Afterward Beulah said the performance seemed so natural that she didn't even think about Charlie's color. I seem to remember there was a great deal of chuckling when Charlie and Beulah came out, all very good natured, for Charlie was respected and admired by the staff.

Knowing that Charlie had ambitions to become a director himself, I felt keenly my responsibility to encourage him and provide opportunities to meet other librarians in the state at conferences and at the meeting of the Texas Council of State College Librarians, a gathering of library directors who work on book contracts and politics with state government staff. I must admit that the first venture to Austin with Charlie for such a meeting gave me pause when we went to the old and fashionable Driskell Hotel. It had not occurred to me beforehand that there might possibly be an incident. So with some apprehension I told Charlie that I would register for us and put the bill on my American Express card. There was no incident at the hotel nor in the local restaurant. The convivial directors welcomed Charlie to our deliberations and some even seemed pleased that we had succeeded in recruiting him to Houston.

To put the above in perspective, I need to say a word about segregated places in Houston. When the Texas Council met in Houston, I told President Hoffman that I wanted to entertain them at dinner (and show off) so could I use the university's membership in one of the fancy clubs downtown (at university expense, of course). He asked me if there would be Negro members and I said "yes." He said, "Well, you won't be able to go to the Petroleum Club, because they still do not admit Negroes. You'll have to go to the Houston Club." I thanked him and told him that the Houston Club was quite satisfactory. Indeed, I preferred the Houston Club. The food was better, and it had the charm of being built before everyone became enamored with stainless steel furniture and cold unfeeling white and black decor. But I was also surprised that the Petroleum Club was still restricted. What with dealing with Arabian sheiks and others in the oil business, I knew that it wouldn't be long before that policy would come to an end.

Charlie will tell you about the desegregating of Houston dining places, along with his friends, Ann and Jim Criswell and Henry Holcomb, reporters for the two Houston newspapers. We were fortunate in our relations with the downtown newspapers and with some of our friends in the business community. While one may get good publicity frequently in a college or university located in a small town, it is very difficult to vie for space in newspapers in large cities. Although I was occasionally annoyed at the newspaper editors who did not use what I thought were newsworthy University of Houston library stories, I know we fared better than most because the librarian of Rice University told me: "I want to hire you as my public relations man." He seemed a little patronizing but also a little envious. As you might guess, the newspapers did feature Charlie's arrival and subsequent departure from Houston. Both were indeed news.

Storm clouds were gathering by the end of Charlie's first year with us. The push for faster integration was on. The University of Houston was located, as I earlier indicated, only four blocks from predominantly African-American Texas Southern University. Since it was also in the Third Ward, which gave to Congress one of its most distinguished Congress persons, Barbara Jordan, it was an obvious place to have experienced the kind of unrest which occurred in many places in the United States. This was especially true since it was also the period of rising unrest over the Vietnam War. It is amazing, in retrospect, how little that affected the UH campus, although there were marches and even an incident of breaking a plate glass window in the new Student Union building. But the University was essentially a conservative place, and that incident really shook many students. Charlie Churchwell, working behind the scenes with the university administration, was especially helpful during that period. He said, somewhat ruefully, that he often spent more time in the administration building than he did in the library, but he had my full encouragement and support.

What might well have been a major crisis, but was not, occurred at the time of Dr. Martin Luther King's assassination. Our dedication ceremonies for the 119,000 square foot addition to the M. D. Anderson Library had been scheduled to begin on the day of Dr. King's funeral, April 9, 1968. Our two-day program was to include a symposium and a Houston Symphony Orchestra performance on campus followed the next day by another symposium and a dedicatory address by Douglas Knight, president of Duke University and chairman of the National Advisory Commission on Libraries. Major eruptions on the Duke campus precluded Knight's attendance. President Hoffman closed the campus on April 9 and we had an abbreviated ceremony the following day. The sense of shock among the students and faculty would have made any other response reprehensible. As I noted in my annual report: "Though it had not worked out as we had planned, our own local problems seemed small indeed compared to the national problems with which the country was confronted." What was to happen in the following years, 1968-70, reflected the national turmoil with demonstrations, pickets, demands, etc., but never, I think, as seriously as what happened elsewhere. Doubtless some of this lack of major confrontations came from the fact that about 80 percent of the students were commuters and did not spend the majority of their time on campus. But the anti-Vietnam sentiment and the interest in further integration were strong among both students and faculty.

From my perspective, the library continued to provide services to an ever-increasing number of faculty and students, all impatient that those resources and services did not keep up with their needs. The new building, the increase in state appropriations for materials, and the support of generous donors helped as did a supportive university administration. But that is a story for another time.

One more illustration of Charlie's helpfulness to the faculty came when one of our white Mississippi born professors began teaching a course in African-American History, an area in which the library had few resources, and, indeed, in which publications were not extensive. The professor, Robert Haynes, urged his departmental colleagues to offer such a course, but they were unsympathetic and said: "Well, if you want it taught, you'll have to do it." Haynes was on the library committee, and he often discussed his problems with Charlie. Haynes spoke often in churches and at other forums in Houston and experienced not only antagonism but incidents resulting in the slashing of his automobile tires during one appearance. Another faculty member who benefited from

Charlie's expertise was our distinguished Latin Americanist, Harvey Johnson. Charlie was dedicated to providing the best possible service to faculty and students, an approach which was strongly supported by our dedicated and well respected library reference faculty.

Charlie continued to do a fine job at Houston and to be active in professional associations both locally and nationally. He participated in Texas Library Association conferences as well as the Southwestern conference, consulted for several libraries, and served on the Advisory Board for his alma mater, Atlanta University (AU). In fact, as I remember, he encouraged that marvelous Dean, Virginia Lacy Jones, to invite me to AU to talk about Library of Congress reclassification, which we had underway at the University of Houston. Alas, that too was not to be as successful as I had hoped. I went on election day 1968. Most of the Atlanta University folks and I, too, were Hubert Humphrey supporters, so the next day, when I was to conduct my program, they and I were downcast about Richard Nixon's election victory. There was an overwhelming sense that the progress in civil rights made under Presidents Kennedy and Johnson would likely be halted under President Nixon, whereas Hubert Humphrey's long commitment to civil rights and education had a history dating back to the late 1940s.

Charles Churchwell, whose career ambition included a directorship, was undoubtedly the target of recruitment efforts by other colleges and universities from the time he came to Houston, including some of the historically Negro colleges and universities who felt he should have come to them instead of the University of Houston. In those days, even with his experience, he would have been unlikely to succeed me at Houston. Chief administrators were still to be white males at most institutions for another decade. For example, the first woman ARL director, Glenora Rossell, was appointed at Pittsburgh in 1969. And A. P. Marshall once told me that Robert Downs had been unsuccessful in encouraging a number of white universities to give Marshall an opportunity to serve in one of their major positions. But Charlie was to have success sooner than I expected.

Miami University was looking for a new director and approached him about joining its staff. One of my staff members argued strongly that I should try harder to get Charlie to remain at Houston. I could not do that. My principle in administration has always been to encourage colleagues to pursue opportunities to advance in terms of their own career goals. Miami University was, and is, a fine university. Recognizing Churchwell's talents, they soon made him an associate provost.

When university faculty, friends, and staff of the University of Houston Library gathered on August 7, 1969, to bid a loving farewell to Charles and Yvonne Churchwell, the respect and admiration for the contributions they had made was very apparent. As I remarked in my annual report, "the staff feels most keenly the resignation of Dr. Charles D. Churchwell to become Director of Libraries at Miami University at Oxford, Ohio. In his two years as Assistant Director for Public Services few people have made as favorable an impact or as much a contribution to the total campus community. We view his departure with mixed emotions, grateful for his professional competence these past two years but happy for him in this significant advancement." In the intervening years, our personal and professional friendship has continued, as he has gone on to other major university administrative posts at Brown University, Washington University in St. Louis, and back to his alma mater, Clark Atlanta University.

Looking back to his time and mine at the University of Houston, I ask if the university was fortunate to have achieved modest desegregation this early with relatively little trauma and without a lot of fanfare? Someone else will have to answer that question. I do not think that I or the other members of the University of Houston library staff had any great feeling that we were crusaders for integration on campus. Most of us did believe in equal opportunity and welcomed the integration of the university, first with students, then with support staff and faculty, and subsequently with administration. We were neither saints nor martyrs, but we did have a strong commitment to librarianship, to its being open to all persons with appropriate credentials, and to the advancement of the university we were privileged to serve. To have had an opportunity to become director of libraries at the University of Houston at an important crossroad in its emergence as a major urban university was both a privilege and a pleasure. And I am certainly grateful to have inherited a remarkable group of capable women librarians (there were few men on the staff) and to have brought to that group a diversified paraprofessional and a superb administrator who just happened to be African American.

Racial Integration at the University of Houston

A Personal Perspective, II[1]

ᘐ Charles D. Churchwell ᘐ

D
r. Edward G. Holley offered me the position of Assistant Director for Public Services of the Libraries of the University of Houston in February 1967. I accepted the offer and reported to work in August of the same year. Holley's appointment of me broke the color barrier for the faculty and administration of the rapidly growing urban university in the segregated city of Houston, Texas, and set the stage for integrating many sectors of life in Houston, still a very segregated city in 1967.

In 1967, some of Houston's residential areas were in a transitional phase, but many hotels and restaurants still did not serve African-Americans. Throughout the state, the system of higher education was segregated—whites and blacks did not attend the same institution. A case in point was Texas Southern University, a black institution, that stood only a few blocks from the University of Houston. It had been opened to prevent a black from attending the law school at the University of Texas in Austin. Moreover, within less than a fifty mile radius of Houston, were the University of Texas at Galveston; Lamar University; and Texas A & M University, clearly all predominantly white institutions; and Prairie View A & M College, a black institution. Texas took its segregation of higher education quite seriously. Dr. Holley changed all this by bringing me in as an associate professor and administrator. His was a courageous decision, to say the least, at a state university in Texas in 1967.

I was welcomed to the faculty and libraries by a group of competent, mature, and secure librarians who had earned the respect of the faculty and administration of the university. Dr. Holley assisted me in many ways but most importantly by being a good supervisor. He did not hesitate to delegate all matters relating to public services to me to handle, and I emphasize *all* matters. He fully supported my decisions.

The most difficult time for me at the University of Houston came during my first days on the job, living with my decision to take the position. Let me try to explain. Like all other African-Americans of my generation, I had been urged many times to return to the black community after I completed my education to help other less fortunate African-Americans get an education. This gnawing feeling of guilt about not having returned proved to be a steady emotional drain. And it was made more acute by the fact that, when Dr. Holley's offer arrived, I was negotiating with officials at Morgan State College and Tuskegee University, both strong historically black institutions looking for a head librarian. I was being recruited by these institutions, and I worried for several days over the choice I had to make but I could not arrive at a decision.

I finally explained my problem to Dr. Robert Downs, then director of the library of the University of Illinois where I was working. Dr. Downs had helped me when I encountered a problem while writing my dissertation, so I knew him rather well and felt sure he would help me again. Dr. Downs asked me what I wanted to do after this first position. I told him I would want to apply for any academic director's position that became vacant and for which I felt qualified. Dr. Downs said if that was my goal, I should not take either of the offers from the black institutions. He named two prominent black librarians who had been working at black institutions for many years and were trying to move to non-black institutions but could not get interviews for positions for which they were qualified. Dr. Downs's advice to go to Houston, though sound, was of little consolation to me during those first few weeks.

With the help of my supervisor and supportive colleagues, I managed to get through this trying period. In addition to them, I was helped by a strong outside support group of white and black friends that included Clara McCleod, who worked with my wife, Yvonne, in the library at Texas Southern University; James McCloud, who was a student at Rice University; Ann Criswell, who was food editor for the *Houston Chronicle*, one of two major newspapers in Houston; James Criswell, who was newspaper librarian of the *Houston Post*, the other major newspaper in Houston; Jean Besant, the wife of Larry Besant, the head of Technical Services at the University of Houston; Henry Orgain, the husband of Marian Orgain, the head of Special Collections at the University of Houston; and of course Bobbie Lee (Mrs. Edward G. Holley). There were also Johnny Brand, the husband of my administrative assistant, Marvine Brand; Rita Paddock, a science librarian at Rice University; Henry Holcomb, a reporter for the *Houston Post* who regularly covered the University of Houston activities; and last, but of course not least, Yvonne, my lovely and wonderful wife.

In order to appreciate what I am going to say next, it is again important to remember just how segregated Houston was. Major restaurants and hotels kept blacks and whites apart. Ann and James Criswell, as I stated above, were among our strong friends outside the university. As the *Chronicle's* food editor, about once a week Ann would choose a restaurant to which we would all go for dinner. Someone in the group other than Ann or Jim would always make reservations. When we appeared there would be a few awkward moments until someone recognized Ann as a member of the party. Many of Houston's finest restaurants served their first black customers in this manner. The group always paid for all its food and services and did not abuse Ann's position.

There is one other incident which caused me a great deal of agony, even though it had nothing to do with my professional duties as a librarian. I relate it only because of the role I played and the insight it may provide about the character of the president of the university, because it was he who ultimately had to approve my appointment. It came to be called the "Bobby Seale problem."

Bobby Seale, as I remember, served as the Minister of Education and Communication of the Black Panther Party. The Black Panthers were composed of many of the most radical blacks of the period, and they openly espoused violence to gain freedom for all black people in America. They had engaged in shoot-outs with the police in Oakland, California, and had threatened to do the same with police in other cities. They were feared by authorities in many large cities, including Houston. The number of black students at the University of Houston was relatively small. They were conservative when compared with the radical white students at the university and the black student leaders at Texas Southern University. Nonetheless, they requested permission from the university to bring Bobby Seale to the campus for a public forum. Their request was granted. Shortly after their request was granted, the Black Panthers had a shoot-out with federal and local officials in Chicago. Fred Hampton, a leading Black Panther in Chicago, was killed. The incident received a great deal of local and national press.

Following the shoot-out, widespread opposition to the visit started to grow. The president of the university, Dr. Philip Hoffman, began to be pressured to cancel the Bobby Seale visit. The opposition came mainly from outside the university, especially from downtown leaders and the police force. President Hoffman stood firmly behind the university's governance process. His refusal to cancel the forum caused the police to insist on being present. President Hoffman was also determined not to allow the police on campus unless they were supervised by university security personnel. As the pressures to cancel the forum mounted, the black students became even more insistent that the university honor its approval of the forum. Negotiations between them and university officials ensued. Because I knew some of the black student leaders, I was pulled into the negotiations. Negotiations lasted for several days and nights, including one long weekend.

The black students began to see the staging of this public forum as the establishment of their legitimacy on campus. Even before I became a member of the university administration's negotiating team, some of the black students had made it clear to me that I should not be at the university. As Dr. Holley had stated, to them I was not the "Oreo." But I had known many of the leaders for quite some time before this incident, and our respect for each other helped us through the negotiations. However, relationships were strained to the breaking point several times after we asked them to consider postponement of the forum because it might bring the police on campus, which even they did not want. Everyone feared the Houston police and the Harris County deputies. But postponement of the forum, for the students, was out of the question.

A compromise was reached after Rev. Lawson, a black minister from the Texas Southern and University of Houston communities joined the discussions and supported the university's position. But postponement was still out of the question. The university made it clear to the black students that it was not considering a postponement of the forum. It did suggest, however, that the site be changed from an outdoor forum to its main auditorium where the crowd could be managed by the university security force and outside help of its choosing. The site the students had chosen was an empty lot located between the University of Houston and Texas Southern University and bordered by a main traffic artery. The forum at this location would have attracted a large crowd which would have been difficult to manage. It would have been a ready-made situation that the Houston city police and the Harris County deputies would have been happy to manage and keep from developing into a riot.

The students accepted the offer of a different site when they were assured that the press and television would be present. The forum was moved on campus and held in the Cullen Auditorium. Henry Holcomb, a *Houston Post* reporter, assured me that his colleagues would definitely be there. The university security force managed the crowd without incident. Newspaper reporters and TV cameras occupied the first two rows in the auditorium. Bobby Seale and the black students were very pleased with the outcome and so were we. There were many plainclothes men, but the Houston police were not visible at all. Bobby Seale presented the Black Panthers's version of the Chicago shoot-out. These statements conflicted with the report of the Chicago police and the FBI. So much for the life of at least one librarian in 1967. What might have happened during the Bobby Seale incident had Ed Holley elected not to bring a black librarian to the university and had he not developed a relationship with the black student leaders of the university?

As we strive to create greater diversity in the workplace, there is a lesson that can be learned from the University of Houston experience. Clear direction and leadership must be provided by top administrators. Choose a place where there is a core of mature staff members who are competent and secure. Choose a workplace where a high premium is placed on trust and respect. Choose a workplace where decision-making is decentralized. All these conditions existed in the libraries of the University of Houston and contributed to their successful desegregation and diversification of the workforce. I was fortunate to be a part of this major change in higher education and to learn so much from it.

NOTE

[1] This chapter is derived from a videotape made by Nick Burckle. The author would like to offer special thanks to Nick Burckle for making this tape and to Ed Holley because he and the Houston experience contributed immeasurably to my accomplishments and career which really began to develop at the University of Houston.

Black Women, Civil Rights, & Libraries

&▲ Jessie Carney Smith &▲

T he first Civil Rights Bill, passed by Congress in 1866, granted blacks the rights and privileges of American citizenship and formed the basis of the Fourteenth Amendment to the U. S. Constitution. This first bill was soon either ignored or subverted. American society began to function as if there were no such civil rights laws and no Constitution. Nearly a century passed before members of the black race throughout this country started to gain certain rights and privileges to which they were entitled as people and as Americans. This essay addresses the work of some black women librarians who have been a part of this constantly changing society and shows how they have been affected by civil rights and how they influenced the development of librarians, libraries, and literature.

The information presented in this essay is based on the files for the author's works, *Notable Black American Women* (Books I and II), published by Gale Research Inc. in 1992 and the sequel volume published in 1996. The research into the lives of black women has been an exciting process, revealing the countless ways in which this neglected group pioneered and helped to shape American culture. The women profiled are women of the struggle, and what they achieved came about through perseverance, determination, courage, and nerve. They often grew weary of oppression, and that oppression resulted from two major factors over which they had no control: gender and race.

The women in the project were born as early as the 1730s and as recently as 1956. They were writers, educators, physicians, politicians, musicians, airline

pilots, entrepreneurs, artists, entertainers, and librarians. They were also abolitionists, Underground Railroad workers, civil rights activists, women's rights
activists, children's rights activists, religious activists, suffragists, and community activists. They were agitators who would not be restricted to the narrow
boundaries that male society and white society set for them because of gender
and race.

Like their sisters in the struggle, librarians among this group devoted time
and energy to civil rights causes. The seven women profiled in this essay are
presented in the order of their birth: Anne Bethel Spencer, Effie Lee Newsome,
Charlemae Hill Rollins, Augusta Baker, Virginia Lacy Jones, Annette L. Phinazee,
and Hannah Diggs Atkins. They were born as long ago as 1885 and as recently
as 1923. Although their protest took different forms, they made a difference in
libraries and in the community.

ANNE SPENCER (1882-1975)

Anne Spencer, poet and librarian, contributed to the Harlem Renaissance
and, like other women writers of that era, remained virtually in the background
until the resurgence of interest in that literary era came in the 1960s. She devoted
at least thirty years to promoting racial pride in her black students through the
reading of black literature. She challenged school integration for what she called
"tokenism" and fought racism by refusing to give in to it and through continuing
work in human relations.

Born Annie Bethel Bannister in Henry County, Virginia, on February 6, 1882,
she was the only child of Joel Cephus Bannister and Sarah Louise (Scales)
Bannister. Her native intelligence was nourished early in life as she learned to
write and as she read the dime novels and newspapers in the home of the refined
black family where she grew up after her parents separated permanently. As a
student at Virginia Seminary (previously the Lynchburg Baptist Seminary), she
demonstrated intellectual rebelliousness, independent thought, and cultural ag-
gressiveness. She, rather than the valedictorian, delivered the valedictory address at her graduation.

After she graduated and married, Spencer established a lifelong residence
on Pierce Street in Lynchburg, Virginia, which became an important site in the
cultural history of black America. Soon after she settled there, her home and
garden became a major rendezvous for blacks traveling to and from the South
and attracted artists, educators, literary figures, and other members of the black
intelligentsia: Sterling Brown, George Washington Carver, W.E.B. Du Bois,
Langston Hughes, Georgia Douglas Johnson, Claude McKay, Adam Clayton
Powell, and Paul Robeson were among the guests. Her home was the black
equivalent of Gertrude Stein's famous salon in Paris in the 1920s. For more than
half a century, her home and garden served as an intellectual oasis for talented
blacks.

From 1923 to 1945, Spencer served as librarian in Lynchburg's all-black
Dunbar High School. Knowing that her students had little or no contact with

books by black authors, she made such books available so that the students would know their own history and culture. She also demonstrated her activist attitude toward segregation. By the late 1950s, when blacks agitated for school integration, she opposed such integration as a form of tokenism, choosing other ways to fight racism. She refused to ride in segregated public transportation or to submit to other Jim Crow laws. Her work on a local human relations committee had led to the founding in 1918 of Lynchburg's NAACP and, thus, to a turning point in her life.

James Weldon Johnson, renowned poet and leader in the NAACP, while visiting Lynchburg to organize the chapter, discovered the talented woman and gave her the pen name Anne Spencer. Johnson introduced her work to H. L. Mencken, who helped launch the careers of black writers, and Mencken published Spencer's "Before the Feast at Sushan," the first of her writings to appear in print. Most of her poems were published in the 1920s, appearing in prominent anthologies. After her cherished friend James Weldon Johnson died in 1938, Spencer gradually withdrew from public life; she died at age ninety-three in 1967 having outlived her literary contemporaries of the Harlem Renaissance. Many of her writings died with her, for Spencer had followed the peculiar and risky practice of making notes on any handy piece of paper—on paper bags, in the margins and fly leaves of books, on bills, in tablets, on the backs of checks, and on envelopes. She used this method to write a new line for a poem, to write an entirely new poem, or to record other thoughts. These papers were overlooked and discarded when her literary works were gathered from her estate.

Effie Lee Newsome (1885-1979)

Effie Lee Newsome, poet, prose writer, illustrator, and librarian, concentrated her efforts on building among blacks two important elements so often destroyed by racial agitation and civil wrongs. She used her writings to instill racial pride in young readers and to help her adult readers understand the realities of race relations.

Born January 19, 1885, in Philadelphia, Newsome was one of five children of Mary Effie Lee and Benjamin Franklin Lee. Her father was the second president of Wilberforce University in Ohio, succeeding Bishop Daniel A. Payne. The Lee family was a reading family. The children spent leisure time reading the *Bible*, poetry, fairy tales, and children's magazines. Effie Newsome was especially fond of books about nature. At age five, she began to write. About this time she also developed a love for the visual arts, and her interest in painting and drawing would manifest itself later in the illustrations she created to accompany her writings for *The Brownies' Book* and *Crisis* magazine.

When she was about eleven years old, Effie Lee's family moved from Philadelphia to Wilberforce. Newsome graduated from Wilberforce University and attended the Oberlin Academy, the Academy of Fine Arts, and the University of Pennsylvania. She married and spent the rest of her life at Wilberforce, where she served as a librarian first at Central State College and then at Wilberforce University. Since books had been a part of Newsome's early life, reading had become an essential part of her whole life; she shared this interest in the reading of good books with the Wilberforce community.

A prolific writer, Newsome directed her prose and poetry primarily at children, reaching a rather wide audience through the magazines that published her works. *The Brownies' Book* and "The Little Page" section of *Crisis* magazine were two important black periodicals. In writing for children, Newsome usually focused on nature as a theme, and she aimed to delight her young audiences and bring happiness to them although she did treat the topic of race in the "Calendar Chat" section of *Crisis*. Newsome also explored racial themes and racial pride in her poetry for adult audiences.

Some scholars refer to Newsome as "patiently political." Her racial sketches were created to teach African-American history and stimulate racial pride. For example, she wrote biographical sketches of black achievers for *The Brownies' Book* and believed they would build self-esteem for black American children. From the 1920s through the 1940s, she was widely respected and she left an extensive body of work. But by her death on May 12, 1979, she, like many other women writers of her time, had largely been forgotten.

CHARLEMAE HILL ROLLINS (1897-1979)

Charlemae Hill Rollins, librarian, storyteller, author, and humanitarian, became an authority on black literature and was a remarkable woman whose life itself was a celebration. She opposed racial stereotypes in children's books and used libraries as well as her own writings to promote the contributions of black people. Rollins sought cultural freedom for black people so that they would not be bound by misrepresentations of them in literature and so that they might know, understand, and appreciate their culture.

Rollins was born in the small farming community of Yazoo City, Mississippi, on July 20, 1897, the child of a farmer and a teacher. Her father was forced to leave Mississippi, yet the family's happiness was not to be interrupted by the new life in the Indian Territory—now known as Oklahoma—where they settled. Rollins grew up with segregation. Her grandmother had been a slave rich in experiences that would influence Rollins's life. The storytelling that was to become a part of her life later on was introduced to her as a child. Her grandmother told stories of her own life as a slave, collected books that had belonged to the master who had fathered her children, and made those books available for her grandchildren to read. That some of them were medical books did not concern Rollins. She enjoyed reading and read these along with the other works in the family's library.

When she was ready for school, Rollins's civil rights were violated in her new town of Beggs. The children had to attend a school for blacks that had been founded by her mother, Birdie Hill, one of the first black teachers in this Indian territory. After completing elementary school, Rollins attended the segregated black secondary schools in St. Louis, Missouri, and Holly Springs, Mississippi. She graduated from yet another segregated school, Western University in Quindoro, Kansas, then taught for a while in Beggs, Oklahoma. She married in 1918, and the next year she and her husband moved to Chicago where she was to spend the rest of her life.

With a love for reading, acquired at an early age, and some teaching experience, Rollins felt compelled to enter the library profession. She joined the Chicago Public Library staff in 1927. As children's librarian in the Harding Square Branch Library, she served a multicultural, multiethnic, non-black population. Her professional training at Columbia and the University of Chicago prepared her for the next assignment as head of the children's department of the George Cleveland Hall Branch, the first branch in the system built in a black neighborhood.

An imaginative, creative, and dedicated librarian with a warm interest in children, Rollins provided inspiration and guidance in the world of books. She encouraged class visits to the library and reached out into the community with library programs. She organized book fairs, reading clubs, black history clubs, and a series of appreciation hours in the library, all aimed at highlighting the contributions of black people. Her storytelling sessions became an important aspect of the library's programs.

In time, Rollins launched a crusade against stereotypical images of blacks in children's literature and wrote her famous book, *We Build Together, A Reader's Guide to Negro Life and Literature for Elementary and High School Use*. She established criteria for evaluating literature and recommended books for libraries and readers. She soon gained national prominence, lecturing widely and reviewing manuscripts on black themes from publishers and authors. In addition to her appointment to numerous councils and committees concerned with children's literature, Rollins continued to write. She published biographical works on black poets and entertainers and made a lasting contribution to literature with her book *Christmas Gif'*.

Augusta Braxton Baker (b. 1911)

Augusta Braxton Baker, storyteller, author, educator, and librarian, made a tremendous impact on literature and libraries as a promoter of accurate portrayals of ethnic, cultural, and religious groups in children's literature. Her concern for images extended beyond those of blacks.

Baker was born in Baltimore on April 1, 1911, the daughter of teachers. We see early evidence of a pattern common in the African-American community— i.e., that storytelling came early, this time from the grandmother who passed along to Baker tales from earlier generations. Baker reflected on the positive values in these stories and, since she had a vivid imagination, the stories helped to strengthen and guide herk understanding.

She had grown up in an all-black community then moved into a predominantly white one when she studied at the University of Pennsylvania. She married early and moved to Albany, New York. When she applied for admission to Albany State Teachers College, the school was reluctant to admit her because of her race. Pressure from the Albany Interracial Council, a branch of the National Urban League, and a number of individuals caused the school to accept her.

Baker entered the library profession in 1937 and from then on dedicated her life to service to children. She began her work at the 135th Street branch of the New York Public Library, renamed the Countee Cullen Branch in 1951 and still later the Schomburg Center for Research in Black Culture. She was in the center of the social, cultural, and educational community in Harlem and in a library which housed the renowned Arthur Schomburg Collection. The library had served the community during the Harlem Renaissance and provided a center for the black artists, poets, writers, and musicians of the era. Baker found that the children in Harlem had little knowledge of their cultural background. She also found that the children's collection in the library lacked materials that focused on racial pride and racial identity and that most of the books that were available portrayed blacks in a stereotypical manner—as shiftless, happy, grinning, dialect-speaking menials. Charlemae Hill Rollins voiced her concern. Baker moved quickly to correct this problem and, with the support of a group of local black women, within two years she had built a collection of books that gave an honest portrayal of blacks that gave young people a positive attitude toward all racial groups.

Baker possessed a special talent for storytelling and held storytelling sessions for children in the community in the library. Her stories, too, gave blacks positive images of themselves. She continued her agitation to remove stereotypical representations of blacks in juvenile literature and spoke widely of her concern before parents, teachers, and various agencies. Publishers began to respond favorably. By 1953, Baker had become a storytelling specialist. In her well-known work, *The Black Experience in Children's Books* she speaks of the impact of books in intercultural education and says that, through them: "The black child is given pride in his heritage at the same time that the white child gains knowledge of another culture and history" (Baker, 1971). Augusta Baker has been a catalyst for social change brought about through books that give a positive portrayal of people regardless of race, culture, or religion.

VIRGINIA LACY JONES (1912-1984)

Virginia Lacy Jones, librarian and educator, was exceptionally well known in the profession for her work to raise the standards of library service for blacks and to enhance the educational level of blacks in the field. Her civil rights were violated by the profession and by the schools where she studied.

Born in Cincinnati on June 25, 1912, of hard working, poor, proud, and ambitious parents, Jones grew up in Clarksburg, West Virginia, a mining town of about 1,200 blacks amid a population of 35,000. Although the family lived in an integrated neighborhood, Jones first studied in racially segregated schools. Not unlike many other blacks who resembled her in appearance, she felt a tinge of discrimination by her own race. The light-complexioned young girl who had long red hair was called "half-white nigger."

Since the local public library was open to all residents, a practice common in some Southern cities, Jones used the library thus beginning a lifelong affair with books and libraries. She moved to St. Louis to enter high school at the institution where her uncle taught and perhaps also because her parents thought the school would offer her more than those in West Virginia. In St. Louis she was a welcome addition to the light-skinned elite which was not uncommon in the black community. The reference librarians in the St. Louis Public Library impressed Jones with their service which appealed to her and encouraged her to become a librarian.

Jones earned a bachelor's degree in library science from Hampton Institute, as it was known then, and worked first at the Louisville Municipal College. She and her fellow black librarians could not join the Kentucky Library Association. When the American Library Association met in Richmond in 1936, Jones was one Hampton student who attended. Due to segregation in the association and in the city, special arrangements had to be made for the students to attend the sessions and special seating was provided. They were barred from the exhibits entirely. Jones used to her advantage her light complexion and thus received hotel accommodations and access to the exhibits. Jones said that she never liked passing for white, had mixed feelings about it, felt shame for her dishonesty, but through it all felt a sense of triumph for outsmarting the racists who thought she was white. In fact, time and time again Jones passed for white to do what she wanted to do in the segregated South.

For a long time racism followed Jones wherever her library career or professional goals took her. When she entered the University of Illinois library school in 1937, she found overt racism. Blacks were not allowed to live on campus and were denied access to local food service. When blacks took meals in the home economics building on campus and sat at a table with whites, the whites left. Social events on campus were generally closed to blacks. As they grew weary of the racial restrictions at the Illinois campus, the black students protested. Jones was one member of the group that joined a protest movement led by the Chicago NAACP to force the campus to change its discriminatory policies. After that, Jones faced stressful and threatening living conditions.

Jones joined the Atlanta University library school faculty and later received her Ph.D. from the University of Chicago. At Atlanta she had been concerned abut the demeaning images of blacks in children's literature and joined Charlemae Hill Rollins of Chicago and Mollie Huston Lee of Raleigh, North Carolina, in a protest to publishers about these images. In 1942, she and Hallie Beachem Brooks conducted a project for the Carnegie Corporation of New York to help the library school assist in improving black schools in the South. In 1945, she visited twenty-two southeastern cities to collect data for her study on black public high schools in certain Southern cities. Thus Jones had first-hand knowledge of the conditions of black libraries and of racial discrimination in travel and living accommodations in the South.

She became the second dean of the School of Library Service at Atlanta University and spent many years there improving library education for blacks, black access to libraries, and in general helping schools, colleges, and public libraries in the South improve service to black users. Jones, a wise counselor, leader, administrator, mentor, and demanding scholar, would not let the fact that white society violated her civil rights interfere with her success.

ANNETTE HOAGE PHINAZEE (1920-1983)

Annette Hoage Phinazee was a trailblazing librarian and educator with a passion for the bibliographical control of African-American materials and for preserving and promoting works by African-American writers. Phinazee was born July 23, 1920, in Orangeburg, South Carolina, to parents who were educators. She attended public schools in Orangeburg and graduated from Fisk University in Nashville, Tennessee. She received a bachelor's and master's degree in library science, and in 1961 she became the first woman and the first black to earn a doctorate in library science from Columbia University. She taught at the Atlanta University School of Library Service under the administration of Virginia Lacy Jones. She also headed the special black collection in the old Trevor Arnett Library at Atlanta University, as it was known then.

She became dean of the School of Library Science at North Carolina Central University and held the position for thirteen years until she died in 1983. Phinazee is known for many notable contributions in library science. She was teacher and counselor to generations of black American librarians. She was a highly respected but concerned member of ALA, attacking the racist attitudes and style of the association beginning with her first meeting in 1948 and escalating at the 1961 annual conference. Soon after, ALA passed stringent resolutions on freedom of access to libraries and refused to recognize those library organizations that remained segregated. Phinazee continued to protest openly and to agitate against ALA's passive attitude toward blacks on committees and in the literature that it promoted. Those who heard her at conferences took notice, and whites who had allowed it to happen felt threatened while blacks who accepted it felt uncomfortable. Gradually the profession changed its posture.

Phinazee was equally known and recognized for her longtime interest in the bibliographical control of African-American library resources. While she was at Atlanta she spearheaded a national conference on the bibliographical treatment of blacks in the literature. She also headed federally funded projects to locate African-American materials in six southeastern states and published the results as a finding aid.

HANNAH DIGGS ATKINS (b. 1923)

Hannah Diggs Atkins, librarian, educator, news reporter, state legislator, and later, the highest ranking woman in Oklahoma state government, was affected personally by the ills of prejudice and became an activist to change politics in America.

Born November 1, 1923, in Winston-Salem, North Carolina, Atkins grew up during the Great Depression, developed a strong work ethic, and learned to appreciate family values and the creative ways in which women contributed to society. She graduated from a black college, St. Augustine's College in Raleigh, and worked as a reporter for the *Winston-Salem Journal and Sentinel*. She taught briefly in Winston-Salem. She earned a bachelor's degree in library science from the University of Chicago and became a school librarian in Winston-Salem. She moved to Oklahoma to serve as a branch public librarian. Then she studied law and later obtained a degree in public administration. She taught library science and law at Oklahoma City University.

Atkins had worked behind the scenes in politics. She worked voter registration drives, aided in campaigns, and then entered the political ring. In 1969, she was elected a state representative, the first African-American woman to sit in her state's legislative body. Now she was ready to make a difference, a difference she had vowed to make early on. Atkins worked to reform legislation for human rights, women's rights, housing, employment, health care, and other areas. She convened the Oklahoma Women's Political Caucus and was instrumental in passing a bill to forbid gender discrimination in employment in state agencies. She helped change House rules that prohibited women from serving as pages. She constantly agitated against injustices of any sort and knew well the problems of discrimination by race and gender. She demanded the elimination of gender designation from state protective labor laws. She worked unceasingly for the ratification of the Equal Rights Amendment. Atkins also chaired the state's Advisory Committee of the U.S. Commission on Civil Rights. Four years after her tenure in the legislature ended, she became Secretary of Human Resources and Secretary of State, making her the highest ranking woman in Oklahoma state government. She held this position for four years.

President Jimmy Carter recognized her successful experiences and dedication to the cause of justice for all people and in 1980 appointed her delegate to the United Nations' Thirty-fifth Assembly. After retiring in 1991 at age sixty-eight, she continued her civil rights activities as a member of the National Board of the American Civil Liberties Union and a member of the NAACP. She never forgot what spearheaded her interest in civil rights: as a child, she had watched her father come home bloody and beaten for attempting to exercise his right to vote. Years later in the Oklahoma legislature, she watched over and protected the rights of all people.

Conclusion

The seven black women profiled here were librarians and, in their own way, civil rights activists. They exemplified black women whose civil rights activities ranged from quiet protest to active militant participation in the movement. These women addressed such issues as removal of stereotypical images in literature, the inclusion of materials on African-American themes in collections, the eradication of racist attitudes and practices of the American Library Association, library services to blacks, and human rights in general. These and other black women dared to speak out publicly or protest quietly in order to cure the ills of society that impact people, civil rights, and libraries.

REFERENCE

Baker, A. (1971). *The black experience in children's books.* New York: New York Public Library.

Unique Gatekeepers of Black Culture

Three Black Librarians as Book Publishers

❧ Donald Franklin Joyce ❧

L ibrarians generally regard themselves as purveyors, classifiers, and mediators of knowledge. They live these roles when they perform tasks associated with the circulation, cataloging, and reference functions in libraries. Some imaginative librarians, in the course of their careers, delve deeper into another role in the sociology of knowledge—they become book publishers. Thus, they become more active agents in the production and distribution of knowledge.

Three black librarians who had distinguished themselves in various areas of librarianship also engaged in book publishing. They utilized their specialized expertise and knowledge as librarians to make unique contributions to the growth and development of black book publishing. A look at the book publishing activities of these black librarians explores a little-known aspect of black librarianship.

THE "REFERENCE SENSE" OF DORIS SAUNDERS & THE BIRTH OF THE BOOK DIVISION OF JOHNSON PUBLISHING COMPANY

In 1961, the Book Division of Chicago's Johnson Publishing Company was established under the direction of consummate librarian Doris E. Saunders. She began her career in the Chicago Public Library System (CPL) in 1942 and rose through positions of increasing responsibility until 1949, when she resigned as a senior reference librarian to accept a position as the first librarian of the fledgling Johnson Publishing Company.

While working as a senior reference librarian in the Social Science Department of CPL's Central Library, Saunders had begun developing a "reference sense," or that ability to identify and anticipate basic reference needs of patrons in a subject area based on repeated requests. As she built the library at Johnson Publishing Company and responded to reference requests from staff and other readers, Doris E. Saunders expanded her "reference sense" to include black materials. This "reference sense," as she related, guided her thinking in the "birthing" of the Book Division of Johnson Publishing Company by helping her to identify the nature of the demand for materials.

> Yes, in the period of time from 1949, when I came to *Ebony*, and in 1961, when we started the Book Division, I had received, not only in person at various library conferences, but I received avalanches of letters from students, teachers, librarians, and from individuals wanting information that was not available at that time. They wanted reprints of articles in *Ebony*.
>
> We had done an article on the fifteen outstanding events in Negro History. We received so many requests for it we finally had it reprinted and sent it to anyone who asked for it.
>
> So it ultimately seemed to us that the best thing to do was to put these things together in a book or booklet. And the more we talked the more we realized that to publish a booklet would be as expensive as to publish a book, if we did it the way we wanted to do it. And it really would not solve our problem. So we decided there were areas. We wanted to do something in politics. We wanted to cover a variety of fields. We saw we really had our initial list. (Doris E. Saunders, interviewed at Johnson Publishing Company, Chicago, Illinois, March 4, 1975)

The Book Division's initial list, which appeared in 1962 and 1963, illustrates how Saunders's reference sense was used to anticipate market demands. This included such informative works of intrinsic reference value as Lerone Bennett, Jr.'s *Before the Mayflower: A History of the Negro in America, 1619-1962* (1962); *The Ebony Cookbook*, by Freda de Knight (1962); *The Day They Marched*, edited by Doris E. Saunders (1963); and *Negro Firsts in Sports*, by Andrew (Doc) Young (1963). Between 1962 and 1966, the Book Division published a plethora of titles which were reflective of Saunders's "reference sense" of black materials, notably *The Negro Politician: His Success and Failure*, by Edward T. Clayton (1964); *What Manner of Man: A Biography of Martin Luther King, Jr.*, by Lerone Bennett, Jr. (1964); and *The Negro Handbook*, compiled by the editors of *Ebony* (1966).

Saunders left Johnson Publishing Company in late 1966 to pursue a growing professional interest in higher education but, at the request of publisher John H. Johnson, returned in 1973 as Director of the Book Division. For the next four years several books were produced by the Book Division illustrative of Doris E. Saunders's special abilities. These titles included *The Ebony Success Library*, by the editors of *Ebony* (1973); *The Ebony Handbook*, edited by Doris E. Saunders (1974); and *Gerri Major's Black Society*, by Gerri Major with Doris E. Saunders (1976). In 1977, after commuting between Chicago and Boston, where she was enrolled at Boston University, Saunders was awarded a master of science in Journalism and a master of arts degree in Afro-American studies. Jackson State University offered Saunders a one-semester writer-in-residence position in January 1978, which she accepted. She remained at the university until 1991 when she retired as professor and coordinator of print journalism.

PROVIDING A PUBLISHING FORUM FOR A GENERATION OF BLACK POETS: DUDLEY RANDALL & BROADSIDE PRESS

University of Detroit poet/librarian Dudley Randall, like most librarians who are knowledgeable about the safeguards of copyright, originally established Broadside Press in 1965 to copyright and publish one of his poems, "The Ballad of Birmingham." A 1951 graduate of the University of Michigan Library School, Randall had worked in the intervening fourteen years as an academic and public librarian at Lincoln University in Missouri, Morgan State College, and Wayne County Federated Library System.

In a 1981 interview, Randall acknowledged that his experience as a professional librarian prompted him to publish a series of broadsides.

> It started almost by accident. I had published a poem (Ballad of Birmingham) on the murder of four girls in a church in Birmingham in 1963 in a local magazine. Some weeks after, folk singer Jerry Moore asked permission to set it to music. I wanted to protect my rights and discovered that a broadside could be copyrighted. So I published it as a broadside.
>
> Later I also published a poem on the assassination of President John Kennedy, so I have two broadsides. Being a librarian (at the University of Detroit), who arranges things, I said, I have a series, and I decided to do a broadside series. I didn't know anything about publishing; I didn't know I was going to start a small press. I named it Broadside Press because we published broadsides." (Kniffel, 1984, p. 17)

Thus, Dudley Randall, prompted by his knowledge of copyright and serial publications and the desire to publish poetry, launched a firm which became one of the major publishing vehicles for a generation of new black poets, Broadside Press. Undoubtedly aware of the few publishing outlets for black poets, Randall developed Broadside into a major vehicle for the publication of a generation of new and established black poets. Broadside Press became an important force in the development of black literature in the United States.

Between 1965 and 1976, Broadside Press published ninety-three broadsides. In the early years, Randall published broadsides once a month and sold them for twenty-five cents. Eventually, the price rose to $10 per broadside. Broadside expanded its publishing activities in 1966 by publishing Marget Danner's *Poem Counterpoem*. A host of other titles, launching new black poets, followed including *Think Black*, by Haki Madhabuti (1967); *Black Judgement*, by Nikki Giovanni (1968); *We a BaddDDD People*, by Sonia Sanchez (1970); and *Poems from Prison*, by Ethridge Knight (1968) (Kniffel, 1984, p. 28).

In 1977, Broadside Press suffered financial trouble. It was sold to the Alexander Crummell Memorial Center, an Episcopal Church in Detroit. Broadside Press, still an active book publisher today and Detroit-based, is currently owned by Don and Hilda Vest.

A LIBRARIAN RESCUING WORKS OF BLACK HISTORY FROM OBSCURITY: W. PAUL COATES & BLACK CLASSICS PRESS

In 1978, when former Baltimore, Maryland, Black Panther leader W. Paul Coates established Black Classics Press in Baltimore to print rare books on black Americans, he knew the book market well. One year after his firm was in operation, Coates was awarded a Masters of Library Science from Atlanta University. He immediately landed a position at Howard University's Moorland-Springarn Research Center as Manuscripts Librarian. Sharpening his reference skills as he matured as a researcher in black history, Coates was eventually promoted to African-American Reference Librarian.

Although some book publishers reprinted many out-of-print titles in black history and literature between the late 1960s and the late 1980s, most of these titles suited students and scholars in higher education or the seasoned researcher and thus were priced for the institutional market. Today, drawing on his expertise as a reference librarian, Coates selects rare out-of-print black titles to be reprinted for the general reader. Through his Black Classics Press, Coates is making these titles available to the general reader at affordable prices. Hence, for the first time in the history of black book publishing, reprints of rare black Americana history and literature are being marketed to the black mass market.

The list of titles selected by Coates for reprinting under the Black Classics Press imprint illustrate his exceptional reference and research skills in unearthing rare out-of-print works of significant value in black history. In 1987, for example, *The Wonderful Ethiopians of the Ancient Cushite Empire*, by Drusilla Dunjee Houston, was reprinted. Originally self-published in 1926 by Houston, a black Oklahoma newspaperwoman, this book received laudatory reviews by J. A. Rogers, A. A. Schomburg, and Robert L. Vann upon its original publication. Other titles reprinted by this firm include George Wells Parker's *Children of the Sun* [1918] (1981); Anna Mellisa Graves's *Africa the Wonder and the Glory* [1942] (1983); and John Coleman De Graft-Johnson's *African Glory: The Story of Vanished Negro Civilizations* [1954] (1986).

CONCLUSION

Doris Saunders, Dudley Randall, and W. Paul Coates made unique contributions to black book publishing in the United States. Doris E. Saunders translated her "reference sense" for black materials into the market demand for books about black Americans. This market demand was not being met by existing publishers. Consequently, her "reference sense" served as a catalyst for the publication of books by the Book Division of Johnson Publishing Company. Some of the reference books which she edited from the Book Division of

Johnson Publishing Company, notably *The Negro Handbook*, have become models for later reference works in black history. W. Paul Coates had operated The Black Book Bookstore in the city's black community for five years before he sold it to start his book publishing firm.

W. Paul Coates's work as a reference librarian in one of the world's largest repositories in black history enhanced his book publishing activities by broadening his knowledge of little-known works in black history. In an interview, Coates assessed the value of his work at the Moorland-Springarn Research Center to his book publishing efforts.

> I enjoy library work, particularly the opportunity to work with a great collection like the Moorland-Springarn Collection. My library work complements publishing, keeping me grounded and rounded out. (Foerstel, 1988, p. 1)

His statement illustrates well the mutually beneficial relationship between black book publishing and black librarianship.

REFERENCES

Bennett, L. (1962). *Before the Mayflower: A history of the negro in America, 1619-1962*. Chicago, IL: Johnson.

Bennett, L. (1964). *What manner of man: A biography of Martin Luther King, Jr.* (2d ed). Chicago, IL: Johnson.

Clayton, E. (1964). *The Negro politician: His success and failure.* Chicago, IL: Johnson.

Danner, M., & Randall, D. (1966). *Poem counterpoem.* Detroit, MI: Broadside Press.

DeGraft-Johnson, J. C. (1986). *African glory: The story of vanished Negro civilizations.* Baltimore, MD: Black Classic Press.

De Knight, F. (1962). *The ebony cookbook: A date with a dish: A cookbook of American Negro recipes.* Chicago, IL: Johnson.

Foerstel, H. (1988). Maryland bookman breaks ground in black publishing. *The Crab, 17,* 1.

Giovanni, N. (1968). *Black judgement.* Detroit, MI: Broadside Press.

Graves, A. M. (1961). *Africa, the wonder and the glory.* Baltimore, MD: Black Classic Press.

Kniffel, L. (1984). Broadside Press, then and now: An interview with Dudley Randall. *Small Press,* (May/June), 17, 28.

Madhubuti, H. (1967). *Think black,* by Don. L. Lee (2d rev. ed.). Detroit, MI: Broadside Press.

Major, C. H, & Saunders, D. E. (1976). *Black society.* Chicago, IL: Johnson.

Parker, G. W. (1981) *The children of the sun.* Baltimore, MD: Black Classic Press (Original work published 1918).

Randall, D. (1965). *Ballad of Birmingham: On the bombing of a church in Birmingham, Alabama, 1963.* Detroit, MI: Broadside Press.

Sanchez, S. (1970). *We a BaddDDD people.* Detroit, MI: Broadside Press

Saunders, D. E. (1963). *The day they marched.* Chicago, IL: Johnson.

Saunders, D. E. (1974). *The* Ebony *handbook.* Chicago, IL: Johnson.

The Ebony *success library.* (1973). *Ebony.* Chicago, IL: Johnson.

The Negro handbook. (1966). *Ebony.* Chicago, IL: Johnson.

Young, A. S. (1963). *Negro firsts in sports.* Chicago, IL: Johnson.

ACRL's Historically Black College & Universities Libraries Projects, 1972-1994

ᘐ Casper L. Jordan & Beverly P. Lynch ᘐ

I n the 1970s, predominantly and historically Black colleges and universities enrolled more than 60 percent of African-American students in higher education in the United States. Black colleges, like others, grappled with the problem of providing library services suitable to support their institutional programs.

The questions of library staff in these institutions resembled those of most small academic libraries, but they were more acute. The proportion of aging administrators in these libraries was larger than in similar predominantly white institutions. Financial problems and personnel shortages had limited the continuing education opportunities for staff members. The "middle management" component in these libraries, through no fault of its own, often had insufficient exposure to the enormous changes occurring in the library and information field. The staff of libraries at black colleges and universities had been rather isolated from the "mainstream" of American librarianship (see Smith, 1977; McGrath, 1965).

INTRODUCTION

Since 1972, the Association of College and Research Libraries (ACRL) has mounted several major programs designed to further the development of the libraries serving the Historically Black Colleges and Universities (HBCUs). This chapter describes these programs, assesses their impact, and proposes strategies for ACRL to consider in future programming (most of the information is drawn from recollections of the authors and information found in the ACRL Archives of the American Library Association at the University of Illinois at Urbana-Champaign. We are indebted to the executive director of ACRL, Althea Jenkins, for her assistance).

ACRL was fortunate that Virginia Lacy Jones, the eminent dean of the Library School at Atlanta University, expressed her concern and strong interest to the association in the early 1970s in furthering the general development of the HBCU libraries. Jones acknowledged that the management of these libraries would be in transformation during the 1980s and 1990s with the looming retirement of many directors. Seeking ways to improve these libraries, Jones focused on those programs that would augment the leadership skills of the librarians in these institutions. Having spent her career recruiting, educating, and mentoring librarians, Jones believed that programs focused on the professional development of librarians in the HBCUs would be central to the development and enhancement of these libraries (Jordan, 1970).

In 1972, Jones was appointed chair of ACRL's ad hoc committee on the HBCU libraries. Also on the committee were Phyllis B. Cartwright, Florida International University; Richard M. Dougherty, University of California, Berkeley; James F. McCoy, Hudson Valley Community College; Annette L. Phinazee, North Carolina Central University; Katherine M. Stokes, U.S. Office of Education; and David Weber, Stanford University. Casper Jordan, associate professor in the School of Library Service, Atlanta University, and the director of the Trevor Arnett Library of Atlanta University, served as ex officio member, as did Beverly Lynch, ACRL's executive secretary.

The committee wrote the proposal to support an internship program for librarians in HBCU libraries and submitted it to the Andrew W. Mellon Foundation. The program goal, to improve the management of libraries at Historically Black Colleges and Universities, was of interest to the Mellon Foundation. The proposal, emphasizing the professional development of librarians, supported the broad purpose of the development of the HBCU institutions since academic librarians perform a teaching and research role as they instruct students formally and informally and advise and assist faculty in their scholarly pursuits.

Virginia Lacy Jones persuaded the Mellon Foundation of the importance of ACRL's project. Over the course of the project, the foundation awarded ACRL $500,000 to implement the internship program. ACRL, the entire library community, and the HBCUs are indebted to Jones for her commitment to these libraries, to the people working in them, and to the Andrew W. Mellon Foundation for its strong and continuing support of these institutions and their libraries.

THE HISTORICALLY BLACK COLLEGES & UNIVERSITIES

Three main groups of institutions constitute the universe of the 104 HBCUs. The private colleges are best identified as the forty-three members of the United Negro College Fund. The public institutions include the seventeen colleges designated in 1890 as "land grants." Fifteen other state-supported colleges and universities are also historically black. Twenty-nine predominantly black colleges include privately supported and quasi-public institutions.

Whatever the pros and cons may be of educational institutions founded for African Americans, the reality is that these colleges and universities do exist. They serve an important purpose, and they have libraries which need strengthening. African-American students, particularly those from rural or disadvantaged backgrounds, still participate less in the American system of higher education than do white students. And for some, attendance at the historically black institutions may be easier financially and sociologically.

Libraries of the HBCUs traditionally are underfunded. Library collections and services have been inadequate in many institutions. These black institutions develop all along the academic procession from the strong libraries to the weakest. Under such financial circumstances, little money has been available for staff travel and professional development. Yet an excellent library requires an excellent staff and a staff that is able to keep current in the fast-changing profession of library and information science. Our universe of libraries includes an Association of Research Libraries library and small libraries of unaccredited institutions. The libraries of these institutions are dedicated and perform miracles with small budgets and small staffs; many had been isolated from much of American librarianship (Jordan, 1974).

THE MELLON INTERNSHIP PROJECT

The Advisory Council, agreeing on the central goal of strengthening the management of the HBCU libraries, proposed an internship program to link librarians from HBCU libraries with directors of libraries well known for their strong management capabilities. The program was intended to accelerate the development of the management ability of librarians in HBCU libraries by providing them with experience in the administration of strong and progressive academic libraries. Between 1974 and 1978, twenty-five managers working in HBCU libraries were identified as potential directors of libraries and given the opportunity to learn about academic library administration in a variety of settings by working directly with the directors of these libraries.

The libraries serving as the host institutions for interns included Austin Peay State University (Tennessee), Eastern Michigan University (Michigan), Emory University (Georgia), University of North Carolina (Chapel Hill), Rhode Island College, the University of Wisconsin (Milwaukee), Oberlin College (Ohio), Stanford University (California), Mount Holyoke College (Massachusetts), State University of New York at Albany, Syracuse University (New York), University of California (San Diego), University of Massachusetts (Amherst), Virginia Commonwealth University, and the University of California (Berkeley). These libraries were selected on the basis of applications identifying leadership qualities. The host libraries received a stipend for their cooperation, and the interns also received their salaries and travel expenses. The interns received an all-expense paid trip to the annual conference of the American Library Association during the year of their Mellon-ACRL Internship (the participants are listed in Appendix A). Funds to employ a substitute librarian were granted to the intern's library. The selection of interns was carried out through a competitive process with the advisory committee serving as the selection committee. Each year there were more applications than available places.

Neither ACRL nor the advisory committee prescribed any model plan for the internship. Each library, with the strong support of the library director, developed individual programs depending upon the knowledge and experience of the intern and the intern's particular interests. The interns studied library administrative methods, exchanged ideas, discussed various managerial problems with staff members in the host institutions, and participated in the day-to-day management of the host library. Strong mentoring developed between some directors and interns and lasting friendships emerged.

The advisory committee conducted annual workshops for the interns and the directors of their host libraries. At these meetings, participants discussed successes and challenges. Joshua I. Smith, executive director of the American Society for Information Science, served as a "consultant in residence" at these workshops throughout the period. Casper Jordan, project director, visited the interns during their experience. At the end of the four years, the complete group of interns, mentors, and advisory committee members met to assess the program. Librarians participating in the 1974-1978 internships are now working at the University of the District of Columbia, University of Maryland Eastern Shore, Florida A&M University, North Carolina A&T University, Jackson State University (Mississippi), Southern University (Louisiana), Alabama State University, Elizabeth State University (North Carolina), Interdenominational Theological Center (Georgia), Langston University (Oklahoma), Howard University (Washington, D.C.), Paine College (Georgia), Fort Valley State College (Georgia), Tougaloo College (Mississippi), and Louisiana State University (Jordan, 1979).

ASSESSMENT OF THE INTERNSHIP PROJECT

A meeting in Atlanta in October 1987, discussed below, featured a general assessment of the 1974-1978 internship program. It was the consensus of the group that the program had involved the appropriate individuals, and that many had remained at their institutions. Thus the general purpose—to strengthen management in HBCU libraries—had been met successfully. Participants completed evaluation forms, and everyone was highly impressed with the results of the project and hoped that a similar project could be continued. Additional ideas included an exchange program and shorter term experiences. Participants felt that the experience was worthwhile for the intern and the HBCU library and emphasized that, in the final analysis, the friendships generated among participants should not be overlooked. The goals and missions were realistic, and the experiences were valuable and worthwhile. The exposure to strong progressive library operations had assisted in moving forward a vitally needed program.

RECENT PROJECTS

In 1986, The Andrew W. Mellon Foundation provided ACRL the funds to undertake a new planning project to consider programs for assisting the libraries of the HBCU. Interest in the development and improvement of HBCU libraries was continuing within the ACRL membership, thus the association sought support from the Mellon Foundation to convene a group of librarians, the majority being from HBCU libraries, in order to solicit further ideas and potential projects. To undertake the task, ACRL President Hannalore Rader appointed an HBCU Library Planning Project Committee chaired by Beverly Lynch, University of Illinois at Chicago, with members Casper Jordan, deputy director of the Atlanta Fulton Public Library; Lorene B. Brown, dean, Atlanta University School of Library and Information Studies; Barbara Williams Jenkins, dean of library services, South Carolina State College; and Joseph Howard, National Agriculture Library. The meeting was held October 18-20, 1987, in Atlanta; the purpose of the meeting was to outline a program that ACRL would mount to improve the libraries in the HBCUs. Samuel Proctor, former president of North Carolina A&T University, keynoted the meeting to which some twenty-five directors of libraries from the three groups of HBCU institutions were invited.

Presentations on previous and ongoing projects related to HBCU libraries were made by Jessie Cottman Smith, University of Maryland Eastern Shore, who had participated in the Mellon ACRL internship program; Casper Jordan; Jessie Carney Smith, Fisk University; and Joseph Howard, National Agriculture Library. The major portion of the three-day meeting was devoted to consideration of various issues before the libraries in these institutions and the identification of possible programmatic initiatives ACRL might undertake to meet the issues.

Following the meeting, the project committee met. The President of ACRL, Joseph Boisse, and the Executive Director, Joan Segal, also participated. Based upon the discussions held over the previous three days, the committee agreed to propose to ACRL three initiatives:

> 1) collect and publish a statistical survey of the HBCU libraries following the model of ACRL's "100" libraries, including data on size of collection, staff, budget;
> 2) seek funding from the National Endowment for the Humanities to carry out a workshop targeted to the HBCUs and their communities on how to do public programming in the humanities, these workshops to be modeled on ACRL's program already in place;
> 3) sponsor a series of accreditation workshops for libraries in HBCUs about to undertake accreditation self-studies.

President Boisse met with the committee during the 1988 Midwinter meeting and supported the proposal that ACRL fund the statistical survey, which it did.

THE STATISTICS PROJECT

At the time of the considerations under discussion, no recent statistics had been compiled on the HBCU libraries although some studies had been undertaken in the 1970s. Jessie Carney Smith (1977), university librarian at Nashville's Fisk University, had written *Black Academic Libraries and Research Collections: An Historical Survey* which included eighty-nine black four-year or graduate degree-granting institutions. Earlier, Casper L. Jordan (1970), associate professor of library services at the Atlanta University School of Library Service, had issued *Black Academic Libraries: An Inventory.* The book discussed eighty-five black four-year degree-conferring institutions both publicly and privately-supported with an emphasis on those institutions subsidized by the United Negro College Fund (UNCF). Jordan (1974) also contributed an article, "Black Academic Libraries—State of Affairs and Selected Annotated Bibliography of Black Academe and Its Libraries" in *Library and Information Services for Special Groups.* The advisory committee felt a pressing need for a new study.

The 1988-89 survey was undertaken by ACRL and designed to follow the conventions and formats of data published by the Association of Research Libraries (ARL) and used by ACRL for its non-ARL University Library Statistics Survey. This allowed HBCU institutions to compare themselves with other groups of libraries. Members of the ad hoc committee provided the expertise and guidance in the important data-collection effort.

In 1991, *ACRL/Historically Black Colleges & Universities Statistics 1988-89: A Compilation of Statistics for Sixty-eight Historically Black College and University Libraries*, compiled by Robert E. Molyneux, was published by ACRL. The study was widely disseminated including a special distribution to the presidents of each HBCU institution, the librarians, the regional accrediting associations, and other interested parties (Molyneux, 1991).

The impact of 1988-89 statistics was immediate: four presidents of HBCUs were among the delegates to the second White House Conference on Libraries and Information Services; they used the statistical data to base their support of resolutions on HBCU libraries. New monies for library collections in HBCU libraries were provided by Mellon. New federal legislation for HBCUs library support was included in funding.

ASSESSMENT OF THE STATISTICS REPORT

The ad hoc committee encouraged the valuable ACRL project to continue. In its final report, submitted to the ACRL Board of Directors July 1, 1991 in Atlanta, the committee:

> recommend[ed] as strongly as it [could] and without reservation that ACRL continue to carry out the statistics project on a regular basis. Over 40% of the African American students graduating from colleges and universities in the U.S. graduate from HBCU institutions. Continuing efforts to improve the libraries in these institutions should be an important goal of ACRL. The Committee notes that an advisory committee comprised of people from HBCU institutions is an important aspect of the data collection process and recommends that the statistics project have an advisory committee for that activity.

Humanities Programming Workshop

The National Endowment for the Humanities (NEH) provided funding to ACRL and the Public Library Association (PLA), two divisions of ALA, to present a Humanities Programming Workshop for HBCUs and their communities in Atlanta, Georgia, on February 22-24, 1989.

The workshop was based on a format developed over the previous five years by ACRL and PLA. It involved teams consisting of an academic librarian, a public librarian, and a humanities scholar. The participating teams learned about the NEH, discovered how to design and carry out high quality humanities programs, gained an understanding of developing a project in a group situation similar to their back-home circumstances, and received information about proposal writing to help them succeed in their efforts to raise funds for such programs.

Over the course of three days, participants heard a major presentation on "What Are the Humanities?" The participants formed teams (HBCU librarian, a humanities scholar from the HBCU, and a public librarian from the HBCU's area) and chose sample projects which differed from those they considered when applying for the workshop. The purpose was to learn the mechanics of developing the idea, understanding the humanities content, and learning the commonalities each member of the group had with the other. A mock review panel considered three real proposals before the entire group. Then small groups convened to prepare proposals for final presentations and critiques. Participants found the workshop valuable. They felt that the librarians' esteem had been heightened on campus, expertise in grantsmanship had been gained, and several of the libraries applied successfully to NEH.

Accreditation Workshops

The October 1987 issue of *Atlanta* carried a story by Tom Junod, "Are Black Colleges Necessary?" Junod discussed the accreditation standards of the Southern Association of Colleges and Schools (SACS), the accrediting body for 760 southern colleges, which had withdrawn accreditation from three historically black colleges and universities: Bishop College, Knoxville College, and Morristown Junior College. Junod quoted the associate executive director of SACS as saying that he expected about half of the eighty black colleges connected with SACS to have accreditation withdrawn as the association began its review of institutions under its newly designed and adopted standards.

The story was distributed to the people attending the planning meeting in Atlanta in 1987; it led to a consideration of the Southern Association's new standards for accreditation and the role the library might play in the outcome of the institutional reviews. In many HBCUs, the librarian serves either as chair or as a member of the self-study committee. It was proposed that ACRL sponsor a series of workshops on accreditation aimed at those institutions about to begin the process leading to reaccreditation.

Two preconferences on accreditation were conducted, the first in Dallas in 1989 and the second in Atlanta in 1991. Funding for the preconferences was provided by registration fees by the Maxima Corporation and by ACRL. Experienced evaluators from HBCU institutions and other institutions discussed the new standards and their shift from input measures to measures of outcome.

The preconferences were well-received, and the advisory committee agreed that they had served a useful purpose. None of the HBCUs lost its accreditation. Although the preconferences were planned for librarians, faculty members on steering committees and presidents were invited and attended the sessions.

CONCLUSION

The Ad Hoc Committee on ACRL's HBCU Planning Project completed its work at the 1991 ALA Conference in Atlanta. At that meeting, the committee conducted the second preconference on accreditation, received copies of the 1988-89 statistics of libraries in the HBCUs published by ACRL, and sponsored a program, "Excellence Through Cultural Diversity" with Huel Perkins, Louisiana State University, as the speaker.

At that program meeting, members of the committee presented brief reports on its work; the three projects, designed in 1987, had been completed. The statistics were distributed to the presidents, librarians, and academic officers in the HBCU institutions as well as to various national higher education associations. A poster session on the statistics followed the 1991 ACRL President's program. The data provided the baseline information the committee had sought. The NEH humanities programming followed successfully ACRL's work in this area. The accreditation workshops had accomplished their purposes.

The one program area the committee did not complete, one which it believes to be very important, was to find ways for ACRL to work closely with the presidents of the HBCU institutions to inform them about the library, its opportunities, and its problems. In the committee's view, the statistics offer one opportunity for ACRL to continue to influence these institutions. But more needs to be done. The committee, anxious that its work with this group of institutions be continued and that other issues of importance to this key segment of the academic library community become a part of the ACRL agenda, suggested to ACRL that it adopt an organizational design appropriate for such programming activities. It urged that ACRL continue its interest in the HBCUs.

During the five years of its work, other possible programs were referred to the committee for comment and advice. The committee was firm in its commitment to complete the three major projects it had identified at the outset and so did not undertake any new ones. The libraries serving the Historically Black Colleges and Universities form an important segment of ACRL institutions. Programs targeted directly to them have been successfully designed and carried out over a period of some twenty years. The emerging issues in librarianship and in higher education offer new opportunities for new designs. We and the many colleagues who have worked on these projects over the years and the librarians working in the libraries of the Historically Black Colleges and Universities, urge that ACRL forge new programs for this important segment of academic librarianship.

APPENDIX A
Mellon-ACRL Internship Project Participants

1974-75

John Page, Jr., University of the District of Columbia
    University of California (Berkeley)

Jessie Cottman Smith, University of Maryland, Eastern Shore,
    Princess Ann, Maryland
    Stanford University

Ida G. Adams, Florida A&M University, Tallahassee, Florida
    University of California (Berkeley)

James R. Jarrell, University of North Carolina (Greensboro)
    Oberlin College

Bernice L. Bell, Jackson State University, Mississippi
    Oberlin College

1975-76

Honor Davenport, Interdenominational Theological Center, Atlanta,
    Georgia
    Oberlin College

Donna Epps, Friendship College, Rockhill, South Carolina
    Oberlin College

Sandra Day, Coppin State College, Baltimore, Maryland
    State University of New York, Albany

Bernice Hawkins, University of the District of Columbia
    Syracuse University, New York

Ella M. Harget, Livingstone College, Salisbury, North Carolina
    University of Massachusetts, Amherst

Adele M. Jackson, Southern University, Baton Rouge, Louisiana
    University of California, San Diego

Ghullam Siddiqui, Wilberforce University, Ohio
    University of Wisconsin, Milwaukee

Patricia M. Singleton, Alabama State University, Montgomery
    Eastern Michigan University, Ypsilanti

Birdie Travis, Florida Memorial College, Miami
    Eastern Michigan University, Ypsilanti

1976-77

Claude W. Greene, Elizabeth City State University, North Carolina
University of North Carolina, Chapel Hill

Rita Jo (Lacy) Bigham, Morris Brown College, Atlanta, Georgia
Austin Peay State University, Clarksville, Tennessee

Brenda Sloan, Virginia State College, Petersburg, Virginia
Mt. Holyoke College, S. Hadley, Massachusetts

Alberta J. Mayberry, Texas Southern University, Houston, Texas
Emory University, Atlanta, Georgia

1977-78

George M. Martin, Howard University, Washington, D.C.
Virginia Commonwealth University, Richmond

Millie M. Parker, Paine College, Augusta, Georgia
Oberlin College

Doris Gosier, Fort Valley State College, Fort Valley, Georgia
Oberlin College

Virgia Brocks-Shedd, Tougaloo College, Tougaloo, Mississippi
Mt. Holyoke College, S. Hadley, Massachusetts

Alma Dawson, Prairie View A&M College, Prairie View, Texas
University of Wisconsin, Milwaukee

REFERENCES

Jordan, C. L. (1970). *Black academic libraries: An inventory*. Atlanta, GA: Atlanta University School of Library Service.

Jordan, C. L. (1974). Black academic libraries—state of affairs and selected annotated bibliography of black academe and its libraries. In J. I. Smith (Ed.), *Library and information services for special groups* (pp. 146-201). New York: Science Associates International.

Jordan, C. L. (1979). *Academic library internship program for administrators of black college libraries: Final report to the Andrew W. Mellon Foundation*. Unpublished report of the Mellon-ACRL Internship Project: A four year evaluation submitted to ACRL (October 1978).

McGrath, E. J. (1965). *The predominantly negro college and universities in transition*. New York: Columbia University Teachers College Bureau of Publications.

Molyneux, R. J. (Comp.). (1991). *ACRL/Historically black colleges & universities statistics 1988-89: A compilation of statistics for sixty-eight historically black college and university libraries*. Chicago, IL: ACRL.

Smith, J. C. (1977). *Black academic libraries and research collections: An historical survey*. Westport, CT: Greenwood Press

ADDITIONAL REFERENCES

The Mellon/ACRL Project at Oberlin College. (1976). *Journal of Academic Librarianship*, (May), 18-21.

$350,000 grant awarded to ACRL for black administrators program. (1974). *College & Research Libraries News, 35*(2), 22.

ACRL internship Program. (1974). *College & Research Libraries News, 35*(9), 220.
ACRL first-year interns. (1975). *College & Research Libraries News, 36*(2), 43.
ACRL internship program. (1975). *College & Research Libraries News, 36*(7), 215.
ACRL internship program. (1976). *College & Research Libraries News, 37*(6), 135.
ACRL internship project extended. (1977). *College & Research Libraries News, 38*(6), 161.
ACRL interns selected. (1977). *College & Research Libraries News, 38*(10), 298.

Liberating & Empowering Minds

The African/Caribbean Canadian Woman Librarian
& the Development of the West Indian/Black Heritage
Collection of the North York Public Library, 1980-1994

❦ Norman Grantley Kester ❦

> The public library has an important role to play in providing resources to counteract past derogatory and biased stereotypes in published materials that have contributed to racism in Canadian society. (Rolfe, 1984, p. 15)

> We are . . . first and foremost, liberators of minds. (Black, 1992, p. xii)

A recent survey reported in *The Globe and Mail* revealed that "86% of Canadians believe that at least 'some racism' exists in Canada, and over 50% believe the level of racism has increased over five years" (Kapica, 1993, p. A1). Much of this concern has been related to media exposure, especially television. Most revealing, too, was the belief that "people of black or African descent faced the greatest discrimination" (Kapica, 1993, p. A2).

Public libraries have done much to encourage diversity and alleviate racism in our society. Our work as librarians has empowered and "liberated," according to African/Caribbean Canadian writer Ayanna Black, and we need to see each other as liberators of minds, both personally and politically. The minority librarian as liberator has done much in the self-assigned role of working with the African/Caribbean Canadian community, and in disseminating and developing the diverse literary, musical, and other artistic works of the black artist and writer.

The development of black special collections in public libraries in Canada has been the story of the development of black people's self-affirmation, self-determination, and the development of African/Caribbean Canadian communities in the cities of Toronto and North York, Ontario. The story of these collections has also been the story of the influential role African/Caribbean Canadian women librarians have played by providing responsive services and collections to the African/Caribbean Canadian community.

This essay discusses the history and significance of the West Indian/Black Heritage Collection of the North York Public Library between 1980 and 1994. Methods of investigation included interviewing black women librarians from two large urban public library systems in North York and Toronto, Ontario. At least two of these women, Laurel Taylor and Rosalind Bryce, had devoted the bulk of their professional lives to provide library services and to develop the West Indian/Black Heritage Collection to meet the diverse needs of a multi-racial African/Caribbean Canadian community. The interviews allowed these women to voice their experiences, speak out on issues, and raise further questions about their roles in developing services and collections within the context of service to the African/Caribbean Canadian community.

Although black librarians, and more specifically black women librarians, have only recently organized a professional forum and association in Toronto for dealing with issues of mutual concern, the pressing information needs of the African/Caribbean Canadian as well as workplace discrimination have resulted in little documentation about the experience of African/Caribbean Canadians as professional librarians. Like Makeda Silvera (1993) who had interviewed black working-class women for a study of domestics who had come to Canada, I adopted the group interview format and the partially unstructured interview as methods for gathering information about African/Caribbean Canadian women librarians.

The survey questions were designed to elicit the interviewee's perceptions about her role as an African/Caribbean Canadian librarian in developing services and collections for the black community. Two colleagues pretested the questionnaire and the instrument was revised. A less structured format for the interview allowed the subjects to feel free to talk about a variety of professional and personal issues as these arose.

The interview itself, was briefly—yet significantly—a liberating and empowering experience. Despite the harsh weather that people had endured in getting to the interview, we were all eager to talk about the subject of the African/Caribbean Canadian librarian in the public library, as well as the development of services and collections especially in North York since 1980. That participants were asked for their opinion about the final transcript of the interview and the final draft of the chapter, spoke much to the idea of inclusion rather than appropriation.

Three essential North York Public Library reports also greatly facilitated my task in this research. Some questions which the interviews and other research hoped to uncover included:

- How did the West Indian/Black Heritage Collection develop, and what social factors led to this development between 1980 and 1994?
- What has been the "role" of the African/Caribbean Canadian woman librarian in the public library?
- What has been the importance of developing nonprint collections?
- What kinds of library programs have been successful for African/Caribbean Canadians over the past decade?
- What has been the importance of "dialect" to black culture and what has been its relationship to the delivery of effective library service to the African/Caribbean Canadian community?

COMMUNITY & COLLECTION HISTORY

The Jane/Finch community has undergone rapid social change and population growth, especially in the 1970s and 1980s. Social and other services have not been able to respond adequately in meeting residents' defined needs. In many cases, residents have "fallen through the cracks" of the social safety net. Many in working-class and racially marginalized communities have felt that the "system" has been working against them. Residents have felt victimized by professional and other social agencies in the community. Establishing trust with the community has thus been an important aim of many social service agencies including libraries.

The community is characterized by a large number of assisted housing projects. Faceless high-rise buildings facilitate the isolation people have felt. Social services in the Jane/Finch corridor have explored various approaches in reaching individuals in the community due to both the perceived and real feelings of isolation and disempowerment. The arrival of additional Caribbean residents in the community over the past two decades has further compounded the problem of the delivery of social, educational, and other services in the community.

Agency outreach, therefore, has been essential in developing links with the community. The same could be said for library services and programs. Outreach to the nonuser would need to be personalized. Hard-to-reach populations might also be interested in non-print media as an alternative to traditional literature. Key to developing good relationships with community residents and users has been the need to be seen as "approachable." Thus, successful outreach has meant planning programs with schools, grassroots community organizations, "moms and tots" groups, or literacy groups, and youth associations. Laurel Taylor has commented that, indeed, over the past decade "many of the people we reach out to are functional illiterates or they read, but they only read newspapers or they read for enjoyment. They want to have personal outreach. They want to see a person" (Laurel Taylor, interviewed by Kester, January 26, 1994).[1]

Twelve years ago, a West Indian, primarily a Jamaican, presence was visible in the community, but this has diminished. Laurel Taylor described the community as a "gateway community" (interviewed by Kester, January 26, 1994).[2] New immigrants settle there and once improved economically, they leave. Today, many African immigrants (Ethiopians, Somalis, and West Africans) have settled in the Jane/Finch corridor, served by the York Woods Regional Library branch. These new groups have just begun to use the library and, although they have seen the West Indian/Black Heritage Collection, they have just started to request materials about authors indigenous to their country of origin.

In November 1981, the West Indian and Black Heritage Collection was established. Two staff members, both from the Caribbean, conceived the idea of such a collection. In 1979, a library science student from the University of the West Indies had visited local social agencies and prepared a bibliography of Caribbean materials. Staff members, including Carmen Amoah and Denise Armstrong, drew up guidelines for the subject coverage of materials in the collection. Other factors were involved in creating the collection. Rosalind Bryce (interviewed by Kester, January 26, 1994) recalled that: "Teachers were having a hard time finding the material to teach and the community at the time was mostly West Indian, Jamaican, immigrant, black, and Italian. There were a lot of community members who came to the library and found that there was nothing for them, and they raised the issue about having materials to reflect their experience." Many West Indian parents had children who would go back to the islands for a visit, yet they had no idea about the culture of their parents. The collection would also be important in providing this information.

In the North York Public Library experience, according to Rob Rolfe (1984), it wasn't until "increasing pressure generated from within the community as well as government studies and the programs and the collection initiated at the York Woods Library" that a climate was created for the library to look seriously at enhancing library services to the African/Caribbean Canadians within the entire library system (p. 3). Rolfe had been one of the first librarians at the York Woods branch to work with the African/Caribbean Canadian community in developing and maintaining the West Indian/Black Heritage Collection during the 1980s.

Rita Cox, currently Branch Head and Specialist of the Black Heritage and West Indian Collection of the Parkdale Branch (Toronto Public Library), was approached by the North York Public Library to purchase a start-up collection of books from the Caribbean. She had previously purchased materials for the York Woods Library. Augusta Baker had earlier influenced Cox to study children's librarianship in New York at Columbia University. Cox agreed to acquire Caribbean materials once purchasing guidelines had been established by the library. At the Toronto Public Library, she had established, beginning in the 1970s, one of the first and most extensive Black Heritage and West Indian Collections in the country. Her expertise in this subject is widely recognized.

Important to the development of library services has been the government policy of "multiculturalism." Developed in the 1970s, this policy was intended to break down discriminatory prejudices as well as enhance cultural diversity in Canadian society generally, not only within Canada's two official speaking groups, English Canadians and French Canadians. In many cases, multiculturalism facilitated the development of multilingual services and collections in public libraries. However, it overlooked the unique needs of the mostly English-speaking African/Caribbean Canadians.

In time, however, multicultural English-language collections developed in the 1970s and 1980s in the metropolitan Toronto area. The West Indian/Black Heritage Collection was developed as one of many multicultural collections in the North York Public Library system. The same could be said for the Black Heritage West Indian Collection of the Toronto Public Library.

Two noteworthy reports influenced the direction of library service to the African/Caribbean Canadian community in the North York Public Library— those by Bryce and Greenidge (1983) and Rolfe (1984). While these reports had been essential in understanding the community's information needs, a separate collection evaluation report, issued in 1991, underscored the need to develop a coherent collection development statement and the importance of marketing the collection by creating a specialized logo (Kester, 1991a, p. 9). Related ideas, evinced in these reports, featured the need for subject specialists assigned to develop both the children's and the adult West Indian/Black Heritage Collections. It was thus important for assigned librarians to develop expertise in these subjects and to select materials from the broad range of information about the African/Caribbean Canadian experience.

According to the collection assessment of adult monographs in 1991, 1,324 books were held in the West Indian/Black Heritage Collection at the York Woods Regional Library (Kester, 1991a, p. 9). Three-fourths of the collection was devoted to the three areas of fiction (25.4 percent), literature and criticism (25.4 percent), and geography and history (20.5 percent) combined (Kester, 1991a, p. 9). The remaining works were in the social sciences. Rosalind Bryce reported that the audio-visual component of the collection (records, audio-cassettes and compact discs) numbered about 300 in 1994 (interviewed by Kester, January 26, 1994).

An important tool in accessing the West Indian/Black Heritage Collection was to create bibliographies and bookmarks. These included, as early as 1984, *Beyond Brer Rabbit: A List of Children's Fiction at the North York Public Library by and About Black People* (Taylor, 1994); *Black History in Canada: An Annotated Bibliography* (Kester, 1991b); *Apartheid: An Annotated Bibliography* (Kester, 1991c); and *Coming of Age Themes in Caribbean Fiction: A Bibliography* (Bryce, 1992). An Indo-Caribbean bookmark has also been prepared.

Laurel Taylor, instrumental in compiling *Beyond Brer Rabbit*, has noted the widespread use of this booklist. It was prepared "so that parents, teachers and adults, who were looking for that material as well as other mainstream material, by and about black people, could find it in the children's collection" (Laurel Taylor, interviewed by Kester, January 26, 1994). These materials were chosen to facilitate positive self-development in African/Caribbean Canadian children. Work with children and youth, the focus of Taylor's and Bryce's professional careers, has been essential in developing services for African/Caribbean Canadians in the public library. Carol Jones Collins (1993) has discussed the significance of making these materials available to African-American young adults. Most noteworthy has been her comment that literature and reading can promote healthy self-concepts and "to be effective, the best books are those which develop empathy, enhance self-image, reflect black culture and tradition, and help in understanding the effects of racism" (p. 383).

Parents typically search for books which reflect something about their children. The children's West Indian/Black Heritage Collection, which Laurel Taylor began managing in 1988 (by 1990 Taylor had also begun to manage the selection and development of the adult West Indian/Black Heritage Collection), has done much to reinforce this idea. Taylor commented that parents "want their children to see people who look like them. They don't always care if [materials] are from the United States, the Caribbean or Africa" (Laurel Taylor, interviewed by Kester, January 26, 1994). *Beyond Brer Rabbit* has been very successful: "So many people not only in the library community, but teachers, parents, educators in the United States and the Caribbean ask for it. It is not strictly West Indian, black history or African materials. It's all inclusive" (Laurel Taylor, interviewed by Kester, January 26, 1994). A fourth edition of this list was published in 1994.

Black History in Canada (Kester, 1991b) and *Apartheid* (Kester, 1991c) resulted from a cooperative work-study project with the University of Western Ontario's School of Library and Information Science. These lists complemented the evaluation of the adult West Indian/Black Heritage Collection. Several smaller bookmarks have been developed to market the collection including those that introduce Caribbean Canadian authors, African authors, Caribbean authors living at home and abroad, and a variety of black and Caribbean musical genres.

The importance of adding nonprint materials to the adult West Indian/Black Heritage Collection was apparent in the work of Rosalind Bryce, the Young Adult Senior Librarian and Audio-Visual Specialist of the West Indian/Black Heritage Collection: "When I got there, looking at the make-up of the community, literacy was a problem, and I thought in order to support the print collection, we should have audio-visuals. Most of the Caribbean people . . . would relate better to the non-print material" (Rosalind Bryce, interviewed by Kester, January 26, 1994). Bryce corroborated with Robert B. Ford (1972) who discussed the inner city library and complained that librarians "are so print-oriented that they fail to explore or see the potential of audio-visual materials" (p. 252). He further observed that enhancing audio-visual materials in the collection would provide for those patrons who were "semi-literate" (p. 252). Bryce has stated further that "some of the musical genres we buy include African, calypso, dub, dub poetry, folk music, pan, rap, reggae, sacred and soka. They are specifically Caribbean—

music of the Caribbean artist" (Rosalind Bryce, interviewed by Kester, January 26, 1994). American works such as jazz and blues are similarly well-represented in the main collection.

Selection for these materials has become quite specialized. Buying trips to Third World Bookstores and Crafts and other book and music stores which deal with Caribbean and black heritage materials have been important in selecting materials. "Direct buying is best" (Rosalind Bryce, interviewed by Kester, January 26, 1994). Acquisition of audio-visual materials has coincided with music and cultural festivals. "I like my buying trips to coincide with the great musical festivals. For instance, Caribana Festival [in Toronto]. So I can get the latest in calypso and pan for the festival, even in Jamaica. So we can have current titles" (Rosalind Bryce, interviewed by Kester, January 26, 1994). Selection can also include browsing through *Share* and other black newspapers for new published local works.

In 1992, the North York Public Library and the Halifax City Regional Library in Nova Scotia supported a one-week employee visit of black librarians who had been coordinating black heritage collections in these systems. Laurel Taylor, the Children's Resource Librarian and Specialist of the West Indian/Black Heritage Collection, was able to meet with Tracy Jones, the Branch Head at Halifax North Library. They discussed issues relating to collection development and community programming. Jones had earlier developed a bibliography on black children's literature for the Halifax City Regional Library.

Today, the West Indian/Black Heritage Collection "is an English language collection specially compiled to highlight materials about the black and Caribbean experience in Canada and elsewhere. It includes books, magazines, pamphlets, records, cassettes and compact discs" (North York Public Library, 1992). The *African American Experience* on CD-ROM is part of the collection in the York Woods Branch Library. While the collection is housed mostly at the York Woods Regional Branch, smaller collections are located at six other branches throughout the city of North York.

COLLECTION DEVELOPMENT

It has not been unusual for librarians to promote and encourage black publishers, booksellers, and authors. Rosalind Bryce's first library report proposed that the library find ways "of aiding, through financial or moral support, the production of such materials" and that maybe it could also offer workshops for writers and artists (Bryce & Greenidge, 1983, p. 72). In the collection's infancy, Canadian writers of African descent were encouraged to bring their works to the York Woods Regional Library, a book here, a work of poetry there. "There weren't publishers like Sister Vision Press [Black Women and Women of Color Press]" (Rosalind Bryce, interviewed by Kester, January 26, 1994). Gloria Reinbergs commented that essentially: "I find that demand drives acquisitions and quite a lot of good black books are coming out, but [librarians] are not buying them" (Gloria Reinbergs, interviewed by Kester, January 26, 1994).

Libraries make selections bureaucratically, hence, many small press materials, especially materials depicting the African/Caribbean Canadian and African-American experience may be missed when selection has not included coverage of these presses.

Inviting African/Caribbean Canadian authors to come to the library and to sell their works expanded their market at a time when many of their manuscripts were not being accepted by publishers. This library-author relationship enhanced the West Indian/Black Heritage Collection, especially in its early years. With the development of black Canadian writing in Toronto and throughout Canada, this level of encouragement has become less important in building collections.

African history and geography have grown as a part of the collection. Laurel Taylor studied African literature at the University of Toronto to broaden her subject knowledge and to further strengthen the collection which has also begun to include materials covering South Africa, especially "apartheid." "For the United States, the fiction is more contemporary and mainstream. We also have to be more selective with black American authors. And it is more difficult to get African and Caribbean materials. We only have a finite budget for a special collection" (Laurel Taylor, interviewed by Kester, January 26, 1994).

It was important to include materials that would cover a broad range of issues or a "representation of issues" as Bryce affirmed (interviewed by Kester, January 26, 1994). For example, a copy of each of James Baldwin's works is included in the fiction part of the collection while duplicates are housed in the main collection. Single copies of Terry Macmillan's and Toni Morrison's novels may also be found in the West Indian/Black Heritage Collection as "black heritage" components. Wole Soyinka's works are included, and "apartheid" materials are split between general and special collections.

The librarians I interviewed believed that non-black librarians were uncomfortable about selecting black books. The interviewees discussed a lack of "confidence" which white librarians felt when selecting black materials. For example, parenting books about blacks might be passed over for the general collection. Laurel Taylor has felt that she is seen too often as being the exclusive selector for black materials. She observed that library colleagues "still look at me as the 'black librarian'" (Laurel Taylor, interviewed by Kester, January 26, 1994). "They don't select it if there is a black kid on the cover. And I'm saying 'well, what's the difference?' And when they think about it, [they say] 'I don't know'" (Laurel Taylor, interviewed by Kester, January 26, 1994). Librarians, in general, might have difficulty selecting black materials, because they might not fully understand which materials would be important to the black user in the public library or they might not see that non-black users might also be interested in these materials. The authors of these works, Taylor believed, "might have something to say regardless of [his/her] apparent skin color" (interviewed by Kester, January 26, 1994). The interviewees also mentioned the lack of culturally specific classification schemes especially for black music and other materials. While some systems like the North York Public Library had classified these materials appropriately, others had not.

ROLE OF THE AFRICAN/CARIBBEAN CANADIAN LIBRARIAN

The role of minority librarians in meeting the needs of the African/Caribbean Canadian community has been quite specific. The librarians interviewed discussed the importance of library users being able to see a minority librarian with the ability to understand their culture. Residents needed to know that the black librarian was interested in acquiring those materials important to the black community. It was important "to let the [members of the] community know that they have representation. We are there for them. We are a link. We are the *broker* for the community between the institution and the community" (Rosalind Bryce, interviewed by Kester, January 26, 1994). The brokerage role might also help the library and its staff (representing the dominant culture) understand the culturally specific needs of the African/Caribbean Canadian user and community and how these have translated into selection, programming, and policy.

The librarian might also need to make the library warm, inviting, and accepting. Library users need to "see someone approachable and who's nice . . . and who sometimes will take the time to talk to them and find a book that they really like" (Laurel Taylor, interviewed by Kester, January 26, 1994). Users need to be educated about how the library works for them, how their ideas about materials would enhance the collection, and that these opinions will be respected by staff members. In fact, over the past fourteen years, the members of the community have "become familiar with the collections, both print and non-print, and they often make suggestions" (Rosalind Bryce, interviewed by Kester, January 26, 1994). Indeed, it would seem that the self-esteem and self-worth of users and community have developed over time.

Interviewees also discussed their function as a positive role model. "The kids see an alternative to being stereotyped. They see a role model who's there" (Laurel Taylor, interviewed by Kester, January 26, 1994). The librarians talked about the significance of showing minority children that librarianship, as a career, was an important way to work with people as well as with African/Caribbean Canadians. The black librarian could serve an essential leadership role in reaching out to the community.

The librarian as "publishing watchdog" was also evinced. Reinbergs commented: "We have to make sure that books they're bringing into the collections are reflective of the groups that are in the community, that there are certain books that are not representative of certain cultures, that have stereotypes, [we need] to make them [librarians] aware that [they] should look at them" (Gloria Reinbergs, interviewed by Kester, January 26, 1994). Rolfe (1984) commented on the "scrutinizing role," observing that librarians and libraries have a social duty to select materials which portray cultural minorities in a positive light (p. 15).

A very special relationship developed among the African/Caribbean Canadian librarian, the community, and the professional writer. Librarians and libraries supported the cultural works of writers. Clarence Hunter (1992) stated that "black librarians have a special responsibility . . . to see that black heritage is passed on" (p. 207). All three groups are symbiotic in strengthening the African/Caribbean Canadian and world black culture. This relationship is enhanced especially by bringing stories to people. "It's an important way of linking the word and the book and the people" (White, 1994, p. C8).

BLACK ENGLISH & DIALECT

Black English and its use (or more specifically, "dialect") were discussed at length. Special dialects can be quite effective for the African/Caribbean Canadian authors establishing the setting of their work. While black English is an American-derived "structure language," dialect, the librarians agreed, was much broader (Haskins & Butts, 1993, p. 44).

Laurel Taylor felt that even the word "black" was American in its usage whereas the West Indian population in Canada was quite "multiracial" and "multicultural." Rosalind Bryce related the value of dialect to the oral tradition, especially in audio-visual materials. "It has to be heard" to make sense culturally and literally. Librarians needed to learn more about the merits of dialects. "And I had to inform my colleagues, that yes, some books are written in black English which to mainstream or traditional people might look ungrammatical, but it is a legitimate form of writing and should not be discounted" (Laurel Taylor, interviewed by Kester, January 26, 1994). Such librarian-storytellers as Augusta Baker and Rita Cox have done much to bring dialect to the public in an easily accessible form. Storytelling materials have been essential to the West Indian/Black Heritage Collection, especially in the children's collection.

The difficulty of rendering an oral story in print and picture, especially in Canada, was illuminated by Laurel Taylor. "And I think that this is where Canadian black children's publishing or African children's publishing, is just starting. So we have Afua Cooper or Itah Sadu . . . putting things out; they're feeling their way along" (Laurel Taylor, interviewed by Kester, January 26, 1994). Toronto poets and dub poets like Clifton Joseph, Lillian Allen, and Itah Sadu have been featured at library-sponsored readings. Marlene Nourbese Phillip, the author of *Harriet's Daughter* and numerous works of non-fiction, visited the library in 1993. Randy Williams, a Bermudian author, employed Bermudian dialect in his presentation at the library. Many Caribbean writers and authors are using dialect in their works, particularly now, thus illustrating the value of this art form to their work and ideas. The world-famous Caribana, a festival of Caribbean music and culture, which attracts over one million travelers to Toronto, will be promoted for an upcoming library program incorporating dialect. It will include "improvising and composing [one's] own calypso. A lot of dialect will be used. Calypsonians will be there to assist [library users]" (Rosalind Bryce, interviewed by Kester, January 26, 1994).

Programs

The most significant community programs over the last ten years have also featured the province of Ontario's first African Canadian Lieutenant Governor, Lincoln Alexander. The premier screening in 1983 of Jennifer Hodge's *Homefeeling*, filmed in the Jane/Finch community, was important for the community as it was held in the York Woods Library theater. "The film was shot in the Jane/Finch area using residents from [the] neighborhood. So a lot of people felt ownership. You know, they felt very close to this film. And, we had two premiere screenings [at the library]" (Laurel Taylor, interviewed by Kester, January 26, 1994). Over 400 people attended. As a focal point for the community's meetings and other forums and library programs, the York Woods Regional Library's theater is undergoing major construction to expand its current size. Wayne Burnett, one of the first African/Caribbean Canadian members of the North York Public Library Board, was influential in moving this process forward despite financial cutbacks in the city. And the Canadian Broadcasting Corporation produced a sequel to *Homefeeling*, ten years after the first film, to observe changes in the Jane/Finch community. The York Woods Library has expressed a fervent interest in having the new film screened in the newly enhanced community theater. A break dance contest in 1985 attracted very large youth audiences, a program that further promoted the audio-visual materials in the collection.

Rita Cox's Kumbaya Storytelling Festival in 1983 featured Canadian, American black, and West Indian storytellers and was quite popular. Augusta Baker attended as did Miss Lou, Paul Keens-Douglas, and Brother Blue from New York City. Libraries in the Metro-Toronto area, including North York Public Library, were also involved in the coordination of this highly successful community event.

Of late, programs about African/Caribbean Canadians in a variety of traditional and nontraditional careers have also been planned. Self-esteem issues for youth have been integrated into these programs. "I also like to do programs that . . . highlight blacks in various careers. Like, I had one black cosmetician and he was male, [and] people in the publishing field, like the editor of *Share*. So the students can get a wide exposure to the types of careers where blacks are found" (Rosalind Bryce, interviewed by Kester, January 26, 1994). Having the editor of Toronto's black community newspaper, *Share*, visit the library during Black History Month was an important way to inspire young African/Caribbean Canadian males to achieve. Having these speakers at the library served as positive role models, according to Charles Boehm-Hill (1993) and could counter "an appalling drop-out rate" (p. 33).

The importance of acquiring appropriate materials for outreach and programming should not be understated. "The collection is used integrally with book display, programming and author visits" (Laurel Taylor, interviewed by Kester, January 26, 1994). In fact, having authors come to the library has also helped to make their words more concrete since their works are housed in the library. It might give incentive for black youths and other users to read.

Laurel Taylor, a member of Black Professionals Reaching Out, has also provided outreach with other professionals in elementary schools. "We're all different kinds of professionals—teachers, real estate people, actors. And we talk about our backgrounds [to students]. This year, I'm having them [members] into the library, mostly talking about helping black children to succeed in school" (Laurel Taylor, interviewed by Kester, January 26, 1994). She has visited schools in her work as a librarian and has drawn positive responses from students. In one instance she reminded a group of students that their local public library had a West Indian/Black Heritage Collection. That afternoon, many of the students had gone to the library and "cleared everything off of the shelves" (Laurel Taylor, interviewed by Kester, January 26, 1994).

Literacy education in the "Leading to Reading" and "Rap n' Read" programs for the community has been ongoing. The latter program, coordinated by Rosalind Bryce, appealed successfully to African/Caribbean Canadian young adults.

> The young adults prefer the student [tutors] to select which books they are going to read. The books that reflect themselves and materials or groups that are indigenous to the Caribbean, they seem to like it because they can match the illustration to the word—and it helps them. The collection really helps and supports the program. (Rosalind Bryce, interviewed by Kester, January 26, 1994)

In the early 1980s, nearly one-half of the participants of the library's literacy program had come from the Caribbean (Bryce & Greenidge, 1983, p. 58).

Attracting speakers and authors of African descent has given credence to the idea that many of these people have made valuable contributions in their fields and to the larger community, an idea that resonated among black students. Bryce has noted the value of having black writers come to the library, especially in the age of television. "To see the contributions we're making in the literature field or the music field [sic]. We are contributing. I think that is important. Because on television who do you see? You don't see black hockey players, you don't see black whatever" (Rosalind Bryce, interviewed by Kester, January 26, 1994). The library has become a valued and much-needed place to launch and showcase the contributory efforts of blacks in writing, in the arts, and in society.

LIMITATIONS OF THE STUDY

The group interview format helped to obtain much information over a short period although at least one key participant was not able to attend. Her presence would have helped in understanding the Toronto Public Library experience. Asking those librarians who were interviewed if they had any other comments about their professional roles at the conclusion of the interview might also have helped in obtaining additional information.

Further research should focus on the specific reading interests of African/

Caribbean Canadian children and youth. Studying literacy work with these groups in the public library might also yield valuable insight into reading levels and reading interests. The use of nonprint materials merits further study as well as the influence of popular culture—such as rap music—in providing educational and cultural programs. A study of the influence of African/Caribbean Canadian women and other minority librarians in a variety of professional settings would also help in identifying their impact on the field and in developing a broader understanding of their work in librarianship and information science.

CONCLUSION

African/Caribbean Canadian women librarians have done much to effect social change in the community and, importantly, they have ensured that the many contributions of those of African descent, in Canada and throughout the world, will be passed on from generation to generation. And in doing so, they have promoted the development of more positive attitudes toward those of African descent in Canadian society.

Over time, the York Woods African/Caribbean community has developed remarkably, and the North York Public Library has provided equitable services and staff for its many users. In October 1992, the library celebrated the tenth anniversary of the establishment of the West Indian/Black Heritage Collection. The community, various groups, teachers, students, and notable authors were invited to celebrate the collection and its significance to the community.

Despite this success in library service in the North York and Toronto Public Library systems, the impulse to grow complacent has not abated. As Stephen Lewis (1992) reported after the wake of the Yonge Street riots in which black and other disempowered youth had participated, "we need to acknowledge the existence of systemic racism in our working and institutional environments and *design approaches for confronting it directly*" (p. 29). Libraries and librarians should take this advice seriously if we would make a difference in confronting and challenging racism.

Why does society need the African/Caribbean Canadian librarian or specialized collections of this nature? Rita Cox summed it up: "I look at children from my race and I want to say to them, 'We are a proud people from a proud race. We've influenced the world with our cultural expressions'" (from a speech in 1993 upon being awarded an honorary doctorate from York University for her inspiring and dedicated work as a public librarian involved in the Parkdale community in Toronto). Nurturing the self-esteem of black children and young adults has been at the heart of the work of African/Caribbean Canadian librarians such as Laurel Taylor and Rosalind Bryce. Common themes are presented within the experience of minorities in the public library. Advocacy, education, and the creation and maintenance of links with the varied members of the African/Caribbean Canadian community should be important aims in furthering minority rights and in affirming minorities as public library patrons. These elements of library service form the basis of empowerment and, ultimately, liberation.

NOTES

[1]In 1996, Rita Cox won Canada's highest civic award, the Order of Canada, for her many accomplishments. She holds the title of Librarian Emeritas for, among other things, founding the Black Heritage and West Indian Collection of the Toronto Public Library.

[2]All Comments (unless otherwise noted) by Laurel Taylor, Rosalind Bryce, and Gloria Reinbergs are from the interviews conducted by Norman Kester, January 26, 1994 during a meeting with Laurel Taylor and Rosalind Bryce (North Public Library) and Gloria Reinbergs (Toronto Public Library) (on audiocassette). These will be cited in the text where they occur as ([name of person interviewed], interviewed by Kester, January 26, 1994).

REFERENCES

Abdullahi, I. (Ed.). (1992). *E. J. Josey: An activist librarian*. Metuchen, NJ: Scarecrow Press.

Black, A. (Ed.). (1992). *Voices: Canadian writers of African descent*. Scarborough, Ontario, Canada: HarperCollins Canada.

Boehm-Hill, C. (1993). Empowering an endangered species: The African/Caribbean/Canadian male. *Education Canada, 33*(2), 31-35.

Braithwaite, R. W., & Benn-Ireland, T. (1993). *Some black women: Profiles of black women in Canada*. Toronto, Ontario, Canada: Sister Vision Press.

Bryce, R. (1992). *Coming of age themes in Caribbean fiction: A bibliography*. North York, Ontario, Canada: North York Public Library.

Bryce, R., & Greenidge, E. (1983). *LIB 2183 practicum in community services: Jane-Finch project: Library/information needs of the black/West Indian population*. Toronto, Ontario, Canada: University of Toronto, Faculty of Library and Information Sciences.

Collins, C. J. (1993). A tool for change: Young adult literature in the lives of young adult African-Americans. *Library Trends, 41*(3), 378-392.

Ford, R. B., Jr. (1972). Farewell to traditionalism: A perspective of the inner city library. In E. J. Josey (Ed.), *What black librarians are saying* (p. 252). Metuchen, NJ: Scarecrow Press.

Haskins, J., & Butts, H. F. (1993). *The psychology of black language*. New York: Hippocrene Books.

Hunter, C. (1992). Passing the torch. In I. Abdullahi (Ed.), *E. J. Josey: An activist librarian* (p. 207). Metuchen, NJ: Scarecrow Press.

Josey, E. J. (Ed.). (1972). *What black librarians are saying*. Metuchen, NJ: Scarecrow Press.

Kapica, J. (1993). Canadians want Mosaic to melt, survey finds. *The Globe and Mail*, 14 December, A1, A2.

Kester, N. G. (1991a). *North York Public Library/York Woods Regional Library: West Indian/Black Heritage Collection assessment*. London, Ontario, Canada: University of Western Ontario, School of Library and Information Science.

Kester, N. G. (1991b). *Black history in Canada: An annotated bibliography: A survey of material from the West Indian/Black Heritage Collection of the North York Public Library*. North York, Ontario, Canada: North York Public Library.

Kester, N. G. (1991c). *Apartheid: An annotated bibliography: A survey of materials from the West Indian/Black Heritage Collection of the North York Public Library*. North York, Ontario, Canada: North York Public Library.

Kester, N. G. (1993). *Trials and celebrations: The African experience in North America: A selected and partially annotated list*. Mississauga, Ontario, Canada: Mississauga Library System. Mississauga Central Library. Social Sciences/Science & Technology Department.

Kester, N. G. (1994). *The African/Caribbean Canadian librarian and the public library: Focus group interview with Laurel Taylor/Rosalind Bryce (North York Public Library) and Gloria Reinbergs (Toronto Public Library), interview by Norman Kester*, audiocassette, 26 January.

Kester, N. G. (1995) Bringing the word and the book to the people: Rita Cox retires from Toronto Public Library, *Feliciter, 41*(2), 26-29.

Lewis, S. (1992). *Report on race relations in Ontario*. Toronto, Ontario, Canada: Government of Ontario.

MacCann, D. (1989). Libraries for immigrants and "minorities": A study in contrasts. In D. MacCann (Ed.), *Social responsibility in librarianship: Essays on equality* (pp. 97-116). Jefferson, NC: McFarland.

North York Public Library (n.d.). *Collections* (pamphlet). North York, Ontario, Canada: North York Public Library.

Philip, M. N. (1992). *Frontiers: Essays and writings on racism and culture, 1984-1992*. Stratford, Ontario, Canada: Mercury Press.

Pierson, R. R.; Griffen-Cohen, M.; Bourne, P.; & Masters, P. (1993). The mainstream women's movement and the politics of difference. In *Canadian women's issues: Volume I strong voices: Twenty-five years of women's activism in English Canada*. Toronto, Ontario, Canada: James Lorimer.

Reimer, D. L. (1984). *Voices: A guide to oral history*. Victoria, British Columbia, Canada: Provincial Archives, Sound and Moving Image Division.

Rolfe, R. (1984). *North York Public Library: Collections and services for the black and Caribbean community*. North York, Ontario, Canada: North York Public Library.

Silvera, M. (1993). Speaking of women's lives and imperialist economics: Two introductions from "Silenced." In H. Bannerji (Ed.), *Returning the gaze: Essays on racism, feminism, and politics* (pp. 197-219). Toronto, Ontario, Canada: Sister Vision Press.

Skrzeszewski, S. (1990). Multiculturalism in Ontario libraries—An overview. In J. Gudnara & C. Mylopoulos (Eds.), *Multiculturalism matters: Reflections on multiculturalism and library practice* (Occasional Paper No. 1) (pp. 19-28). Ontario Library Association. Multicultural Services Guild.

Speller, B. (1991). *Educating black librarians*. Jefferson, NC: McFarland & Company.

Taylor, L. (1994). *Beyond Brer Rabbit: A list of children's fiction at the North York Public Library,* 4th ed. North York, Ontario, Canada: North York Public Library.

Taylor, S. (1992). *Many rivers to cross: The African-Canadian experience, The National Tour 1992-1994*. Toronto, Ontario, Canada: Multicultural History Society of Ontario.

White, N. (1994). Sadu's stories come to life with a Caribbean lilt. *The Toronto Star,* February 13, C8.

Uprooting Black Heritage

Lessons from an African-American
Collection at Auction[1]

ε❧ Detine L. Bowers ❧ε

N o incident demonstrated more clearly the lack of collective buying power among those who would preserve African-American culture than the Alex Haley estate auction in October 1992. For less than a half million dollars, the entire manuscript collection could have been preserved, but there was no collective African-American purchase. This article focuses on the auction, its significance, and on projects that attempt to preserve the history of important black schools.

African-American archives nationwide confront economic challenges. Preservation strategies must be implemented to avoid the current organizational and financial struggles of the Martin Luther King, Jr., Center for Nonviolent Social Change Library (Chepesiuk & Kelley-Palmer, 1994), one of the largest African-American archives in the country, and scattered materials and archives in poor condition across the country (Lee, 1994, pp. 224-41). Building a supportive network among existing collections could be one solution to the problem of limited resources. The success of the acquisition and preservation of African-American archives will depend upon increased fundraising efforts and strong community networking to build collective buying power.

THE AUCTION

The Conference Center of the University of Tennessee—Knoxville housed scores of boxes of Haley's manuscript collections. On the day of the Haley auction, I heard two Anglo-American women, who appeared to have walked into the center off the streets of Knoxville, exclaim: "All of this material, just out here for people to pick through, it's a disgrace!" Indeed, it was a sad day, not just because Haley's debts led his brother to auction the estate that included more than 500 lots of books and manuscripts or because the auctioneer handled the materials unprofessionally, reducing the sale of Haley's estate to that of any other Tennessean. No collective effort was made to recover African-American roots.

Just over 100 people attended the manuscripts auction. A small percentage of the attendees who purchased items were African American: a handful of black book dealers, four or five African-American library and museum collectors, and a few black celebrity representatives and private collectors exemplified the low buying power and lack of collective interest in the Haley legacy. A few other blacks were with the media covering the occasion. Anglo-Americans from around the nation came and waited for the manuscripts auction block to open.

Where were African-American scholars, Afrocentrists, African-American studies departments, university archivists, African-American colleges and universities, and "heritage collectors?" Where were the Malcolm X scholars who are concerned about preserving the Malcolm X papers—those who seek a central Malcolm X archive?

As I listened to the bids roll, I awaited an offer from a single African-American buyer who would bid and place the collection in a single repository; just one person who appreciated the collective value of Haley's estate, with all the contents intact; someone willing to preserve most of this collection for posterity. Aside from purchasing a few of his books and some letters written to Malcolm X about his September 12, 1964, *Saturday Evening Post* article, I felt helpless. I was a newly appointed assistant professor of communication studies, sitting on the block, watching the disintegration of the African-American family. I never met Haley, but found myself feeling trapped as thoughts whirled through my mind about what could be done at this late date—the first day of auctioning was already underway.

Meanwhile, I thought about how slaves must have felt when they had been auctioned. Images of the helpless slave family, separated at auction by buyer greed and lust flashed repeatedly before my eyes. The entire manuscript collection that included research notes, Malcolm X papers, rare photographs, and several award plaques was dispersed, garnering less than a half million dollars, a modest price for African-American roots.

A few special items went to African-American individuals and archives. Detroit-based entertainment attorney, Gregory J. Reed, bought edited manuscripts of the *Autobiography of Malcolm X*. A large collection of *Roots* research materials went to an African-American book dealer, some items to the New York Public Library Schomburg Center for Research in Black Culture, and others to the National Afro-American Museum in Wilberforce, Ohio. Files, photos, and other precious memories found numerous private homes. Haley's estate was auctioned and dispersed, as American black culture has always been.

The basic question is two-fold: first, why wasn't there a collective claim to African-American roots through stronger organizational support for buying the materials? For example, a special fund from a handful of celebrities could have kept the manuscript portion of the Haley estate intact. Second, there is a fundamental question of value. How much value does the broader African-American community, including black celebrities, place on historical and cultural preservation? These questions could open dialogue among black archivists about a collective agenda, a network that fosters more aggressive acquisition strategies with black donor support. The research community needs to ensure continuity in accessing and maintaining African-American archives.

For over 200 years, the history of African-Americans has been either dispersed or denied a place of record by Anglo-Americans who auctioned slaves and denied freedom of speech and basic citizenship for African Americans. This has resulted in an almost irretrievable scattering of African-American roots. As a communication scholar involved in historical-critical analysis, I know the painstaking effort required to conduct historical research on African Americans because of the issue of preservation. The nineteenth-century works of Nathaniel Paul, Henry Highland Garnet, Frederick Douglass, Alexander Crummell, Martin Delany, William Whipper, David Ruggles, Jermain Loguen, James Forten, Robert Purvis, Amos Beman, William Watkins, and other African-American human rights leaders is extremely difficult to uncover because the materials are scattered or in extremely poor condition. That the community allowed such a scattering to happen in 1992 is untenable. One hundred years after Frederick Douglass, the cycle of destruction Douglass warned about remains unbroken. What was most unfortunate was its dispersal among Anglo-Americans, not because of their race, but because the estate should mean much more to the black community.

The auction stopped me dead in my Afrocentric footsteps. I questioned the future of African-Americans' archival buying power and collective agendas as well as the relationship of potential donors to predominantly black archival institutions such as the Martin Luther King, Jr. Center for Nonviolent Social Change, the Schomburg Center for Research in Black Culture, and the Moorland-Spingarn Research Center at Howard University.

The irony of the scattering of *Roots* should provoke remedies. Where should archives of blacks who achieve celebrity status be housed? Should archives go to already consolidated African-American collections? Should these institutions establish more aggressive recruiting efforts and legally ensure the acquisition of collections from potential donors early in their careers? The answer to all of these questions is a resounding "yes." Alex Haley had donated most of his *Roots* research to the University of Tennessee-Knoxville, and many of his other prized manuscripts were available for a black collection there or elsewhere. But then we must ask, do existing archives have the financial footing necessary to survive and enjoy growth? A key concern should be strong infrastructures that ensure longevity of the archives through consolidation and more aggressive grant acquisition.

IMPORTANT BLACK ARCHIVES

Upon a recent visit to an African-American college in Virginia, I found poorly maintained book and photograph archives. Rare books and photographs were openly accessible to the public, and much of the material showed tremendous wear from inadequate preservation methods. Perhaps small black colleges might consider consolidating some of their collections with larger black archives such as the Martin Luther King, Jr. Center or Schomburg and increasing both African-American community-based funding and corporate funding. Exhibits could be interchanged among African-American collections and collective organizational fundraising efforts initiated to generate maximum support. Whatever the mechanism, immediate change is required to ensure long-term preservation of a rich cultural heritage.

Lessons from the Alex Haley auction have been invaluable to my work related to African-American archives in my local community and will hopefully serve as a model for other communities. As founder of Project CI (Christiansburg Institute) at my university, I seek ways to recover African-American artifacts related to southwest Virginia's African-American school that operated from 1866 to 1966 and to share these artifacts with other African-American museums and archives.

Project CI is a partnership among Virginia Polytechnic Institute and State University and the Christiansburg Institute Alumni Association, Inc. (CIAA), Radford University, and other community organizations to establish a museum and community education center, develop programming, accumulate an archival collection, and create exhibits of the African-American high school that served southwest Virginia and children from neighboring states for 100 years. The project aims to bring local and national attention to the school's visionary supervisor, Booker T. Washington, and the model of industrial education for African-Americans in the state of Virginia at the turn of the century. The following mission statement was adopted in December 1994:

> The mission of Project CI is to facilitate the development of programs that encourage local and national awareness of the Christiansburg Institute, an African-American educational institution founded in 1866, and to promote and preserve the unique history of African-American education in Virginia. Project CI is a partnership between the Christiansburg Institute Alumni Association, Incorporated, and Virginia Tech. (Swain, 1995)

As a pilot program, Project CI offers students from a variety of disciplines, including communication studies, architecture, horticulture, engineering, etc., an opportunity to participate in restoring and maintaining an important cultural enterprise. This will unite local college students and community members with the community's African-American heritage, thus institutionalizing a relationship with an important segment of the community.

CIAA has managed to organize alumni in a way that few other black schools have. Because of this, alumni have gathered numerous artifacts and have preserved a collection of memorabilia, photographs, and documents. Although CIAA represents collective action, a lack of financial resources has limited its opportunities. CIAA now owns and operates a small museum of these artifacts at the site of the Christiansburg Institute. In 1996, the remaining building and land was donated to the alumni but a developer purchased the school property in the 1960s.

With the assistance of local universities and the community, the organization is undertaking a "Reclaiming Our Heritage" project aimed to recover artifacts such as photographs and documents, some of which are scattered throughout the country. The CIAA story, similar to that of many other stories of African-American collections, involves members of the community entrusting graduate student researchers with valuable artifacts. Ultimately, the alumni and others connected with the school gloaned researchers' oral histories, historic photographs, and other documents pertinent to the school without a clear understanding of what would happen to the materials they contributed. They provided some researchers with some of the best historic documents about the community. This story is a cliché about African-American artifacts and about the potential for abuse of community trust. Consequently, like many American Indian artifacts, black artifacts are held hostage within mainstream America, awaiting public recognition or continued obscurity.

The future of preserving the rich heritage of the Christiansburg Institute now rests with a partnership with local universities, community organizations, and an organization committed to the school's legacy of hard work, commitment, and service. Communicating this heritage must include other national African-American museum projects such as the National Afro-American Museum in Wilberforce, Ohio, so as to ensure that some key documents about Christiansburg Institute are donated to national African-American collections. While the National African-American Museum Project, a Smithsonian Institution project, might have been a crucial location for Christiansburg Institute artifacts, controversy over congressional funding for this project has thwarted its full realization. However, the effort must be one that offers its story to other national African-American collections through donations of photographs and duplicate documents and video documentaries as well as opportunities for traveling exhibits at other national African-American collections.

The rich heritage of another African-American industrial school in Manassas, Virginia, Manassas Industrial School, is also being recovered. Industrial education was generally prescribed for African Americans at the turn of the century with Booker T. Washington as black industrial education's primary national advocate. Few extant artifacts remain from this school founded in 1894 by an ex-slave, Jane (Jennie) Serepta Dean. Irony explains best the fact that Jennie Dean's school for the industrial and social training of blacks stood near a crucial site of the Civil War, Bull Run. The Manassas Museum pursued the recovery of the lost heritage, raising millions to establish a monument to this school and its founder.

The Manassas Museum currently houses a few extant artifacts of the school and its students. Phase one of the museum's memorial to Jennie Dean includes outlines of buildings from the Industrial School, historic markers, landscaping, an information kiosk, and a model of the original campus. Phase two of the project includes a performing arts center, which would seat 500 and is intended to be used for community programs and the arts. The Manassas Museum's effort has emerged as a model for other communities where African-American history, including valuable artifacts, is obscured due to lack of financial resources required to collect remnants of the material culture.

With future efforts to preserve African-American artifacts comes the question of how to work collectively to ensure that the community becomes the keeper of the tradition. Collaboration through partnerships and African-American community networking to ensure adequate funding for training and proper preservation equipment is the challenge. It is time for African-Americans to place a high value on a community's rich heritage, to strengthen strategies. Jennie Dean's creed that each of us needs to do our part is sound advice for organizing today.

NOTE

[1] This article is an adaptation of an earlier published essay. See Bowers, D. L. (1992). Disintegrating *Roots*: African-American life and culture returns to the auction block. *Black Scholar, 22*(4), 2-5.

REFERENCES

Bowers, D.L (1992). Disintegrating *Roots*: African-American life and culture returns to the auction block. *Black Scholar, 22*(4), 2-5.

Chepesiuk, R., & Kelley-Palmer, G. (1994). The Martin Luther King Library and Archives at the crossroads. *American Libraries, 25*, 148-151.

Coughlin, E. K. (1992). Malcolm X: A barometer of today's racial climate. *The Chronicle of Higher Education, 39*(7). A8, A14.

Halley, A. (1976). *Roots,* 1st ed. Garden City, NY: Doubleday.

Lee, R. (1994). As curator of a black heritage collection. In E. J. Josey (Ed.). *The black librarian in America revisited.* pp. 224-241. Metuchen, NJ: Scarecrow Press.

Lewis, S. J. (1942). *Undaunted faith: The life story of Jennie Dean.* Catletts, VA: "The Circuit" Press.

Smith, J., & DeHart, A. E. (1991). *Christian[s]burg Institute: A proud heritage.* Petersburg, VA: Westar Publishing Co.

Swain, A. (1995). *Christiansburg Institute: From Freedmen's Bureau enterprise to public high school.* Unpublished master's thesis, Radford University, Radford, Virginia.

Civil Rights, Libraries, & African-American Librarianship, 1954-1994

A Bibliographic Essay

ᔔ Edward A.Goedeken ᔔ

T he modern era in the African-American experience began with the U. S. Supreme Court's 1954 decision, *Brown vs. The Board of Education of Topeka, Kansas*, outlawing the long-established principle of "separate but equal" that had governed race relations since the end of the nineteenth century. For African-American librarians, however, the effects of the 1954 ruling would not begin to be realized for another decade as the American Library Association (ALA) came to terms with the burgeoning civil rights movement that had begun in the mid-1950s. Only in the mid-1960s did southern state library associations allow blacks to join. Like much of the nation as a whole, ALA was not in the forefront of the movement. The path from exclusion to inclusion in professional librarianship has, in many respects, mirrored the experience of African-Americans and the expansion of civil rights in post-World War II American society.

Despite its reticence, ALA possessed leaders such as Eric Moon and E.J. Josey who sought to enlighten the library community on the issues of race and librarianship. Such groups as the Black Caucus, founded in 1970, have served as important forums for this effort. And in 1976, Clara S. Jones became the first African-American President of ALA. Nevertheless, much work remains if we are to improve African-American participation in American librarianship by the end of the century. One approach for improving our understanding of the present is to perceive more clearly the past, a task accomplished by becoming more familiar with the major writings on the history of black librarianship since 1954. This chapter provides guidance for such a journey in scholarship.

GENERAL SOURCES

Familiarity with the larger context of African-American history should facilitate an understanding of the history of African-American librarianship. Although a vast literature awaits anyone interested in pursuing this topic, competent guides aid the novice. John Hope Franklin (1994), one of the foremost African-American historians, has published seven editions of his classic, *From Slavery to Freedom: A History of African Americans.* Franklin (1993) elaborates his views further in *The Color Line: Legacy for the Twenty-First Century.* Lerone Bennett, Jr. (1993) provides another useful survey, *Before the Mayflower: A History of Black America*, and Vincent N. Parrillo (1994) treats the larger aspects of race in America, extending beyond African-American groups, in *Strangers to These Shores: Race and Ethnic Relations in the United States.* August Meier (1986), another well-regarded historian, discusses the historical profession's relationship with African-American issues in *Black History and the Historical Profession.* John H. Bracy, Jr., August Meier, and Elliott Rudwick (1972) edited an important collection of primary materials in *The Afro-Americans: Selected Documents.*

BROWN VERSUS THE BOARD OF EDUCATION OF TOPEKA, KANSAS

The definitive history of the Brown decision, published by Richard Kluger (1976) and entitled, *Simple Justice: The History of Brown v. Board of Education and Black America's Struggle for Equality*, is complemented by the edited work of Mark Whitman (1993), *Removing a Badge of Slavery: The Record of Brown vs. Board of Education.* The significance of this case for the future of race relations is outlined in an article by Michael J. Klarman (1994) who also summarizes nicely the historiography of this important ruling.

MARTIN LUTHER KING, JR. & THE CIVIL RIGHTS MOVEMENT

The volume of writings on the Civil Rights Movement is truly daunting to any scholar. Indeed, the amount of research and writing in the past few years on Martin Luther King, Jr. alone could be described as a minor industry. Carlson Publishing, for example, has produced an eighteen-volume set of dissertations, master's theses, and journal articles published between 1950 and 1985 entitled *Martin Luther King, Jr. and the Civil Rights Movement* (Garow, 1989).

Fortunately, much scholarship has been identified in numerous bibliographies. Paul T. Murray's (1993) *The Civil Rights Movement: References and Resources* provides a compass for the major literature and should be consulted at the beginning of any serious research on the subject. His introduction, surveying the major writings, is especially helpful to those new to this field. Steven F. Lawson (1991) has analyzed the recent literature in an essay for the *American Historical Review.* Researchers of the Civil Rights Movement will also benefit from the selective bibliography by Thura Mack and Janette Prescod (1991). Of the many histories of the movement, Robert Weisbrot's (1990) *Freedom Bound: A History of America's Civil Rights Movement* is among the most readable and reliable. Any study of Martin Luther King, Jr. must begin with the first volume of Taylor Branch's (1988) magisterial *Parting the Waters*, a comprehensive history of civil rights from 1954 to 1963. Branch is complemented by two other prominent historians, David J. Garrow and Stephen B. Oates. Garrow's (1986) *Bearing the Cross* and Oates's (1982) *Let the Trumpet Sound* are essential for a broader understanding of the man and the movement. In 1992, the University of California Press began publishing King's papers, greatly improving scholarly access to significant primary material (King, 1992-).

HISTORIES OF AFRICAN-AMERICAN LIBRARIANSHIP: SOURCES

Three important reference works assist library historians in their quest for printed information. Wayne A. Wiegand and Donald G. Davis, Jr. (1994) have recently edited the *Encyclopedia of Library History* which brings together dozens of essays on a wide-range of topics relating to the history of librarianship. A second source, indispensable to library history scholarship, is the monumental bibliography by Donald G. Davis, Jr. and John Mark Tucker (1989), *American Library History*. The Davis-Tucker volume updates the earlier *American Library History: A Bibliography* by Michael H. Harris and Donald G. Davis, Jr. (1978) and surveys the literature through 1986.

The Davis-Tucker bibliography incorporates the citations, without the annotations, of a third highly useful reference work, Arthur P. Young's update of Michael H. Harris's (1974) *A Guide to Research in American Library History*. Young's (1988) guide to dissertations and theses contains references to over thirty master's theses produced for the Atlanta University library school during the 1950s and 1960s on public library service to African Americans in a number of communities throughout the South in the years following World War II. These theses remain an untapped mine of material for anyone interested in learning how public libraries served minorities in the pre-Civil Rights era.

HISTORIES OF AFRICAN-AMERICAN LIBRARIANSHIP: SPECIFIC WORKS

Although broad histories of African-American librarianship are rare, their quality is quite high even though they appear in article, rather than in monographic, form. The best work thus far is that of Rosemary Ruhig Du Mont. In "Race in American Librarianship: Attitudes of the Library Profession," Du Mont (1986a) provides an illuminating analysis of the faltering steps of the American Library Association as it moved toward accepting and incorporating African-American librarians into full participation. (Du Mont has continued her interest in the issues of diversity and librarianship. See for example, Du Mont & Caynon, 1994. In this work, she has a chapter on the history of multiculturalism.) It is by no means a proud history. A.P. Marshall (1976) adds another overview; he begins his survey at the end of the Civil War, whereas Du Mont treats the twentieth century only. To these essays should be added E.J. Josey's (1994) "Race Issues in Library History" which summarizes succinctly the major historical points. Josey and Shockley's (1977) *Handbook of Black Librarianship* contains an excellent chronology by Josey and Casper LeRoy Jordan identifying pioneer African-American librarians and significant developments. Josey, discussed below, has emerged as a major figure in African-American librarianship. Finally, Davis and Tucker (1992) evaluate the contributions of Arthur Shomburg, Monroe Nathan Work, and Dorothy Porter Wesley in their study of African-Americans and academic libraries.

Mary Lee Bundy and Frederick J. Stielow (1987) have edited an important collection of essays on librarianship in the 1960s. Contributions include William Cunningham's comments on the early years of the ALA's Black Caucus. Other chapters feature an interview with the outspoken editor of *Library Journal*, Eric Moon, and Helen Williams's overview of the African-American experience in white library schools during the 1960s. The volume concludes with Stielow's learned summary of the decade's historical implications. For a flavor of the period, one can consult Eric Moon's (1993) most significant writings reprinted in *A Desire to Learn*. Moon persistently and articulately promoted library involvement in contemporary social issues and became an early advocate of equality for African-American librarians.

Memoirs and reminiscences have become building blocks for narrative syntheses. With only a few scholarly studies having appeared, researchers continue to require primary sources. In addition to the underutilized master's theses cited in the Young bibliography, one can consult with Annie L. McPheeters's (1988) autobiography which traces her professional life as a public librarian in Atlanta, Georgia, in the 1950s and 1960s. Annette L. Phinazee (1980) edited the proceedings of a 1976 conference at North Carolina Central University, which includes, among others, essays by A.P. Marshall, Clara S. Jones, Casper LeRoy Jordan, and Robert Wedgeworth with an emphasis on African-American librarians in the Southeast. Phinazee's work should be supplemented by Carole Taylor's (1980) survey of library service in black academic libraries in the South from 1940 to 1970.

Jessie Carney Smith, editor of the outstanding reference sources, *Notable Black American Women* and *Notable Black American Women Book II*, summarized the contribution of a group of significant African-American women librarians whom she refers to as her "Sweet Sixteen" (Smith, 1993). Smith discusses Sadie Delaney, Vivian Harsh, Nella Larsen, and Catherine Latimer. Also noteworthy is Smith's (1977) historical work on African-American academic librarianship, *Black Academic Libraries and Research Collections*. A general source that complements Smith for biographical information is Darlene Clark Hine's (1993) two-volume *Black Women in America* which relates the lives of seventeen African-American women librarians. A major sourcebook, providing bibliographic access to entries in more than 300 biographical dictionaries and directories, is the three-volume guide by Randall K. Burkett et al. (1991), *Black Biography, 1790-1950* (some libraries have acquired the microfiche collection on which the bibliography is based, thus providing scholars with access to thousands of previously inaccessible biographical articles).

A scholarly approach, taken by Lelia Rhodes (1975), featured interviews of a number of prominent female African-American librarians. Rhodes's subjects include: Clara S. Jones, Virginia Lacy Jones, Annette L. Phinazee, Jessie Carney Smith, and Eliza Atkins Gleason. An example of a recent book-length biography is Kirkland Jones's (1992) study of Arna Wendell Bontemps, an important writer and long-time director of the library at Fisk University. An earlier essay on Bontemps by Jessie Carney Smith (1978) for the *Dictionary of American Library Biography* remains quite useful. Avril Johnson Madison with Dorothy Porter Wesley (1995) and Helen H. Britton (1994) add recent essays on Wesley, a seminal figure among African-American bibliographers.

E. J. JOSEY

The foremost advocate for African-American librarianship during this period is without doubt the indefatigable activist, E.J. Josey. Any scholarly investigation of the subject cannot proceed without taking into account Josey's involvement as a speaker, writer, conciliator, and coalition builder. Born in Virginia in 1924, he earned an undergraduate degree from Howard University in 1949 and a master's in history from Columbia University the next year. In 1953, he completed his master's in librarianship at the State University of New York at Albany. He subsequently worked at the Free Library of Philadelphia and directed the libraries at Delaware State College and at Savannah State College. From 1966 to 1986 he served the New York State Library, first as chief of the Bureau of Academic and Research Libraries and then as chief of the Bureau of Specialist Library Services. Since 1986, he has taught at the University of Pittsburgh's School of Library and Information Science.

His professional career is intertwined inextricably with the issues of civil rights and minority librarianship. Josey gained national visibility in 1964 by protesting vigorously ALA's decision to honor the Mississippi Library Association for its National Library Week activities when that state had elected to withdraw from ALA in order to maintain separate library associations for its black and white members. In 1970 he founded ALA's Black Caucus and in 1983 became ALA president. Since his writings are voluminous, only the four monographs Josey edited on African-American librarianship will be mentioned. Researchers interested in the larger corpus of Josey's scholarship should consult the bibliography by Ismail Abdullahi (1992) in the essays he edited honoring Josey's career.

During the 1970s, Josey edited or co-edited three books that capture the essence of African-American library thought in the aftermath of the heady 1960s. Already by 1970, disillusionment had set in due to the lack of progress in mitigating pervasive racism. Josey (1970) introduced his landmark collection, *The Black Librarian in America*, noting the failure of the Nixon Administration to advance Lyndon Johnson's civil rights agenda. Nevertheless, Josey's volume mixed optimism with pessimism as described by twenty-five prominent African-American librarians representing a broad spectrum of library practice. Calls for continuing the struggle were intertwined with the personal histories of long-time activists like Virginia Lacy Jones, Miles M. Jackson, and Augusta Baker. A. P. Marshall provided a historical context in "The Search for Identity," and Jessie Carney Smith related her now-famous view on "The Four Cultures," her perspectives as a librarian, a woman, a black, and a Southerner. Josey divided his book into five parts according to type of library or activity: library education; public; academic; special; and federal, state, or city; and concluded with an informative autobiographical sketch.

Josey (1972) followed his first collection two years later with *What Black Librarians Are Saying*, a collection that, with some of the same authors, continued Josey's goal of disseminating the thoughts and opinions of prominent contemporary African-American librarians. Less autobiographical and historical than the 1970 book, this collection focused on other issues including the information needs of African-American communities, intellectual freedom, and professional aspects of African-American librarianship. A dominant theme was the balancing act performed by African-American librarians as information professionals in their communities on one side and, on the other, as articulate representatives of racial interests in these same communities.

In 1977, a different type of book appeared, *Handbook of Black Librarianship*, compiled by Josey with Ann Allen Schockley (1977), which sought to incorporate into one volume a wide range of materials relating to African-American culture and librarianship. Besides the historical essays by Casper LeRoy Jordan and Lucy Campbell, the *Handbook* contained information on various state library associations and featured Josey's recollection of the founding of the Black Caucus of ALA in 1970. This volume also reflected Josey's growing interest in identifying and promoting the vast range of literary and historical sources that undergird the study of the African-American experience. Lists of periodicals and books written by or for African-Americans were buttressed with information locating archival collections of African-Americana (for more on Josey's interest in developing collections of ethnic literature, see Josey & DeLoach, 1983). Finally, Josey and Shockley identified undergraduate and graduate library programs in predominantly black institutions as well as libraries that served African-American populations (Josey & Peeples, 1977). The *Handbook* serves as a remarkable snapshot of African-American book culture in the late 1970s and remains a valuable compendium nearly twenty years after its publication.

Twenty-four years after his first collection, Josey (1994) returned with *The Black Librarian in America Revisited*. Of his thirty essayists, only eleven had contributed to the 1970 volume. The arrangement is the same—by library type or activity—although the new edition adds a section on profiles and issues. Jessie Carney Smith reexamined her four cultures, while Casper LeRoy Jordan profiled the career of Virginia Lacy Jones. Although Josey remained troubled by the lack of progress in reducing racism in our culture, he was cautiously optimistic that the new democratic administration of Bill Clinton would provide new energy in the civil rights arena. He happily pointed to the 1976 election of Clara Jones as the first African-American president of ALA and of his own election to that post in 1983. Josey's new collection highlighted the continued valiant efforts of African-American librarians throughout the nation to improve ethnic relations not only within librarianship but within the culture as a whole.

Josey has continued his interest in exploring various aspects of the African-American library experience as a dissertation advisor at the University of Pittsburgh. For example, in the past few years, his students have investigated racism in California academic libraries and analyzed African-American male library directors. These carefully crafted works demonstrate some of the possibilities for research in the area of African-American librarianship (see Fisher, 1991; Ball, 1992).

OTHER HISTORICAL ASPECTS OF AFRICAN-AMERICAN BOOK CULTURE

Throughout American history, African-Americans have served prominently in publishing and book collecting. Of the many bibliophiles and collectors who worked over the decades to preserve and promote the African-American literary and cultural heritage, the most important was Arthur Alfonso Schomburg (1874-1938) whose vast collection became the nucleus for the Schomburg Center for Research in Black Culture, a special collection of the New York Public Library. Access to Schomburg's collections is greatly enhanced by the *Kaiser Index to Black Resources, 1948-1986* (1992). The center is discussed by Glendora Johnson Cooper (1996), and Schomburg's life is treated capably in Elinor Des Verney Sinnette's (1989) biography. Sinnette has also co-edited essays on black bibliophiles and collectors (Des Verney et al., 1990).

The story of African-American publishing is told by Donald Franklin Joyce in *Gatekeepers of Black Culture* (1983) and *Black Book Publishers in the United States* (1991). Especially pertinent for civil rights issues are Carl Senna's (1993) *The Black Press and the Struggle for Civil Rights* and Henry L. Suggs's (1983) volume on the black press in the South.

HIGHER EDUCATION FOR AFRICAN AMERICANS

General histories of African-American higher education include studies by J. B. Roebuck and K. S. Murty (1993), Charlene Hoffman (1992), and a volume by Walter R. Allen et al. (1991). Frederick Chambers (1978) has produced an extensive bibliography of writings on this topic. Statistical data on traditionally black institutions is featured in Susan Hill's (1985) compilation. And the Association of College and Research Libraries (1991) collected and published African-American library statistics for 1988-1989.

LIBRARY EDUCATION FOR AFRICAN AMERICANS

General overviews of library education include those by Sarah K. Vann (1961), Donald G. Davis, Jr. (1976), C. Edward Carroll (1970), and Charles D.

Churchwell (1975). In addition to her seminal essay on race in American librarianship, Rosemary Du Mont (1986b) produced another important study focusing on African-American library education entitled "The Educating of Black Librarians: An Historical Perspective." Du Mont explained the background for the Hampton Institute and Atlanta University, both significant training facilities for African-American librarians. Du Mont's later essay with William Caynon (1990) for the *Encyclopedia of Library and Information Science* expanded her 1986 contribution. Shifflet (1994) looked at the debate surrounding the establishment of the Hampton Institute (see also Martin & Shiflett, 1996). Arthur C. Gunn (1986) produced a detailed study of the history of the Hampton Institute and the early years of the Atlanta University Library School. More on the school in Atlanta can be learned from its long-term dean Virginia Lacy Jones (1979) and from Casper LeRoy Jordan's (1991) lecture. Kathryn Stevenson (1991) outlined the history of the North Carolina Central University Library School in Benjamin F. Speller Jr.'s recent collection of essays devoted to African-American library education. An example of efforts to continue library education for African-American librarians was offered in the proceedings of the 1973 institute at Alabama State University (Robinson, 1974).

SUGGESTIONS FOR FUTURE RESEARCH

Approximately ten years ago, Rosemary Du Mont (1986a) called for more historical research and more sophisticated methods of investigation into public library service to southern blacks. Who assisted African-Americans in meeting their information needs, and how did the attitudes of information providers fit into the overall framework of southern racial attitudes? Taking advantage of the cluster of master's theses completed at Atlanta University in the 1950s should make it possible for scholars to build on the solid foundation of Eliza Gleason's (1941) study of the public library in the South.

Possibilities for future research seem almost endless. For example, solidly researched biographies are lacking for nearly every major African-American librarian in this century, from Virginia Lacy Jones to Clara S. Jones to A. P. Marshall to Sarah Butler. These are just a few of the individuals whose stories ought to be told by qualified biographers. What do we know about the various African-American state library associations that existed side by side with the white ones in the South? How did African-American rural library services differ from those in urban areas? How was racism in librarianship reflected in northern states? What role did African-American librarians play in the civil rights movement? Much more can be learned about how the American Library Association dealt with the issue of race and American librarianship. The ALA archives have yet to be exhausted on these topics. Moreover, we still need a synthesis of existing studies of African-American library education. Library history remains wide-open for capable scholars willing to dig into the past. This essay has highlighted some of the sources relating to the African-American library experience since 1954. The history itself remains to be written.

REFERENCES

Abdullahi, I. (1992). Bibliography of works by and about E. J. Josey. In I. Abdullahi (Ed.), *E.J. Josey: An activist librarian* (pp. 231-254). Metuchen, NJ: Scarecrow Press.

Allen, W. R.; Epps, E. G.; & Haniff, N. Z. (Eds.). (1991). *College in black and white: African American students in predominantly white and in historically black public universities.* Albany, NY: State University of New York Press.

Ball, P. B. H. (1992). *African-American male library administrators in public and academic libraries: A descriptive study.* Unpublished doctoral dissertation, University of Pittsburgh.

Bennett, L., Jr. (1993). *Before the Mayflower: A history of Black America,* 6th rev. ed. New York: Penguin Books.

Bracey, J. H. Jr.; Meier, A.; & Rudwick, E. (Eds.). (1972). *The Afro-Americans: Selected documents.* Boston, MA: Allyn and Bacon.

Branch, T. (1988). *Parting the waters: America in King years, 1954-63.* New York: Simon and Schuster.

Britton, H. H. (1994). Dorothy Porter Wesley: A bio-bibliographic profile. In O. Williams (Ed.), *American black women in the arts and social sciences* (3d ed.) (pp. 3-23). Metuchen, NJ: Scarecrow Press.

Brown versus The Board of Education of Topeka, Shawnee County, Kansas. (1954). 347 *U. S. Reports,* 483, pp. 483-500.

Bundy, M. L., & Stielow, F. J. (Eds.). (1987). *Activism in American librarianship, 1962-1973.* Westport, CT: Greenwood Press.

Burkett, R. K.; Burkett, N. H.; & Gates, H. L., Jr. (Eds.). (1991). *Black biography, 1790-1950* (3 vols). Alexander, VA: Chadwyck-Healey.

Carroll, C. E. (1970). *The professionalization of education for librarianship with special reference to the years 1940-1960.* Metuchen, NJ: Scarecrow Press.

Chambers, F. (1978). *Black higher education in the United States: A selected bibliography on negro higher education and historically black colleges and universities.* Westport, CT: Greenwood Press.

Churchwell, C. D. (1975). *The shaping of American library education.* Chicago, IL: ALA.

Cooper, G. J. (1996). African-American historical continuity: Jean Blackwell Hutson and the Schomburg Center for research in black culture. In S. Hildenbrand (Ed.), *Reclaiming the American library past: Writing the women in* (pp. 27-51). Norwood, NJ: Ablex.

Davis, D. G., Jr. (1974). *The Association of Library Schools, 1915-1968: An analytical history.* Metuchen, NJ: Scarecrow Press.

Davis, D. G., Jr. (1989). *American library history: A comprehensive guide to the literature.* Santa Barbara, CA: ABC-Clio.

Davis, D. G., Jr., & Tucker, J. M. (1992). Before the waters parted: Minority leadership in academic and research libraries. In T.G. Kirk (Ed.), *Academic libraries: Achieving excellence in higher education* (pp. 48-53). Chicago, IL: ACRL.

Des Verney, E.; Coates, W. P.; & Battle, T. C. (Eds.). (1990). *Black bibliophiles and collectors: Preservers of black history.* Washington, DC: Howard University Press.

Du Mont, R. R. (1986a). Race in American librarianship: Attitudes of the library profession. *Journal of Library History, 21*(3), 488-509.

Du Mont, R. R. (1986b). The educating of black librarians: An historical perspective. *Journal of Education for Library and Information Science, 26*(4), 233-249.

Du Mont, R. R., & Caynon, W. (1990). Education of black librarians. *Encyclopedia of Library and Information Science, 45,* 109-124.

Du Mont, R. R., & Caynon, W. (1994). *Multiculturalism in libraries.* Westport, CT: Greenwood Press.

Fisher, E. M. (1991). *Modern racism in academic librarianship towards black Americans: A California study.* Unpublished doctoral dissertation, University of Pittsburgh.

Franklin, J. H. (1993). *The color line: Legacy for the twenty-first century.* Columbia, MO: University of Missouri Press.

Franklin, J. H., & Moss, A. A., Jr. (1994). *From slavery to freedom: A history of African Americans,* 7th ed. New York: McGraw-Hill.

Garrow, D. J. (1986). *Bearing the cross: Martin Luther King, Jr., and the Southern Christian Leadership Conference.* New York: William Morrow.

Garrow, D. J. (Ed.). (1989). *Martin Luther King, Jr. and the Civil Rights movement* (18 vols.). Brooklyn, NY: Carlson Printing.

Gleason, E. A. (1941). *The Southern negro and the public library: A study of the government and administration of public library service to negroes in the south.* Chicago, IL: University of Chicago Press.

Gunn, A. C. (1986). *Early training for black librarians in the U.S.: A history of the Hampton Institute Library School and the establishment of the Atlanta University School of Library Service.* Unpublished doctoral dissertation, University of Pittsburgh.

Harris, M. H. (1974). *A guide to research in American library history,* 2d ed. Metuchen, NJ: Scarecrow Press.

Harris, M. H., & Davis, D. G., Jr. (1978). *American library history: A bibliography.* Austin, TX: University of Texas Press.

Hill, S. (1985). *The traditionally black institutions of higher education, 1860 to 1982.* Washington, DC: U.S. Department of Education, Office of Educational Research and Improvement.

Hine, D. C. (Ed). (1993). *Black women in America: An historical encyclopedia.* New York: Carlson Publishing.

Hoffman, C. M. (1992). *Historically black colleges and universities, 1976-90.* Washington, DC: U.S. Department of Education, Office of Educational Research and Improvement.

Jones, K. C. (1992). *Renaissance man from Louisiana: A biography of Arna Wendell Bontemps.* Westport, CT: Greenwood Press.

Jones, V. L. (1979). Atlanta University School of Library Service. *Encyclopedia of Library and Information Science,* vol. 2, pp. 82-87.

Jordan, C. L. (1991). With twenty-five carefully selected students: An informal account of black library education. *The Georgia Librarian, 28*(3), 61-67.

Josey, E. J. (Ed.). (1970). *The black librarian in America.* Metuchen, NJ: Scarecrow Press.

Josey, E. J. (Ed.). (1972). *What black librarians are saying.* Metuchen, NJ: Scarecrow Press.

Josey, E. J. (1994). Race issues in library history. In W. A. Wiegand & D. G. Davis, Jr. (Eds.), *Encyclopedia of library history* (pp. 533-537). New York: Garland Publishing.

Josey, E. J. (Ed.). (1994). *The black librarian in America revisited.* Metuchen, NJ: Scarecrow Press.

Josey, E. J., & DeLoach, M. L. (Eds.). (1983). *Ethnic collections in libraries.* New York: Neal-Schuman.

Josey, E. J., & Peeples, K. E., Jr. (Eds.). (1977). *Opportunities for minorities in librarianship.* Metuchen, NJ: Scarecrow Press.

Josey, E. J., & Shockley, A. A. (Eds.). (1977). *Handbook of black librarianship.* Littleton, CO: Libraries Unlimited.

Joyce, D. F. (1983). *Gatekeepers of black culture: Black-owned book publishing in the United States, 1817-1981.* Westport, CT: Greenwood Press.

Joyce, D. F. (1991). *Black book publishers in the United States: A historical dictionary of the presses, 1817-1990.* New York: Greenwood Press.

The Kaiser Index to Black Resources, 1948-1986. (1992). (from the Schomburg Center for Research in Black Culture of the New York Public Library). Brooklyn, NY: Carlson.

King, M. L., Jr. (1992). *The papers of Martin Luther King, Jr.* (C. Carson et al. eds.). Berkeley, CA: University of California Press.

Klarman, M. J. (1994). How Brown changed race relations: The backlash thesis. *Journal of American History, 81*(1), 81-118.

Kluger, R. (1976). *Simple justice: The history of* Brown vs. Board of Education *and black America's struggle for equality,* 1st ed. New York: Knopf.

Lawson, S. F. (1991). Freedom then, freedom now: The historiography of the Civil Rights Movement. *American Historical Review, 96*(2), 456-471.

Mack, T., & Prescod, J. (1991). The struggle for Civil Rights: A selected, annotated bibliography of research collections and U.S. government documents, 1963-1985. *Choice, 28*(6), 887-892.

Madison, A. J., & Wesley, D. P. (1995). Dorothy Burnett Porter Wesley: Enterprising steward of black culture. *Public Historian, 17*(Winter), 15-40.

Marshall, A. P. (1976). Service to Afro-Americans. In S. L. Jackson, E. B. Herling, & E. J. Josey (Eds.), *A century of service: Librarianship in the United States and Canada* (pp. 62-78). Chicago, IL: American Library Association.

Martin, R. S., & Shiflett, O. L. (1996). Hampton, Fisk, and Atlanta: The foundations, the American Library Association, and library education for blacks, 1925-1941. *Libraries & Culture, 31*(Spring), 299-325.

McPheeters, A. L. (1988). *Library service in black and white: Some personal recollections, 1921-1980.* Metuchen, NJ: Scarecrow Press.

Meier, A., & Rudwick, E. (1986). *Black history and the historical profession, 1915-80.* Urbana-Champaign, IL: University of Illinois Press.

Molyneaux, R. J. (Comp.). (1991). *ACRL/historically black colleges & universities library statistics, 1988-1989.* Chicago, IL: ACRL, American Library Association.

Moon, E. (1993). *A desire to learn: Selected writings.* Metuchen, NJ: Scarecrow Press.

Murray, P. T. (1993). *The Civil Rights Movement: References and resources.* New York: G. K. Hall.

Oates, S. B. (1982). *Let the trumpet sound: The life of Martin Luther King, Jr.* New York: Harper and Row.

Parrillo, V. N. (1994). *Strangers to these shores: Race and ethnic relations in the United States,* 4th ed. New York: Macmillan Publishing Co.

Phinazee, A. L. (Ed.). (1980). *The black librarian in the Southeast: Reminiscences, activities, challenges* (papers presented for a colloquium sponsored by the School of Library Science, North Carolina Central University, October 8-9, 1976). Durham, NC: North Carolina Central University.

Rhodes, L. G. (1975). *A critical analysis of the career backgrounds of selected black female librarians.* Unpublished doctoral dissertation, Florida State University.

Robinson, H., Jr. (Ed.). (1974). *Lift ev'ry voice and sing* (papers presented at an Institute for Training Librarians for Special Black Collections and Archives, April 12-14, 1973). Montgomery, AL: Alabama State University.

Roebuck, J. B., & Murty, K. S. (1993). *Historically black colleges and universities: Their place in American higher education.* Westport, CT: Praeger.

Senna, C. (1993). *The black press and the struggle for civil rights.* New York: Franklin Watts.

Shiflett, O. L. (1994). The American Library Association's quest for a black library school. *Journal of Education for Library and Information Science, 35*(1), 68-72.

Sinnette, E. D. (1989). *Arthur Alfonso Schomburg, black bibliophile & collector: A biography.* New York and Detroit, MI: New York Public Library and Wayne State University Press.

Smith, J. C. (1977). *Black academic libraries and research collections: An historical survey.* Westport, CT: Greenwood Press.

Smith, J. C. (1978). Arna Wendell Bontemps (1902-1973). In B. S. Wynar (Ed.), *Dictionary of American library biography* (pp. 44-47). Littleton, CO: Libraries Unlimited.

Smith, J. C. (Ed.). (1992). *Notable black American women.* Detroit, MI: Gale Research.

Smith, J. C. (1993). Sweet sixteen: Black women librarians, 1882-1992. In S. F. Biddle (Ed.), *Culture keepers: Enlightening and empowering our communities* (proceedings of the First National Conference of African American Librarians, Sept. 4-6, 1992, Columbus, Ohio) (pp. 118-126). Newark, NJ: Black Caucus of the American Library Association.

Smith, J. C. (Ed.). (1996). *Notable black American women book II.* Detroit, MI: Gale Research.

Stevenson, K. C. (1991). Annette Lewis Phinazee and the North Carolina Central University School of Library and Information Science. In B. F. Speller, Jr. (Ed.), *Educating black librarians* (papers from the 50th Anniversary Celebration of the School of Library and Information Sciences, North Carolina Central University) (pp. 113-139). Jefferson, NC: McFarland & Company.

Suggs, H. L. (Ed.). (1983). *The black press in the south, 1865-1979.* Westport, CT: Greenwood Press.

Taylor, C. R. (1980). *Contributions of black academic libraries in providing services to the black community.* Unpublished doctoral dissertation, Florida State University.

Vann, S. K. (1961). *Training for librarianship before 1923: Education for librarianship prior to the publication of Williamson's report on training for library service.* Chicago, IL: American Library Association.

Weisbrot, R. (1990). *Freedom bound: A history of America's Civil Rights Movement*, 1st ed. New York: W. W. Norton.

Weigand, W. A., & Davis, D. G., Jr. (Eds.). (1994). *Encyclopedia of library history*. New York: Garland Publishing.

Whitman, M. (Ed.). (1993). *Removing a badge of slavery: The record of* Brown v. Board of Education. Princeton, NJ: Markus Wiener Publishing.

Young, A. P. (1988). *American library history: A bibliography of dissertations and theses*, 3d rev. ed. Metuchen, NJ: Scarecrow Press.

Contributors

ROSIE L. ALBRITTON is Assistant Professor of Library and Information Science at Wayne State University. She holds a B.S. in Biology and Psychology from Tennessee State University, an M.A. and A.B.D. in Educational Psychology from the University of Chicago, an M.A. in Human Development from Governors State University, and a Ph.D. in Library and Information Science and a CLR Fellowship Certificate in Research Library Management from the University of Michigan. Her teaching and research interests include academic library management and evaluation, leadership theory and development, the impact of technology on minority populations, and the historical contributions of African Americans to librarianship. Her publications include "Transformation Leadership in Academic Libraries" in *Advances in Library Administration and Organization* (vol. 13, 1995); *Developing Leadership Skills: A Sourcebook for Librarians* with Thomas Shaughnessy (Libraries Unlimited, 1990), and "Continuing Professional Education: A Management Development Approach," *Reference Librarian* (no. 30, 1990).

DETINE L. BOWERS is the founder of Harmony Blessings, an organization dedicated to communicating inner peace and instituting global transformation through peace communication. She holds a B.A. from Virginia State University, an M.A. from Colorado State University, and a Ph.D. in Communication from Purdue University. Her research and publication interests include Africentric rhetoric and spiritual and intercultural communication.

CHARLES D. CHURCHWELL is retired Dean of the School of Library & Information Studies at Clark Atlanta University and former Director of the Robert W. Woodruff Library at Atlanta University Center. He earned a B.A. in Mathematics from

Morehouse College, an M.S.L.S. from Atlanta University, and a Ph.D. from the University of Illinois. He served as Assistant Director for Public Services at the University of Houston, as Director of the Library at Miami University (Ohio), and as Dean of Library Services at Washington University in St. Louis. His research interests include library administration and education for librarianship. His publications include *The Shaping of American Library Education* (American Library Association, 1975).

DONALD G. DAVIS, JR. is Professor of Library & Information Science at the University of Texas. He holds a B.A. in history from UCLA, an M.A. in history, an M.L.S. from the University of California, and a Ph.D. from the University of Illinois at Urbana-Champaign. Editor of *Libraries & Culture*, a quarterly issued by the University of Texas Press, he has published widely on topics related to library history. He co-edited the *Encyclopedia of Library History* with Wayne A. Wiegand (Garland, 1994) and *American Library History: A Comprehensive Guide to the Literature* with John Mark Tucker (ABC-Clio, 1989).

EDWARD A. GOEDEKEN is Humanities Bibliographer and Associate Professor at Iowa State University. He holds a B.A. from William Penn College, an M.A. in history from Iowa State University, an M.L.S. from the University of Iowa, and a Ph.D. in history from the University of Kansas. He devotes most of his scholarly energies to the maintenance of bibliographies in library history; these are published as columns in the *LHRT Newsletter* and as bibliographic essays in *Libraries & Culture*. Goedeken also dabbles in citation studies of humanities literature.

EDWARD G. HOLLEY is William Rand Kenan, Jr. Professor Emeritus, School of Information and Library Science at the University of North Carolina. He earned a B.A. *magna cum laude* from David Lipscomb University, an M.A. from George Peabody College for Teachers of Vanderbilt University, and a Ph.D. from the University of Illinois. As Director of Libraries at the University of Houston and Dean and Professor at North Carolina, he has published numerous articles and books on academic libraries as well as on library biography and history. His numerous awards include the Melvil Dewey Medal and the Lippincott Award. His monographs include *Charles Evans: American Bibliographer* (University of Illinois, 1963), *Raking the Historical Coals: The ALA Scrapbook of 1876* (Beta Phi Mu, 1967), and *The Library Services and Construction Act: An Historical Overview from the Viewpoint of Major Participants* with Robert F. Schremser (JAI Press, 1983).

JAMES EDGAR HOOPER, Director of Instructional Technology, Baylor School, Chattanooga, Tennessee, received a B.A. from Southwestern at Memphis (Rhodes College), an M.S.L.S from the University of North Carolina, and an M.A. in history from the University of Illinois. His research interests include libraries, the early republic, and twentieth-century U. S. history.

CASPER LEROY JORDAN is retired and former Associate Professor of Library Services at Atlanta University School of Library Service and Deputy Director of the Atlanta-Fulton County Public Library. He holds an AB from Case Western Reserve University and an M.S. in Library Science from Atlanta University. His research interests include minority academic librarianship and African-American bibliography and studies. His publications include *A Bibliographic Guide to African American Women Writers* (Greenwood Press, 1993) and *Black Firsts: 2000 Years of Extraordinary Achievement* edited with Jessie Carney Smith and Robert L. Johns (Gale Research, 1994).

DONALD FRANKLIN JOYCE is Dean, Library & Media Services, Austin Peay State University, Clarksville, Tennessee. He holds a B.A. from Fisk University; an M.L.S from the University of Illinois; and a Ph.D. from the University of Chicago. Joyce's research interests are African-American book publishing and African-American bibliography. He has published *Gatekeepers of Black Culture: Black-Owned Book Publishing in the United States, 1817-1981* (Greenwood Press, 1983); *Blacks in the Humanities, 1750-1984: A Selected Annotated Bibliography* (Greenwood Press, 1986); and *Black Book Publishers in the United States: A Historical Dictionary of the Presses* (Greenwood Press, 1991). Joyce is presently engaged in updating *Blacks in the Humanities* covering the years from 1985 through 1997.

NORMAN G. KESTER is Reference Librarian and social sciences book selector for the Mississauga Central Library, Mississauga Library System, Ontario. A social activist on many fronts, he edited *Liberating Minds: The Stories and Professional Lives of Gay, Lesbian and Bisexual Librarians and Their Advocates* (McFarland, 1997). A number of minority librarians are included in *Liberating Minds*. He contributed to James V. Carmichael, Jr.'s *Daring to Find Our Names: The Search for Lesbigay Library History* (Greenwood Press, forthcoming) and serves as "Lead Thread" columnist for Canada's national library press, *Feliciter*. Finally, an excerpt from a chapter of his post-modern South African-Canadian gay memoir is included in *MA-KA, Diasporic Juks: Contemporary Writings by Queers of African Descent* (Toronto, Ontario: Sister Vision Press, January 1998).

DAN R. LEE is Reference Librarian at Lander University, Greenwood, South Carolina. He holds a B.A. from Eastern Kentucky University and an M.L. from the University of South Carolina. His research interests include the history of library services for southern African Americans; his publications include "Faith Cabin Libraries: A Study of an Alternative Library Service in the Segregated South," *Libraries & Culture,* 26 (Winter 1991).

BEVERLY P. LYNCH is Professor, Graduate School of Education & Information Studies, UCLA, and former dean of UCLA's Graduate School of Library and Information Science. She holds a B.S. from North Dakota State University, an M.S. from the University of Illinois, and a Ph.D. from the University of Wisconsin. Her current work includes an international survey on standards for libraries. Her most recent book is *Information Technology and the Remaking of the University Library* (Jossey-Bass, 1995).

CHERYL KNOTT MALONE is assistant professor in the Graduate School of Library and Information Science at the University of Illinois. She holds a B.A. from the University of Houston, M.L.S and M.A. degrees from the University of Arizona, and a Ph.D. from the University of Texas. Her research interests include the history of public libraries and librarians in the United States and the dynamics of race, gender, and class in the information professions. Her publications include "Women's Unpaid Work in Libraries: Change and Continuity" in *Reclaiming the American Library Past: Writing the Women In*, edited by Suzanne Hildenbrand (Ablex Publishing, 1996).

KLAUS MUSMANN is Library Director of the Armacost Library of the University of Redlands in Redlands, California. He holds a B.A. from Wayne State University, an M.L.S. from the University of Michigan, an M.A. from Michigan State University, and a Ph.D. from the University of Southern California. His research focuses on the diffusion of technological innovations in libraries. His most recent book is entitled *Technological Innovations in Libraries, 1860-1960: An Anecdotal History* (Greenwood Press, 1993).

MARILYN H. PETTIT is University Archivist at St. John's University, Jamaica (Queens), New York. She received a B.A. from the University of Texas, an Archives Certificate and M.A. and Ph.D. degrees in U. S. history from New York University. She has served as an archival educator at New York University and the University of Maryland. Her research interests focus on the culture of gendered literacy and the origins of public schooling for females. Publications include *New York University and the City: An Illustrated History, 1831-1996* co-authored with Thomas J. Frusciano (Rutgers University Press, 1997).

JESSIE CARNEY SMITH is University Librarian and William and Camille Cosby Professor in the Humanities at Fisk University. She holds a B.S. from North Carolina Agricultural & Technical State University, an M.A. from Michigan State University, an M.A.L.S. from George Peabody College for Teachers of Vanderbilt University, and a Ph.D. from the University of Illinois. She focuses her research on African-American themes, particularly women. Her publications include *Notable Black American Women,* and *Notable Black American Women, Book II* (Gale Research, 1992 and 1996), *Epic Lives: One Hundred Black Women Who Made a Difference* (Visible Ink Press, 1993), *Powerful Black Women* (Visible Ink

Press, 1996), *Black Firsts: 2,000 Years of Extraordinary Achievement* with Casper LeRoy Jordan and Robert L. Johns (Gale Research, 1994), and *Black Heroes of the 20th Century* (Visible Ink press, 1998).

JOHN MARK TUCKER is Humanities, Social Science, & Education Librarian and Professor of Library Science at Purdue University. He holds a B.A. from David Lipscomb University, M.L.S. and Ed.S. degrees from George Peabody College for Teachers of Vanderbilt University, and a Ph.D. from the University of Illinois. His research interests include the history and biography of academic librarianship especially the period of the late 19th and early 20th centuries. His publications include *Reference Services and Library Education: Essays in Honor of Frances Neel Cheney* with Edwin S. Gleaves (Lexington Books, 1983) and *American Library History: A Comprehensive Guide to the Literature* with Donald G. Davis, Jr. (ABC-Clio, 1989).

ANDREA L. WILLIAMS is Curriculum Materials Librarian at Midwestern State University in Wichita Falls, Texas. She holds B.A. and M.A. degrees in English literature from Midwestern State and an M.L.S. from Texas Woman's University, and she writes reviews for *Appraisal: Science Books for Young People.*

Index

⋙ Compiled by Jennifer Young ⋘

The Publications Office of the Graduate School of Library and Information Science at the University of Illinois at Urbana-Champaign produces a variety of scholarly and practical publications for library and information science professionals. The office's catalog includes subscription journals, books, conference proceedings and monograph series.
For more information, contact

The Graduate School of Library and Information Science
University of Illinois at Urbana-Champaign
501 E. Daniel St.
Champaign, IL 61820
Voice: (217) 333-1359
Fax: (217) 244-7329
E-mail: puboff@alexia.lis.uiuc.edu
World Wide Web: http://edfu.lis.uiuc.edu/puboff

Consistently ranked as one of the top three library and information science programs in the U. S., the Graduate School of Library and Information Science, founded in 1893 at the Armour Institute in Chicago, maintains a reputation of excellence and quality. The University of Illinois at Urbana-Champaign was founded in 1867, and is regularly cited among leading universities in the United States.